Great Men of
the Bible

GREAT MEN

of the

BIBLE

by

DR. JOHN R. RICE

SWORD OF THE LORD PUBLISHERS
Murfreesboro, Tennessee 37130

ISBN 0-87398-314-9

Printed and bound in the United States of America

Table of Contents

Introduction

The stories of great men in the Bible make a fascinating book. What color! What charm! What intriguing interest there is in the way God dealt with great men in the Bible!

"One example is worth a thousand arguments," and a vivid example makes more impression than a simple precept.

"Blessed is the man that walketh not in the counsel of the ungodly, nor standeth in the way of sinners, nor sitteth in the seat of the scornful," says Psalm 1:1, but when we see that heathen wives led Solomon, the wisest man who ever lived, into idolatry, the truth is more striking and impressive.

Proverbs 13:24 says, "He that spareth his rod hateth his son: but he that loveth him chasteneth him betimes"; but the lesson of undisciplined sons is more strikingly pressed on our hearts when we see the tragedy of Eli's sons who "made themselves vile, and he restrained them not" (I Sam. 3:13). Death to the sons and disgrace to Israel and a curse on all future generations of Eli!

The colorful, unforgettable victory of Gideon and his three hundred with lamps and pitchers, tends to build more faith in God than the simple command, "Have faith in God."

It is wonderfully true God has invited us, "Draw nigh to God, and he will draw nigh to you" (Jas. 4:8); but how powerful is the lesson when we see the heathen army captain, Cornelius, seeking God, and God sending an angel to tell him of a preacher, then by multiple visions He prepares that preacher, Peter, to give up his racist Jewish prejudice and preach the Gospel to Gentiles! And Cornelius and his family and friends are saved and filled with the Spirit.

Of course we know Jesus said, "I am the way, the truth, and the life: no man cometh unto the Father, but by me," and surely Old Testament saints had to be saved by coming to trust in the Saviour who had been promised; but how much clearer, more easily understood and believed when we see that Abraham "believed in the Lord; and he counted it to him for righteousness" (Gen. 15:6), and as Jesus said, "Abraham rejoiced to see my day: and he saw it, and was glad" (John 8:56).

Do all things work out for our good? Does God control kings and circumstances in history? Yes. We see it so clearly when we study the great first world emperor, Nebuchadnezzar, perhaps unwittingly the tool and agent of God and controlled by God.

So we bring to you these studies of great Bible characters.

In another book, *Bible Giants Tested,* we gave case histories of Jacob, Caleb, King Saul, Jehoshaphat, Elijah, John the Baptist, Peter and Paul, as each one faced some great crisis in his life. This book is different, since it gives a study of character and the life story of these great men, not based on a particular incident, or fact.

May these stories make the Bible more interesting than ever and set your heart to seeking all the more wonders in that wonderful Book!

Murfreesboro, Tennessee   John R. Rice
1976

1

Abraham, Friend of God

The first chapters of Genesis tell briefly the whole story of creation, of millions of people who died in the worldwide flood, the Tower of Babel and confusion of tongues, and the scattering of Noah's descendants over the world. It is about the whole human race thus far. Then in chapter 12 Abraham takes the center of the stage, and he and his family fill the last 38 chapters of Genesis. Then most of the Old Testament is about his descendants, the nation Israel.

Abraham was a friend of God. To him and his seed was all Palestine given. Through him all the nations were to be blessed. Through him was to come the Messiah.

Abraham was a wonderful Christian, not only the fountainhead of a nation but an example of salvation by grace through faith, described in Romans, chapter 4. Next to Moses, perhaps, Abraham may have had more constant and intimate touch with God than any other Old Testament character.

My book, *Seeking a City,* tells the life and teachings of Abraham in a historical novel, portraying the rich life of this man and how much he knew about God, about Christ, about the Second Coming and the millennium.

I. GOD'S COVENANT WITH ABRAHAM

God had great plans for Abraham, and you can understand that it took a great many years for Abraham to understand God's plan, to believe it, to grow to it and to be willing to make the day-by-day sacrifice of everything he had held on to in order to have God's best for him.

1. God Called Abraham to Separate From Wickedness of People Around Him

Genesis 12:1-3 tells us:

> *"Now the Lord had said unto Abram, Get thee out of*

thy country, and from thy kindred, and from thy father's
house, unto a land that I will shew thee: And I will make
of thee a great nation, and I will bless thee, and make thy
name great; and thou shalt be a blessing: And I will bless
them that bless thee, and curse him that curseth thee:
and in thee shall all families of the earth be blessed."

God made something of this clear to Abraham while he was
still in Ur of the Chaldees. Abraham did not make an immediate
break with his family, his father, his brother's son, Lot. He did
not immediately go on down to Palestine, the place God had appointed. When he went to Palestine, and the drouth came, he
went down to Egypt for a time. But he made the break, a start,
toward the total separation from worldly things and former ties
which God had called upon him to make. That was a step in the
way to becoming a great nation, although it would be twenty-five
years before God began to work out His plan with the birth of
Isaac. Abraham was seventy-five years old when he left Haran
for Palestine (Gen. 12:4). He was a hundred years old when Isaac
was born (Gen. 21:5). Oh, the road to becoming a great nation
and blessing millions of people was a long road and Abraham had
much to learn.

2. God Promised Abraham All the Land of Palestine, and Descendants to Occupy It

In Genesis 13:14-18 we read:

"And the Lord said unto Abram, after that Lot was
separated from him, Lift up now thine eyes, and look
from the place where thou art northward, and
southward, and eastward, and westward: For all the land
which thou seest, to thee will I give it, and to thy seed for
ever. And I will make thy seed as the dust of the earth: so
that if a man can number the dust of the earth, then
shall thy seed also be numbered. Arise, walk through the
land in the length of it and in the breadth of it; for I will
give it unto thee. Then Abraham removed his tent, and
came and dwelt in the plain of Mamre, which is in
Hebron, and built there an altar unto the Lord."

Notice, it is the literal land of Palestine. Abraham was to walk through the length and breadth of it, and the land he saw and walked upon was to be given him.

Note also that it was to be an everlasting possession.

I think that the heart of Abraham may have been sad because he had just separated from his nephew Lot whom he loved so much. He had taken responsibility for Lot, when Lot's father died. He took Lot with him and evidently Abraham helped make Lot rich. But God let him know there would be children of his own and descendants. These descendants would be "as the dust of the earth," literally great numbers of Israelites that could not be counted through the centuries.

3. God Promised Abraham Spiritual Descendants, Like the Uncounted Stars

Abraham was getting on in years. He had no heir but Eliezer, his servant. And with deep question in his heart he called on the Lord: "Lord God, what wilt thou give me, seeing I go childless, and the steward of my house is this Eliezer of Damascus?" We read then in Genesis 15:3-6:

> "And Abram said, Behold, to me thou hast given no seed: and, lo, one born in my house is mine heir. And, behold, the word of the Lord came unto him, saying, This shall not be thine heir; but he that shall come forth out of thine own bowels shall be thine heir. And he brought him forth abroad, and said, Look now toward heaven, and tell the stars, if thou be able to number them: and he said unto him, So shall thy seed be. And he believed in the Lord; and he counted it to him for righteousness."

The descendants, then, are to be literal, physical descendants, and while he had been promised literal, physical descendants as the dust of the earth, now there is a promise of descendants like the stars above!

We believe it is a spiritual lesson that God is making known to Abraham. Some way He is making clear to Abraham that the Messiah will come and that multitudes will be blessed and be forgiven and saved through this Messiah.

Galatians 3:29 tells us, "And if ye be Christ's, then are ye Abraham's seed, and heirs according to the promise." If we know that, and it is revealed in the New Testament, did not God show Abraham that, too?

For here is the time Abraham was converted. "He believed in the Lord; and he counted it to him for righteousness," says verse 6. "For there is none other name under heaven given among men, whereby we must be saved" (Acts 4:12). Abraham must have understood that those heavenly seed, the children of Abraham by faith in the coming Messiah, would be Christian people of all ages. So Abraham understood that through the child who was to come of his body would be a line from which the Saviour would come. And it was this that would bring the spiritual blessing to many nations through Abraham.

4. God Revealed to Abraham That Through Christ, His Greater Seed, Abraham and His Spiritual Seed Would Inhabit Palestine Forever

I do not wonder that Abraham was slow to grasp the immensity of the promises God gave! Looking back, we who already have the Saviour and have seen how God worked out His wonderful plans and the coming of the Lord Jesus, can see it. Hindsight is so much easier than foresight.

So Abraham either did not fully understand or could hardly believe the wonderful things God had promised: "He that shall come forth out of thine own bowels shall be thine heir" (Gen. 15:4).

Oh, perhaps he thought it could not be through Sarah. Now Sarah was getting old. Already the age for childbearing was gone. Abraham felt he must some way make arrangements. So Sarah, burdened always as was a childless, barren woman in Bible times, thought to help God out. She proposed that Abraham should take her maidservant Hagar and through Hagar raise up a seed. Thus it came that Ishmael was born. But he was not the child of the promise! God would not have Ishmael in the ancestral line of the Saviour. And in Genesis 17, when Abraham was ninety-nine years old, God appeared to him again and in Genesis 17:2-8 God said:

> *"And I will make my covenant between me and thee, and will multiply thee exceedingly. And Abram fell on his face: and God talked with him, saying, As for me, behold, my covenant is with thee, and thou shalt be a father of many nations. Neither shall thy name any more be called Abram, but thy name shall be Abraham; for a father of many nations have I made thee. And I will make thee exceeding fruitful, and I will make nations of thee, and kings shall come out of thee. And I will establish my covenant between me and thee and thy seed after thee in their generations for an everlasting covenant, to be a God unto thee, and to thy seed after thee. And I will give unto thee, and to thy seed after thee, the land wherein thou art a stranger, all the land of Canaan, for an everlasting possession; and I will be their God."*

Abraham was to be the father of many nations, not only the nation Israel, descended through Jacob, but the Edomites through Esau and the Arab people through Ishmael. But God repeats His great covenant:

> *"And I will give unto thee, and to thy seed after thee, the land wherein thou art a stranger, all the land of Canaan, for an everlasting possession; and I will be their God."*

We will note that somewhere in these promises, and perhaps in verse 8 here, God used the word "seed" in the singular, not plural, for He now refers to Abraham and Christ inheriting the land and not simply unconverted Jews alone.

Galatians 3:16 says, "Now to Abraham and his seed were the promises made. He saith not, and to seeds, as of many; but as of one, And to thy seed, which is Christ." So the promise is for far more than a Jewish state. The promise is that one day the Lord Jesus Himself will sit on David's throne and will have a kingdom on this earth, with Abraham's Seed, the Lord Jesus Christ, as King.

5. God Gave Abraham Circumcision as Mark
of Covenant of Separated People

Now Abraham has a son, Ishmael. He is not the son of the promise, but he is a son of Abraham, and Abraham is responsible for him. So now God gives to Abraham the covenant of circumcision. In Genesis 17:9-14 the Lord explained circumcision:

"And God said unto Abraham, Thou shalt keep my covenant therefore, thou, and thy seed after thee in their generations. This is my covenant, which ye shall keep, between me and you and thy seed after thee; Every man child among you shall be circumcised. And ye shall circumcise the flesh of your foreskin; and it shall be a token of the covenant betwixt me and you. And he that is eight days old shall be circumcised among you, every man child in your generations, he that is born in the house, or bought with money of any stranger, which is not of thy seed. He that is born in thy house, and he that is bought with thy money, must needs be circumcised: and my covenant shall be in your flesh for an everlasting covenant. And the uncircumcised man child whose flesh of his foreskin is not circumcised, that soul shall be cut off from his people; he hath broken my covenant."

And following in the same chapter we learn where Abraham, ninety-nine years old, was circumcised and his son, thirteen years old, and all the men of his house, that is, his servants, were circumcised also.

This ceremonial circumcision was given to Abraham after he had learned to trust the Lord. "And he believed in the Lord; and he counted it to him for righteousness" (Gen. 15:6). And so we believe Abraham knew the spiritual meaning of the rite. In Romans, chapter 4, we learn how Abraham was saved by faith before he was circumcised: "And he received the sign of circumcision, a seal of the righteousness of the faith which he had yet being uncircumcised: that he might be the father of all them that believe, though they be not circumcised; that righteousness might be imputed unto them also."

So circumcision is a spiritual picture, a ceremony, meaning that one who trusts in Christ is born again, now has a different destiny, a different nature, a different father. Abraham was circumcised as a seal marking his conversion and picturing that others need to be circumcised in heart, that is, converted. And Romans 2:28, 29 says, "For he is not a Jew, which is one outwardly; neither is that circumcision, which is outward in the flesh: But he is a Jew, which is one inwardly; and circumcision is that of the heart, in the spirit, and not in the letter; whose praise is not of men, but of God."

The rites of the ceremonial law were not empty gestures nor ceremonies. They were pictures of great spiritual truth. And the Lord promised in Deuteronomy 30:1-6 that He would one day regather Israel, would turn their captivity, bring them back to Palestine "and the Lord thy God will circumcise thine heart, and the heart of thy seed, to love the Lord thy God with all thine heart, and with all thy soul, that thou mayest live."

Oh, wonderful covenant God made with Abraham, and that covenant is with us, the spiritual seed of Abraham, too!

And Hebrews 11:39,40, telling the heroes of the faith, including Abraham and others, says, "And these all, having obtained a good report through faith, received not the promise: God having provided some better thing for us, that they without us should not be made perfect."

II. THE DRASTIC COURSE:
LEAVING ALL FOR GOD'S WILL

Jesus said once that "if any man come to me, and hate not his father, and mother, and wife, and children, and brethren, and sisters, yea, and his own life also, he cannot be my disciple. And whosoever doth not bear his cross, and come after me, cannot be my disciple" (Luke 14:26, 27).

Again He said, "So, likewise, whosoever he be of you that forsaketh not all that he hath, he cannot be my disciple" (Luke 14:33).

We need not be surprised, then, that God expected of Abraham a drastic course of forsaking his land, his people, his comfort, his riches, and long years of toilsome waiting and praying to God for the fulfillment of God's plan in his own life.

God had said, "Get thee out of thy country, and from thy kindred, and from thy father's house, unto a land that I will shew thee." He was to leave his country. He was to leave his kinfolks. He was to leave his father's house.

1. Abraham Left Ur of the Chaldees

We may suppose that Abraham was rich. In the first place, he had flocks and herds wherever he went, and he was a thrifty, sober, businesslike, godly man. Back in Ur of the Chaldees he would have plenty—a home with all comforts; it may be a palace. It is not for nothing that God reminds us that "by faith he sojourned in the land of promise, as in a strange country, dwelling in tabernacles with Isaac and Jacob, the heirs with him of the same promise." Note they lived in tents, and it is obviously meant that Abraham and Sarah left a settled house and abode in Ur of the Chaldees. They were to be pioneers. They were to cook over campfires. They were to live in tents. They were to go among strangers. They were to say good-by to all their friends. So Abraham left Ur of the Chaldees. That was a step of faith.

2. Father Terah Was Hard to Leave

God had told Abraham to leave his kindred and his father's house. But instead of complete obedience we see in Genesis 11 that Abraham let Terah, his father, take things in his own hand. "And Terah took Abram his son and Lot the son of Haran his son's son, and Sarai his daughter in law, his son Abram's wife; and they went forth with them from Ur of the Chaldees, to go into the land of Canaan; and they came unto Haran, and dwelt there." Not willing to make the sacrifices necessary, yet the father wants to be in on the blessing.

So he loads up and they make their caravan. Are they going to Canaan? That is where they intended to go. But no doubt the old man Terah got tired of the journey. He was seventy years old when his first son was born, 130 when Abraham was born. And they come to Haran and stop on the way, instead of going on to Canaan.

Abraham, why don't you go on to Canaan as you started and as God instructed? What? And leave my old father? This is the same problem that James and John had when Jesus called them by the Sea of Galilee to leave their father and the ship and the nets to follow Him.

So Terah stopped in Haran instead of going on to Canaan where God had said they should go. Ah, Abraham, if you had left your father back in Ur of the Chaldees you would have been better off. You did not leave "your kindred and your father's house," as God commanded. There is more to learn, Abraham, before you enter into the great blessing God has for you.

3. Abraham Took With Him Nephew Lot

Lot was the son of Haran, Abraham's brother. Since Haran was dead, Abraham felt a need to take the young man under his wing to help him, to protect him, and, no doubt, to enjoy the fellowship and love he had for this dear kinsman. God had said, "Get thee out of thy country, and from thy kindred, and from thy father's house." But Abraham took Lot along with him.

But we must remember that Lot did not feel the same burden to seek God as did Abraham. He grew rich and he was selfish. There came a time when there must be a parting of the ways.

"And the land was not able to bear them, that they might dwell together: for their substance was great, so that they could not dwell together. And there was a strife between the herdmen of Abram's cattle and the herdmen of Lot's cattle: and the Canaanite and the Perizzite dwelled then in the land. And Abram said unto Lot, Let there be no strife, I pray thee, between me and thee, and between my herdmen and thy herdmen; for we be brethren. Is not the whole land before thee? separate thyself, I pray thee, from me: if thou wilt take the left hand, then I will go to the right; or if thou depart to the right hand, then I will go to the left. And Lot lifted up his eyes, and beheld all the plain of Jordan, that it was well watered every where, before the Lord destroyed Sodom and Gomorrah, even as the garden of the Lord, like the

> *land of Egypt, as thou comest unto Zoar. Then Lot chose*
> *him all the plain of Jordan; and Lot journeyed east: and*
> *they separated themselves the one from the other.*
> *Abram dwelled in the land of Canaan, and Lot dwelled*
> *in the cities of the plain, and pitched his tent toward*
> *Sodom. But the men of Sodom were wicked and sinners*
> *before the Lord exceedingly."*—Gen. 13:6-13.

Ah, and Lot pitched his tent toward Sodom and soon landed in Sodom. There he took up the drinking of the Sodomites, called them brethren, did not lead his family to know the Lord and serve Him, and soon, when the destruction of the city came, Lot lost wife and all his children but the two daughters at home, and those two daughters had absorbed the wickedness of Sodom. He got the girls out of Sodom, but he didn't get Sodom out of the daughters. So they got their father drunk and he became the father of their illegitimate children.

Abraham would have done better had he left Lot back in Ur of the Chaldees, as God had told him.

4. Hard for Abraham to Believe That From His Own Body and From Womb of Sarah Would Come Promised Child

There is a wonderful lesson here. If Abraham and Sarah had had a child born in their young days and through natural process, then it would not have been miraculous. It would not have been such a wonderful answer to prayer. But God had them wait until it takes a miracle. So Abraham, as good as dead, and Sarah, an old, old woman of ninety, are to have a child!

God must test Abraham. Abraham, do you think you must get the Egyptian woman Hagar to bear the son God has promised? Could you not trust Him?

Again, we must remember that only by long praying and waiting on God are many of His blessed plans accomplished in us. And so the twenty-five years from the time Abraham left Haran and went into Canaan until the child Isaac was born are years to grow in Abraham a certain great character, depending on God.

Did Abraham doubt that the land of Canaan would be his future home? Well, when famine came he went down to Egypt and used human subterfuge to save his life. He got himself and Sarah into serious trouble, but God delivered him. Then he went back to the land of Canaan.

God has taken time to develop this man, the friend of God, and make him fit to be the blessing God has promised he shall be.

III. ABRAHAM'S GROWTH IN FAITH

It took God many long years to develop Abraham's faith. First, back in Ur of the Chaldees, God had already told Abraham he should leave his father's house, his kindred, and go to a land that God would show him, evidently to Canaan. Father Terah insisted on going, too, and he went as far as Haran, and they all stopped there and stayed for some time.

We are sure there was always an unrest in Abraham's heart. At last he went on to Canaan, when he was seventy-five years old. It was twenty-five years more before Isaac was born. Note the progress in Abraham's faith.

1. Faith to Leave Home, Country, Kinfolks, Security, and All Things, Developed Slowly

We have no doubt that Abraham honestly wanted to please the Lord and intended to go to any length to do the will of God. But no Christian in the world turns out to be a full-grown, greatly-developed Christian the day he is saved. Some people foolishly think that to be saved means to be automatically right about everything. That is not true.

God had a period of time in preparing Moses to lead Israel out of Egypt at eighty years of age. God took long years to get David ready to be king of Israel. The way the apostles grew under the three years or more of teaching with Jesus is an illustration. Paul, later to be an apostle, after barely escaping with his life at Damascus and being poorly received by the Christians in Jerusalem, and threatened with death, went back to his old home in Tarsus and, as far as we know, preached no more for a time until Barnabas went for him and led him back into a glorious ministry.

Then we need not be surprised that step by step God led Abraham to a greater faith. At last God took away the father and

Abraham left his body at Haran. Then circumstances and perhaps Lot's selfishness made it so he and Abraham must part company. After many, many repetitions of the sweet promises by the Lord, Abraham came to believe that he would really father a great nation and that they would inherit Palestine.

2. At Last Gospel Broke Through Into Abraham's Heart, He Trusted Coming Messiah and Was Saved

It is a very simple statement we have in Genesis 15:6, "And he believed in the Lord; and he counted it to him for righteousness." And what was the message that stirred that saving faith? It was very simple. God "brought him forth abroad, and said, Look now toward heaven, and tell the stars, if thou be able to number them: and he said unto him, So shall thy seed be." We are sure that there were a great many more words from God than this simple statement. There was enough to make clear that the seed promised would involve the Lord Jesus Himself, a Messiah who would save people. There was enough said, surely, that Abraham would understand that now God is talking about a Heavenly Seed of born-again people who would be saved through Abraham's greater Son, the promised Seed, the Saviour!

That is made quite clear, I think, in Galatians 3:6-9:

> "*Even as Abraham believed God, and it was accounted to him for righteousness. Know ye therefore that they which are of faith, the same are the children of Abraham. And the scripture, foreseeing that God would justify the heathen through faith, preached before the gospel unto Abraham, saying, In thee shall all nations be blessed. So then they which be of faith are blessed with faithful Abraham.*"

Read again verse 8, "And the scripture, foreseeing that God would justify the heathen through faith, preached before the GOSPEL unto Abraham, saying, In thee shall all nations be blessed." So Abraham heard the Gospel. God made clear through the Spirit in his heart and through other words that are not recorded that He spoke of a coming Saviour who would be able to save people from sin.

Oh, when Abraham had met God at many an altar and sought His face many, many times for some years, you may be sure that God would not leave him without the truth. He who would see that the truth was brought to Cornelius, the seeking centurion, would not leave the hungry heart of Abraham without knowing the truth about the Saviour. It was true then as now, "Draw nigh to God, and he will draw nigh to you," and, "Those that seek me early shall find me." But Abraham had the Gospel preached to him.

God had preached the Gospel to Adam and Eve as He made coats of skins, showing that the innocent sacrifice must die for the guilty sinner. God had told them that the Seed of the woman should bruise the serpent's head and it would bruise His heel. He had someway explained to Abel that the dying lamb from his flock pictured the coming Saviour so that "by faith Abel offered unto God a more excellent sacrifice."

We are never to think that God had two plans of salvation. The only salvation that any sinner in this world can ever have is through the Lord Jesus Christ. People trust Him now who never saw Him. People trusted Him then when they never saw Him but when His coming was foretold and the atoning grace of God was made known to them in some way.

We cannot believe that a spiritually-minded man, seeking the face of God, would look again and again on a smoking sacrifice and not see something there of an atoning Saviour who was promised.

Abraham had the Gospel preached to him. When he looked at those stars and thought of the unseen multitudes who would be saved through the Messiah, "Abraham believed God, and it was accounted to him for righteousness." He put his trust in the Messiah not yet born but who already in the mind and plan of God was crucified for sinners. Now Abraham stepped over the line. Instead of a seeking sinner, now he is a believing child of God.

3. Climax of Faith for Abraham Was When He Offered Isaac as Sacrifice

What a trial and temptation it was when God said to

Abraham, "Take now thy son, thine only son Isaac, whom thou lovest, and get thee into the land of Moriah; and offer him there for a burnt-offering upon one of the mountains which I will tell thee of."

So Abraham rose early the next morning to do it. He took two servants and Isaac. He chopped some wood for a burnt offering, that wood representing the human works that will be burned and that for which Jesus died.

Did Abraham tell Sarah? We do not know. Probably the lad Isaac did not at first know that awesome, secret thing gnawing at the heart of Abraham as he took the three days' journey from Beersheba, in Southern Palestine, up to Mount Moriah, that ridge that runs now through the city of Jerusalem and on which the Temple eventually would be built. There Abraham left the servants and donkey below, the wood was bound on Isaac's back and they went up on the hill and there an altar was prepared. The startled son was bound upon the altar and Abraham raised his knife to strike it in the heart of that boy for whom he prayed twenty-five years and for whom he would have gladly died! Oh, but he must please God at any cost!

What was in Abraham's mind then? That is made clear in Hebrews 11:17-19:

> "By faith Abraham, when he was tried, offered up
> Isaac: and he that had received the promises offered up
> his only begotten son. Of whom it was said, That in Isaac
> shall thy seed be called: Accounting that God was able to
> raise him up, even from the dead; from whence also he
> received him in a figure."

And why did he think God would raise him from the dead? Well, in the first place, God had made a promise that He must keep. The multitude innumerable should come through this boy Isaac. So, if Abraham killed him, he must be raised from the dead. And Abraham believed it.

Oh, yes, and Abraham knew more than that, too, for in that lad he saw the Lord Jesus Himself. So in cryptic words he said to Isaac, "My son, God will provide himself a lamb for a burnt-offering." Abraham saw Jesus there. That is what the Lord Jesus Himself said about it in John 8:56, "Your father Abraham rejoiced to see my day: and he saw it, and was glad."

And Abraham knew more than that. When he dwelt in tents and slept on goatskin pallets, and when Sarah and her servants cooked by a campfire, Abraham had holy thoughts. He had left Ur of the Chaldees, and he realized that he was a sojourner, a stranger, a temporary dweller in Palestine. So instead of going back to the country from which they came out, Abraham and his descendants desired "a better country, that is, an heavenly: wherefore God is not ashamed to be called their God: for he hath prepared for them a city" (Heb. 11:16). And before that is stated, "For he looked for a city which hath foundations, whose builder and maker is God" (Heb. 11:10).

Ah, the spiritual mind, then, can begin to see that Abraham himself was a good Christian, a spiritually-minded Christian, looking forward to seeing Jesus in person and Christ's heavenly reign on earth!

4. Character of Abraham Most Commendable

Abraham appears to have a certain gentleness. What Christian virtues he showed! We might criticise him for lying about Sarah, calling her his sister when, in fact, she was his half-sister; we may think he was unwise to go down into Egypt when perhaps he should have stayed in Palestine. If they were errors, they were the errors of a good man.

It is amazing the respect people had for him. First, the love story of Abraham and Sarah is wonderfully sweet. "Even as Sara obeyed Abraham, calling him lord," we read in I Peter 3:6. His love and protection for his nephew Lot were touching. His unselfishness in gladly offering Lot whatever part of the country he should choose. Actually it was promised to Abraham—he had a right to pick and choose, but he sought first the welfare of Lot.

When Sarah died, the respect of the neighboring heathen people and the sons of Heth was very obvious.

Abraham had a great manliness about him also when the five kings fought and took Sodom, Gomorrah, Admah, Zeboim and

Zoar, and took Lot and his family captives. Abraham gathered together his own servants, got his friends at Mamre and they pursued headlong after these kings, came upon them and slew them and delivered Lot and his family and brought back the captured stuff. Then most generously he refused to take anything for himself of what he had rescued for others.

In his old age, Abraham was determined that Isaac should stay separated from the heathen world, so he sent Eliezer back to Padan-aram for a bride. God was in it and the bride was secured who would fit God's plan.

Now let me say to every person whose eyes fall upon this passage. Can it be said of you as of Abraham that "he believed God, and it was accounted to him for righteousness"? Can you say that all your sins are laid on the Saviour and that when you put your trust in Him, all Christ's righteousnesses are thus ascribed to you? Can you say that "Christ died for me; I take Him as my Saviour"?

Oh, above everything else, make sure that you have trusted Christ, as did Abraham and thus you can have salvation by grace through faith, as he did.

2

The Story of Joseph

The Shepherd Boy, Beloved of His Father, Hated by His
Brethren, Sold Into Slavery, a Spirit-Anointed
Prophet of God Who Came to Be Prime
Minister of Egypt, Saved Millions
From Starvation

The last fourteen chapters of the book of Genesis have the
fascinating story of Joseph who is the hero of most of it.

Once when I was pastor in Dallas, Texas, I pressed upon the
people, "You cannot claim to be a good Christian without daily
reading the Bible. You can read the Bible through by reading
four chapters a day."

Mr. Tom Patton, then owner of Machinery Sales and Supply
Company, protested to me he was so busy he hardly had time to
do his necessary work, much less read the Bible. But, vexed at
my insistence and yet feeling guilty, he set out to read the Bible
through.

That week he read the story of Joseph, and he came to me in a
great flurry Sunday morning. "Why didn't you tell me the Bible
was like that?" He had gotten into this story and couldn't lay the
Bible down until past midnight, so interested was he in seeing
how it came out with this boy so blessed of God!

God would not have put such details in Holy Writ if there were
not charm and sweet counsel and warning and edifying riches in
the story for us.

We remember that Jacob had twelve sons. He had fallen in
love with Rachel and made a bargain with her scheming father
Laban, his uncle, that he would work seven years for her. That
seemed but a little while—he loved her so much. Then in the
night crooked Laban brought to him Leah, her weak-eyed sister,
for the wedding bed, and behold, the cheated husband found he

must work seven years more for Rachel! A week later he married Rachel and faithfully worked out the long years. And theirs was a great love.

For some years Rachel was barren. At last, after much prayer and heart-searching, God gave her the child Joseph. As far as we know, all Jacob's other ten boys and the daughter Dinah had been born before, from Leah and the two handmaids or slave wives, Bilhah and Zilpah. Then after about six years Rachel bare Benjamin and died. Then Jacob hugged to his heart this fine boy Joseph, favored him, made him a coat of many colors, and no doubt taught him many spiritual truths that the other boys did not know.

Joseph was a spiritual lad. God revealed to him in dreams that he would have a place of authority and importance. His brothers hated him all the more because his father loved him and because of his dreams. Eventually, when he came to seek them out for a report for his father, he was first put into a pit, then sold as a slave to a Midianite caravan, and down in Egypt he was sold as a bondslave to Potiphar, the captain of Pharaoh's guard.

There he was greatly blessed. Soon he was in charge of all the household. The scheming and wicked wife tried to seduce him and then falsely accused him to her husband. Joseph was put in jail. Soon the jail was left in his care. It was obvious that he was a prosperous man, that the blessing of God was on this young man. Two of Pharaoh's servants, the butler and baker, were put in jail by the angry sovereign. They had dreams and Joseph, with the Spirit of God upon him, revealed their dreams: one was to be restored to power and the other was to be executed. It happened as he had prophesied.

Two years later Pharaoh had dreams of seven fine fat cattle down on the bank of the Nile; they were followed by seven scrawny, ill-favored cattle that swallowed them up and were no better yet! What did it mean? In another dream seven fat ears of grain were swallowed up by seven scrawny, withered ears that were no good. What did it mean?

The butler remembered how the hand of God was upon Joseph. So he was brought to Pharaoh and Joseph was able to tell Pharaoh the meaning of the dreams. God meant it for good—there would be seven years of plenty and seven years of famine. But who would organize the people, save up the surplus crops and so keep the people through seven terrible years of famine? Pharaoh knew at once that here was the man for him, with wisdom and the blessing of God. So Joseph became prime minister.

We remember how his brothers came down from famine-stricken Palestine to buy grain in Egypt. We know how he knew them, how he first kept Simeon prisoner, then demanded to see Benjamin. Eventually he revealed that he was their brother and he sent for Jacob. Jacob and the family came down to Egypt for the long sojourn till God should deliver the nation Israel under Moses.

What a charming, blessed story of how God was with Joseph! He was one of three Jewish men of whom it is recorded that they each went into a foreign nation a captive, and, by their character and the blessing of God, were led into places of great usefulness.

After Joseph there came the time when Daniel was carried captive into Babylon and came to be there next to Nebuchadnezzar, and finally, under Darius the Median, president or the chief of the presidents of the counsel.

Then there came a time when the Jew Mordecai, in the reign of Ahasuerus in Babylon, rose to power and led in the overthrow of Haman's wicked plot to kill all the Jews, and then became in political power next to the king himself.

I. JOSEPH HATED BY BROTHERS

There may have been a number of reasons for the hatred of the brothers who plotted to kill Joseph and then after protests by Judah and Reuben, was sold into slavery in Egypt.

1. Brothers Jealous of Joseph

"And when his brethren saw that their father loved him more than all his brethren, they hated him, and could not speak peaceably unto him" (Gen. 37:4). Joseph was the son of Jacob's old age, and Jacob made him a coat of many colors and loved him "more than all his children."

This jealousy was principally by the sons of the two slave wives, Bilhah and Zilpah. Joseph was with Dan and Naphtali, Bilhah's sons, and with Gad and Asher, sons of Zilpah.

It was natural that the children of these bondservant wives, or concubines, not equal to Rachel and Leah—whose maidservants they were—would feel inferior and jealous. We can remember how Hagar, Abraham's servant wife, and her son Ishmael, were jealous when Isaac was born to Sarah, Hagar's mistress. She rebelled and ran away and then came back and when the boy Ishmael mocked at the baby Isaac, they were sent away again. Note that both Reuben and Judah, Leah's sons, tried to save Joseph from the wrath of the other brothers. Those two bondwomen, maidservants to Leah and Rachel, were wives but in a sense second-rate wives, and their jealousy was some way imbibed by their sons who also felt their inferior standing to Joseph and perhaps to Benjamin.

2. Inevitably There Was Friction Between Older and Younger Brothers

Joseph, the beloved of the father, was sent to check on the flocks, herds and the work of these brothers. Genesis 37:2 tells us how he was with the sons of Bilhah and Zilpah, "and Joseph brought unto his father their evil report."

Does it mean they had been lazy in camp in taking care of the flocks? Did beasts of prey take some animals they left unguarded? The report was an "evil report," so they hated Joseph and would not speak peaceably unto him.

3. A Spiritual Barrier Between Older and Younger

Joseph had dreams that he and his brothers shocked wheat together. Their shocks of wheat bowed before his. He dreamed that eleven stars bowed to his star, as well as the sun and moon. Obviously God intended to set his dreams going about a future of usefulness. But his brothers hated the idea that he should ever have pre-eminence over them.

Besides that, they evidently were not good men, nor spiritual. And it was obvious that God was with Joseph, and Joseph knew it.

Not only the sons of the two bondwomen, but no doubt Leah's sons also were jealous. They were not spiritual men. In a murderous rage over their sister Dinah, Simeon and Levi had deceived and then killed a whole town of men at Shechem. Judah later committed adultery with Tamar, his daughter-in-law. Reuben committed adultery with the bondwoman Bilhah, Jacob's slave wife or concubine. And the character of the four sons of Bilhah and Zilpah was shown in their determination to murder Joseph.

So there was not a spiritual kinship between Joseph and the older brothers. Joseph was on the side of the Lord. He sought the will of God and had God's blessings. That made him all the more hateful to these men.

It seems that the hand of God was on the boy Joseph even when he was only seventeen and showed him he would one day rule.

When we follow Joseph in Egypt, we see he would not be seduced by Potiphar's wife; we see that God was with him. God revealed His will to Joseph always. Joseph prospered in whatever he did. So it is clear that Joseph was a godly man.

We can see that the brothers had been jealous over Jacob's love for Joseph, which love and trust seems to have been honestly deserved by this young man.

So we believe the brothers hated him because he was good, even as Cain, the carnal and wicked son of Adam, hated Abel, his righteous and godly brother, the one called a prophet of God (Luke 11:50,51). Joseph's brothers hated him, and between the lines we see God taking Joseph's side.

II. JOSEPH IN GOD'S WILL, WITH GOD'S CONSTANT BLESSING

Joseph is sometimes spoken of as a type of Christ. Of him and Daniel it has been well said that it is difficult to find a single record of any of their sins and failures. God was with Joseph.

1. How Did Joseph Know About God?

There was no written Bible in those days, but God had made

many precious promises with Abraham. Through Abraham there should come a multitude of seed as the sand of the sea for multitude, and spiritual descendants as the stars of the sky. And through him would come blessing to the world.

God had even revealed to Abraham the coming of the Saviour, the Christ, for Jesus said, "Abraham rejoiced to see my day: and he saw it, and was glad" (John 8:56). We know that Abraham was converted: ". . . he believed in the Lord; and he counted it to him for righteousness" (Gen. 15:6). Romans 4:3 also tells us Abraham was converted, saved by grace, and thus is a pattern for New Testament Christians. Abraham, who faithfully worshiped God and met Him in a secret place again and again, had left a great imprint on Isaac and other descendants.

God had made the same covenant with Isaac, then repeated that covenant with Jacob more than once. He had called Jacob back to Bethel and they all went back there to worship at that place which Jacob had called "the house of God." And no doubt Jacob had offered sacrifices because he had promised God, ". . . of all that thou shalt give me I will surely give the tenth unto thee." From Genesis 49:8-10 we see that Jacob knew about the coming of the Messiah, "Shiloh," and he spoke as a prophet of God. We can be sure that of the traditions, down from the time of Eden when God said to the serpent, "I will put enmity between thee and the woman, and between thy seed and her seed; it shall bruise thy head, and thou shalt bruise his heel," people learn from their fathers and by tradition handed down about God's dealings, God's prophecies and the future He had planned of the coming Messiah through Abraham's seed.

2. Then as Now, God Loved Men and Met All Who Sought His Face

When Cornelius sought the face of God and had no Bible, God sent an angel to tell him where to find a messenger, and so Cornelius heard the Gospel and was saved, and also his family (Acts 10).

The Bible promises, "Draw nigh to God, and he will draw nigh to you." And that was true before it was written in our Bible.

"For God so loved the world, that he gave his only begotten Son
. . ."; but that was true about God long before John 3:16 was
written, and Jesus is "the Lamb slain from the foundation of the
world." We may be sure that God did not leave Himself without
a witness and that every hungry heart that sought Him could
find Him.

In Romans 10:13 we are told, "For whosoever shall call upon
the name of the Lord shall be saved." Whatever limitations there
were in men's knowledge of God, yet men could find God, could
get forgiveness of sins, and could have God's favor. We know that
Joseph did know about God and did find His favor. God, who
had revealed Himself to Abraham and to Isaac and to Jacob, did
not leave the boy Joseph without light in the dark and without a
knowledge of God and the way to peace and forgiveness.

3. We Believe Joseph Was a Born-Again Christian

We know Abraham was saved. We know that by faith
righteous Abel offered a more excellent sacrifice than Cain, and
so he knew about the coming Saviour and was accepted of God
and is named one of the heroes of the faith in Hebrews 11.

In Romans, chapter 2, we find that God watches carefully and
"will render to every man according to his deeds," and to those
who do well and seek God, He gives "glory and honour and immortality, eternal life" (Rom. 2:7). And we learn that those who
do not have the law have their conscience to judge them and
teach them. One could not be saved without the Gospel, but
whatever Gospel Joseph needed it was revealed to him through
the teaching God had given Abraham, Isaac and Jacob and the
teaching God gave to him.

There was no Bible, but God dealt with people and made
Himself known then just the same.

4. Joseph Sought and Earned Blessing of God

Joseph did not earn salvation—nor does anyone else. But he
did earn the favor of God by his deeds.

When God called David to have him anointed as king, who

later was to take the place of King Saul who proved unworthy, Samuel said to him, "But now thy kingdom shall not continue: the Lord hath sought him a man after his own heart, and the Lord hath commanded him to be captain over his people" (I Sam. 13:14). God sought and found one with a heart anxious to please God and so He put His blessing on David and used him.

The prophet of God said to King Asa, "For the eyes of the Lord run to and fro throughout the whole earth, to shew himself strong in the behalf of them whose heart is perfect toward him" (II Chron. 16:9). David had sought God's help when he killed the bear and the lion. David gave God the glory and sought His help when he slew Goliath. Then we dare not think that it was the arbitrary choice of God alone without some fitness on David's part.

Between Jacob and Esau God chose Jacob to be in the ancestral line of Christ, but we must remember that Esau despised his birthright and Jacob sought it earnestly. It was not a whim of God but a proper choice.

So we may be sure that God sought some lad with a heart of devotion, loyalty and character that He could grow, through suffering, trouble, circumstances and trial, into the mighty man who would save millions of lives in the great famine that was to come.

We must remember God's law of sowing and reaping. When Jesus said, "But seek ye first the kingdom of God, and his righteousness; and all these things shall be added unto you" (Matt. 6:33), He expressed a law of God. See Joseph's loyalty to Potiphar, whose slave he was; see his virtue in rejecting all the advances of Potiphar's wife; see his humility in giving God the glory—"Do not interpretations belong to God?" (Gen. 40:8). Then to Pharaoh he said in Genesis 41:16, "It is not in me: God shall give Pharaoh an answer of peace." We must admire his forgiveness and love for his wicked brothers, saying, "Fear not: for am I in the place of God? But as for you, ye thought evil against me; but God meant it unto good, to bring to pass, as it is this day, to save much people alive" (Gen. 50:19,20).

III. GOD USED ENEMIES, TROUBLES, DELAYS FOR GOOD OF JOSEPH AND OTHERS

Life is not a bed of roses for any good one. "All that will live godly in Christ Jesus shall suffer persecution" (II Tim. 3:12). Paul and Barnabas went back to retrace their missionary journey and to teach the young converts "that we must through much tribulation enter into the kingdom of God" (Acts 14:22). Then we should not be surprised when for Joseph or for ourselves God uses some hardship, some trouble, some enemy, some delay, to bring good to us.

In preparing Joseph for great usefulness and happiness, the hand of God is easily seen now. No doubt for Joseph there were years when he had to take these things by faith.

1. Hatred of Brothers Brought Him to Egypt

How Jacob grieved when he thought he had lost Joseph! The brothers brought that bloody garment of many colors which they had dipped in the blood of a kid to pretend that Joseph had been slain. Jacob grieved and grieved. Some of the brothers had wanted to kill Joseph, but God had to intervene, through the protest of Reuben, then through the coming of a Midianite caravan; so he went down to Egypt.

How sad Joseph must have been to be taken from Palestine, away from family, sheep and country, to Egypt, the most powerful nation in the world, and among heathen strangers! But there were millions of people to save in Egypt. The famine would reach all the nations nearby, but only in Egypt would there be a Nile River with millions of acres that could be watered those seven years of plenty.

We learn there was a canal dug for the water of the Nile which approximately doubled the amount of land that could be cultivated and watered. Even today the remnant of it is called "Joseph's Canal," and only in Egypt was a king who could order all the surplus saved through the seven years. So to Egypt went Joseph as a slave.

In Potiphar's house, God had training for Joseph. There he grew and pleased his master. He had more and more of the household affairs. The servants were turned over to him. The business of the home of this important man was in his care. He learned to manage people and money. As a shepherd boy in the fields of Palestine, perhaps he would not have had, working under his brothers, the experience, authority, the solid growth that he had here in Potiphar's house.

2. Wicked Wife of Potiphar Tempted Joseph, Then Falsely Accused Him

Our sense of justice rebels when we see Joseph falsely accused and sent to jail when he was perfectly loyal to his master, clean in his life, and blameless in his behavior. The wicked woman who could not seduce him to adultery now charged him with attempted rape and had him put in jail.

But Potiphar's wife did not know what she did for Joseph. First, the testing not only proved him in character but helped make him the man he ought to be—a mature man for leadership. James 1:2 says, "Count it all joy when ye fall into divers temptations." Perhaps the word "temptation" here has more of the meaning of trial than of being tempted to sin, but the experience of Joseph was both temptation and trial. And God meant it for good. Now his character is somewhat congealed, set, and developed for the decision not to yield to the tempting woman. When he said no that time, he said it for the rest of his life, to this kind of sin.

When Daniel "purposed in his heart that he would not defile himself with the portion of the king's meat, nor with the wine which he drank," he was setting a course of action that would make him bold to continue to pray to the God of Israel when it meant the lions' den. Early fundamental decisions are the stuff of which character is made.

The loyalty of Joseph to his master Potiphar was getting Joseph ready to be loyal to Pharaoh when he would rise to great authority. God was getting him ready.

Jail! In the plan of God? Again he earned and took over leadership in the jail. We are told, ". . . and whatsoever they did there, he was the doer of it" (Gen. 39:22). There is something about his solid character, his eagerness to work, his under-standing of men, his loyalty to authority, that earned him the confidence of jailer and helpers. However wicked people are, they must respect character.

Dr. Bob Jones, Sr., used to say, "You cannot compel love but you can compel respect." So Joseph was soon running things at the jail and proving himself and growing himself for the authority that was to come later.

When one day the butler and baker came under the anger of Pharaoh and were sad about their dreams, Joseph had concern over their sadness. He was something of a chaplain, a father, a spiritual fountain for all with whom he came in contact. God is getting him ready for all the poor famine-stricken people in Egypt to whom he will be physically the lord and saviour in the awful time of need that is ahead.

3. God Allowed Him to Be Forgotten Two More Years

When Joseph was given the answer and the meaning of the dreams of the butler and baker—the butler to be released in three days, the baker to be put to death—he earnestly said to the butler:

> "But think on me when it shall be well with thee and shew kindness, I pray thee, unto me, and make mention of me unto Pharaoh, and bring me out of this house: For indeed I was stolen away out of the land of the Hebrews: and here also have I done nothing that they should put me into the dungeon."—Gen. 40:14,15.

But, alas, verse 23 says that after the baker was hanged and the butler was restored to his job, "yet did not the chief butler remember Joseph, but forgat him."

Alas, how frail are human friendships! One would think the grateful butler would go out of his way to help this good man to be released from false accusation and unearned imprisonment. But no, he forgot!

He forgot because God remembered! There is some maturity that comes with trouble, and God is getting Joseph ready.

A little later when it is time for the seven years of plenty and time for the seven years of famine, God will bring Joseph to the attention of Pharaoh; meantime, he is forgotten.

Let us always remember that when friends forget, God does not! Let us remember that when men do not repay good for good, God always pays back.

When I was an evangelist and having the blessing of God on my ministry, my younger brother, Evangelist Bill Rice, also became an evangelist. Men advised him to set some minimum price per week on his services. (It is true that often pastors and churches do not adequately care for the full-time evangelist.) But I told Bill, and he agreed with me, "Your contract is with the Lord. You must depend on Him. If men do not always treat you well, God will see that you get what you need and what you deserve. Your contract is with Him."

How often God has proved it to me and to my brother and to others.

So here, with Joseph in prison and the butler forgetting his intention to help him, Joseph still languished in prison. As he ran things there he wondered, "What will the future be?" But it takes years to grow a great oak. And God is now growing a tree, Joseph, to be king of the forest.

Country hams grow better when they are cured long.

Years ago I conducted a citywide revival campaign in Winston-Salem, North Carolina, with forty or more churches involved, in the Liberty Warehouse seating thousands. I was invited to breakfast with Dr. B. H. Stevens, then president of Piedmont College and pastor of the Salem Baptist Church. What a fine breakfast we had—hot biscuits, country-cured ham, eggs, grits, honey with the hot, buttered biscuits! I enjoyed it so much that Dr. Stevens took me to his basement to see country hams hanging there, some for two years!

But if it takes time to cure a ham in the traditional country fashion, it takes time for God to cure a man into what he ought to be.

God took plenty of time to ripen David for the kingdom with years of serving, then fleeing from Saul when in danger of his life!

Abraham and Sarah had long years of prayer, waiting and

testing before they were ready to receive the baby Isaac, long promised but not given until Abraham was one hundred and Sarah was ninety!

Moses matured for forty long years in the wilderness by tending sheep, before God sent him to deliver Israel. Some would have thought eighty years was too late to begin, but God knew.

4. Sorrow, Poverty, Enslavement Built Joseph's Character

No doubt Joseph grieved for his father Jacob and his brother Benjamin. His mother was dead. We know something of how Joseph felt when they were threatening to kill him, then when he was sold as a slave to the Midianites going down to Egypt. Would he ever see his father again? How would he fare among these heathen people of another race, country and language? He protested and pleaded so earnestly that those wicked brethren had it on their conscience long later. After twenty or twenty-one years, they still remembered their sin; now when they face the stern prime minister in Egypt, they do not know it is their brother. But we read in Genesis 42:21,22:

> "And they said one to another, We are verily guilty concerning our brother, in that we saw the anguish of his soul, when he besought us, and we would not hear; therefore is this distress come upon us. And Reuben answered them, saying, Spake I not unto you, saying, Do not sin against the child; and ye would not hear? therefore, behold, also his blood is required."

Oh, he had pleaded!

How indignant he must have felt at the false accusations! But since he was to be greatly exalted, he first must be abased. Like the Apostle Paul, he must have a "thorn in the flesh" or the equivalent, or at least sorrow and limitation and delay, because "tribulation worketh patience; and patience, experience" (Rom. 5:3,4).

Joseph, since you must rule over a nation of poor and troubled people, you too must be poor, you too must be the underdog, you too must be helpless until God opens the right door and raises you up.

Sorrow is often of God. It is one of the schools through which God puts the choicest servant. It is one way that the dross is melted out of the gold and one is humbled and taught compassion.

My mother died when I was less than six years old. Without a mother, how many times in the rough West Texas country I grieved and thought, "I could have been a better man had my godly mother lived!" When Mother's Day came, I would wear a white flower and spend a lonely day realizing my loss. I did not know that God was preparing me to minister to multitudes.

Oh, how many deathbeds, how many open graves have I stood by! How many broken homes have I tried to mend! How many drunkards and fallen women have I told that the mercy of God offers peace and pardon! How long have I held open wide the door of salvation for sinners and pleaded with them to come! I know God has given me some compassion. I thank God that I early learned to weep.

Dr. George W. Truett had a heart-breaking tragedy. His dearest friend was the Dallas Chief of Police. Once they went hunting together. Going through a fence, I believe, the gun was accidentally discharged and his friend was killed. Oh, it put long pain into his heart, pathos into his magnificent voice, and a seriousness and compassion that all who knew him felt.

Charles H. Spurgeon once preached in Surrey Music Garden in London when some 22,000 people crowded to hear him. Oh, he might have been greatly exalted but some fool in jest cried, "Fire!" and a plunging, frightened tumult came as people tried to flee. Some were trampled to death in that useless and foolish tragedy. Spurgeon was so broken by it that his mind tottered for days. He thought at first he could never preach again! But God puts gold through the flames to refine it.

Joseph, opportunities, obligations, powers are coming to you that no normal man would be ready for. Do not hasten, then, to possess the land. Joseph, you must be fit to govern all Egypt. The lives of multitudes in Egypt and in many nations are to be in your hand.

Let us not be impatient, then, when God gets Joseph ready

with serious schooling. In many cases, it takes years, and sorrow, and poverty, and misunderstanding, and suffering to make us fit for what God wants us to do.

IV. LESSON FOR ALL IN LIFE OF JOSEPH

In these beautiful fourteen chapters closing the book of Genesis, God has surely many blessings for us. This is the inspired Word of God. Not only is it a most charming story but it is rich with meaning for the humble heart who observes and meditates on these Scriptures.

1. Character, Righteousness Certain to Receive Reward

Remember, God is a just God, and He does not forget His own who serve Him.

What a clean and godly man was Joseph! He would not listen to the temptress. He could have been resentful of his master Potiphar and eager to take advantage of him. This young man would have the normal pressure of sex attraction and desire. We suppose Potiphar's wife was young and attractive, too; but Joseph felt he must do right. The fact that he snatched himself away and ran, leaving his garment, would indicate that the temptation was great and he feared it. But God must reward that virtue, and God will.

How gently Joseph forgave his brothers who had nursed murder in their hearts and sold him as a slave! Resentment would be normal; forgiveness and gentleness here are great marks of godly character.

He was humble. He gave God the glory for God's interpretation of the dreams for the butler and baker and Pharaoh. He said, "God shall give Pharaoh an answer of peace." He knew his circumstances were controlled of God, and he said to his brethren in Genesis 45:5, "Now therefore be not grieved, nor angry with yourselves, that ye sold me hither: for God did send me before you to preserve life." And in the same chapter, in verse 8, "So now it was not you that sent me hither, but God: and he hath made me a father to Pharaoh, and lord of all his house, and a ruler throughout all the land of Egypt."

He knew his life was in the hand of God. How happy is the Christian who knows that and relies upon it!

So we learn that God cares for His own. The sower is certain to reap. Those who "seek . . . first the kingdom of God, and his righteousness" will have all they need supplied according to the promise in Matthew 6:33.

2. God's Answer Comes in Plenty of Time

Oh, Joseph may have been greatly vexed and impatient in his heart many a time in those long years while he waited for his release and exaltation. How could we blame him if he thought the years were going by and he had no home, had no future and was only a slave, falsely accused and in jail! But God always does things in plenty of time.

We remember that the young King Saul was impatient when the Philistines were threatening Israel, the people were going away from him, as he waited for Samuel. After seven days he precipitately offered a sacrifice himself. He must surely get some answer from God, and right now!

But he was not a priest. He had no authority to offer sacrifices. It was forbidden. And when it was done, Samuel arrived. In I Samuel 13:13,14, Samuel rebuked Saul:

> "And Samuel said to Saul, Thou hast done foolishly: thou hast not kept the commandment of the Lord thy God, which he commanded thee: for now would the Lord have established thy kingdom upon Israel for ever. But now thy kingdom shall not continue: the Lord hath sought him a man after his own heart, and the Lord hath commanded him to be captain over his people, because thou hast not kept that which the Lord commanded thee."

Abraham was so anxious for a son. God had promised him that through this son all the nations of the earth should be blessed, and surely he knew that meant the coming Messiah. But Sarah was barren after long years of prayer. Now Sarah was past the child-bearing age. So she and Abraham agreed he would take the slave girl Hagar as a wife and perhaps God would count the child of this union as the promised son! So Hagar bare Ishmael, and these two became thorns in the sight of Abraham and Sarah. God would not count Ishmael the promised son through whom the Messiah would come to bless all nations. And how surprised were Sarah and Abraham when God made Sarah young again; and at ninety was able to bare the child Isaac! They ran ahead of God. God's plane always comes in on schedule. Not our schedule, but God's!

Dr. Ian Paisley, pastor of Martyr's Memorial Presbyterian Church in Belfast, Ireland, was sent to jail for having public meetings in that strife-ridden North Ireland. In jail he wrote a commentary on Romans. But in due season he was released. The people rallied to him. He was elected to the Parliament of North Ireland and then to the House of Commons in the Parliament of Great Britain, representing Ireland! Oh, if he were willing to wait, God had the time of vindication and help.

Oh, Joseph, do not fret, for "in due season we shall reap, if we faint not." Godly sowing is followed with godly reaping (Gal. 6:9).

3. Compassion of God for Troubled People Shows in Life of Joseph

Oh, it is obvious that God looked upon Joseph with tender compassion when he was hated by his brethren. God gave him dreams of the future. When he was in Potiphar's house, God prospered him as a slave. When he was put in jail, God was with him there. And in due time the pity of God for troubled hearts was shown and He gave great advancement and blessing to Joseph.

We note the kindness of God to Joseph's brothers. These wicked men came to humiliation! Oh, yes! They had times of great anxiety as they faced the stern, young prime minister and remembered their sins. Yes, but remember they had forgiveness both from Joseph and from God. They had comfort and food and homes provided for them and their families. God is great to forgive sins. "He will not always chide: neither will he keep his anger for ever. He hath not dealt with us after our sins; nor rewarded us according to our iniquities" (Ps. 103:9,10).

And then how great was the mercy of God on all the people saved from the famine! The tender heart of God cared about hungry children and desperate men who wondered what would become of their families. He cared about those in foreign countries and had them come to Egypt. He had Joseph help the people lay by enough so there would be food for famine years. God had compassion then as He does now. He who notes the fall of every sparrow and clothes every wild flower has compassion on His people.

We find that Jesus "was moved with compassion on them, because they fainted, and were scattered abroad, as sheep having no shepherd" (Matt. 9:36).

4. In Joseph, Prophecy Was Fulfilled

God had revealed to Abraham the time of Israel's sojourn in Egypt in Genesis 15:13: "And he said unto Abram, Know of a surety that thy seed shall be a stranger in a land that is not their's, and shall serve them; and they shall afflict them four hundred years." That four hundred years, from the time of Abraham to the exodus under Moses, was foretold, and it included Jacob and his family down in Egypt where eventually they were all enslaved when a king arose who knew not Joseph.

God had long-range plans and they were being fulfilled.

5. Let Us Come With Holy Joy to Serve Such a God!

The story of Joseph makes sure that it is worthwhile to serve God. Always those who please Him turn out well. And let every man in his heart feel a holy allegiance and glad joy to resist temptation, to forgive enemies, to make good where you are, to be patient in trouble, until God works out His perfect plan in each life.

3

Moses, Man of God

It is very difficult to judge the comparative greatness of men in the Bible. Jesus said that never was greater man born of woman than John the Baptist (Matt. 11:11).

To Ezekiel, pleading for wicked Israel, God said that though Noah, Daniel and Job were to intercede, He would not hear their prayer for these, which indicates that in God's sight these three were very great men of prayer, great men of holiness and righteousness.

But Moses stands out with many amazing characteristics. He was the divinely-inspired author of the first five books in the Bible. He led the children of Israel out of Egypt and for forty years in the wilderness. God gave him all the ceremonial laws, the priesthood, the Tabernacle, the furniture and the ordinances.

It is the blasphemy of infidels to mock at Moses as the author of the Pentateuch. For years they even said that Moses couldn't even write. Then came an infidel doctor, Astruc, associate of harlots and other wicked doers in France, who formed the opinion that the books of Genesis, Exodus, Leviticus, Numbers and Deuteronomy were a hodge-podge collected from oral tradition, handed down by word of mouth, then written by a number of various authors, and that some holy hypocrite of an "adapter" or editor had gathered these fragments together and made them into a whole and that they were perhaps written about the time of the captivity of Israel! That is silly. The Graff-Wellhausen group decided they could figure, by the terms used for God and such things, what part was written by a certain priestly group and what part by other writers.

In the first place, the infidels are not scholarly. That foolish theory has been proven false by Allis in *The Five Books of Moses*, and by many other scholarly writers.

But we don't need to try to find proof that Moses wrote these books. Again and again in the New Testament, Jesus referred to these first five books in the Bible and said, "Moses said . . . ." He said that many times referring to all the books of the Pentateuch as the writings of Moses. (See Mark 7:10; 10:3; 12:20; John 3:14; 5:45; 7:19.) Honest Christians who believe the Bible, believe that.

I. CONSIDER DISTINCTIONS THAT MEASURE MOSES' GREATNESS

1. He is named 658 times in the Old Testament and 78 times in the New Testament. Only David is mentioned more times in the Bible—972 times; Abram about 320 times; Paul some 162 times. Checking the number of pages in a Bible without notes, I find that Moses was inspired to write 189 pages, with Luke giving only 63½ pages; John with the Gospel, Revelation and the three letters, only 44 pages. All the epistles written by the Apostle Paul, including Hebrews, whose authorship some question, have only 66½ pages.

2. Moses seemed to be on a more intimate relationship with God and for longer periods than any other man. He spent forty days in Mount Sinai with the Lord once, then forty days more. He talked to God face to face, not by parables nor with intermediaries. His face glowed as he came down from the mount and from the presence of God, a little like the face of Jesus glowed in the book of Revelation when John fell at His feet as dead.

3. The miracles God worked at the hand of Moses are beyond number. Count all those plagues in Egypt, count the giving of the Law, instruction about the ceremonies, about the priesthood, the Tabernacle, the sacrifices, the moral laws. The divine revelation and supernatural expression of God's power and miracles appeared more often with Moses than with any other man mentioned in the Bible.

4. He took a race of slaves and made them into a nation with God's leadership. He was with them forty years and he had the power of a dictator, power of life and death. He was in a far more

definite way the father of the nation Israel than was George Washington the father of his country.

5. But Moses is a type and likeness of Jesus Christ. The Lord promised him, "The Lord thy God will raise up unto thee a Prophet from the midst of thee, of thy brethren, like unto me; unto him ye shall hearken" (Deut. 18:15). We are not told that anyone else was particularly to be a likeness of Jesus.

1. God's Care in Moses' Birth, Preservation, Rearing

It is a wonderful story in Exodus 2:1-10, and we give it here in the very words of Scripture:

> "And there went a man of the house of Levi, and took to wife a daughter of Levi. And the woman conceived, and bare a son: and when she saw him that he was a goodly child, she hid him three months. And when she could not longer hide him, she took for him an ark of bulrushes, and daubed it with slime and with pitch, and put the child therein; and she laid it in the flags by the river's brink. And his sister stood afar off, to wit what would be done to him. And the daughter of Pharaoh came down to wash herself at the river; and her maidens walked along by the river's side; and when she saw the ark among the flags, she sent her maid to fetch it. And when she had opened it, she saw the child: and, behold, the babe wept. And she had compassion on him, and said, This is one of the Hebrews' children. Then said his sister to Pharaoh's daughter, Shall I go and call to thee a nurse of the Hebrew women, that she may nurse the child for thee? And Pharaoh's daughter said to her, Go. And the maid went and called the child's mother. And Pharaoh's daughter said unto her, Take this child away, and nurse it for me, and I will give thee thy wages. And the woman took the child, and nursed it. And the child grew, and she brought him unto Pharaoh's daughter, and he became her son. And she called his name Moses: and she said, Because I drew him out of the water."

There had risen a king who knew not Joseph. The marvelous

way God had preserved the nation in time of famine through that Hebrew was not now appreciated. The Israelites had multiplied until now they were counted a menace by the rulers. What if all these Jews, so thrifty, so hard working, should rebel or betray them to outside enemies? And the natural hatred that worldly people have for the people of God no doubt made them envious of the Jews. So the Jews were made slaves.

But since the children of Israel multiplied so rapidly, Pharaoh passed a law that Jewish boy babies were to be put to death by the midwives. But God put it in the heart of the midwives to make excuses, and some boy babies who were born were preserved.

When Moses was born, his mother saw "that he was a goodly child." I wonder, did she not have in her heart some inkling, some moving of the Spirit of God, showing her that her prayers were answered and that God would use this lad? She hid the child for three months and then, no doubt, after prayer, she committed him to a little ark of bulrushes daubed with pitch so as to be leak proof, and committed him to the River Nile, hiding him among the bulrushes. And there Pharaoh's daughter, coming to bathe, heard the cry of the little one, which cry God used to reach her heart.

So she reared the child as her own, and God provided it so his mother could be his nurse. We do not know all the details, but the character of Moses must have been largely built by the teaching and ministration of this mother who acted as nurse, although Moses was counted legally the son of Pharaoh's daughter!

We remember the mighty influence of the mother and grandmother of Timothy and that through them he learned the Holy Scriptures (II Tim. 1:5). I have no doubt that the godly influence of Hannah on Samuel, and of Elisabeth on John the Baptist, was here repeated in the influence of this good woman who, by faith, saw that her boy lived and was reared. Hebrews 11:23 says, "By faith Moses, when he was born, was hid three months of his parents, because they saw he was a proper child; and they were not afraid of the king's commandment." That faith of godly parents was back of the great man that Moses became under God's blessing.

2. "When He Was Come to Years"

When Moses was forty years old, there came a great time of decision and realigning of his life's purposes.

Spirit-filled Deacon Stephen says much about Moses in Acts 7. There he reminded the Jews that in rejecting Christ they were following the willful sinfulness of the nation Israel and were rejecting the teaching of God through Moses when they rejected Jesus. And he tells us of the baby Moses,

> *"Pharaoh's daughter took him up, and nourished him for her own son. And Moses was learned in all the wisdom of the Egyptians, and was mighty in words and in deeds. And when he was full forty years old, it came into his heart to visit his brethren the children of Israel. And seeing one of them suffer wrong, he defended him, and avenged him that was oppressed, and smote the Egyptian: For he supposed his brethren would have understood how that God by his hand would deliver them: but they understood not. And the next day he shewed himself unto them as they strove, and would have set them at one again, saying, Sirs, ye are brethren; why do ye wrong one to another? But he that did his neighbour wrong thrust him away, saying, Who made thee a ruler and a judge over us? Wilt thou kill me, as thou diddest the Egyptian yesterday? Then fled Moses at this saying, and was a stranger in the land of Madian, where he begat two sons."*—Acts 7:21-29.

Hebrews 11:24-27 tells us of this great time of crisis in the life of Moses, "when he was come to years." Stephen says that was when he was forty years old.

Exodus does not tell us all that was in the mind of Moses. But here we learn that he had deliberately chosen to turn his back on the riches and culture of Egypt, on his position in the king's household. Perhaps he even turned away from the possibility that one day he would take the throne as Pharaoh of Egypt. No!

He "refused to be called the son of Pharaoh's daughter." He told the people plainly that he was an Hebrew and not of the Egyptian race and not of the Egyptian religion. He rather chose "to suffer affliction with the people of God, than to enjoy the pleasures of sin for a season."

We can understand how Moses looked with sorrow on these, his own people whom he now openly acknowledged as his own, being oppressed as slaves in Egypt. And when an Egyptian oppressed a Jew, Moses intervened and killed the Egyptian. But the Jews were jealous of him. He had grown up in the palace. He was accustomed to riches. He was no slave, as they were. He was a man of culture and learning and not of their class of learning and possessions. They doubted him, and Pharaoh would have killed him had he not fled. Although Moses had hid the slain Egyptian in the sand, it was widely known and "when Pharaoh heard this thing, he sought to slay Moses. But Moses fled from the face of Pharaoh, and dwelt in the land of Midian" (Exod. 2:15).

Here we learn from Hebrews more explicitly the spiritual experience of Moses. When he turned back to be an Hebrew and openly avowed his connection with the race of slaves, he turned to Israel's God, too. He chose "to suffer affliction with the people of God." He regarded joys of the life as an Egyptian prince as the life with "the pleasures of sin," and so he renounced them.

Better than that, we are told that he esteemed "the reproach of Christ greater riches than the treasures in Egypt: for he had respect unto the recompence of the reward."

How much did Moses know about the Saviour? Well, he knew about the "reproach of Christ." He knew that the Saviour was coming. That means he had learned the promises God gave Abraham, Isaac and Jacob. He knew that Greater Son of Abraham who would come. And we are sure that when God gave Israel the passover forty years later, Moses knew the meaning of the blood, of the slain lamb, "for . . . Christ our passover is sacrificed for us" (I Cor. 5:7).

But Moses would now have delivered Israel if he could. That was in his heart but they would not unite under him. They were

hardened in heart. It would take miracles before they would
believe Moses would have the power to break the rule of Pharaoh
and deliver this whole race of slaves from their hard masters!
"For he supposed his brethren would have understood how that
God by his hand would deliver them: but they understood not"
(Acts 7:25).

No, first Moses must go to the backside of the desert of Midian, and Acts 7:30 says, "When forty years were expired," God
appeared to him in a flaming bush in the desert.

But why must forty years expire before the deliverance?

God had planned the thing out and said to Abram in Genesis
15:13,14:

> "Know of a surety that thy seed shall be a stranger in a
> land that is not their's, and shall serve them; and they
> shall afflict them four hundred years; And also that na-
> tion, whom they shall serve, will I judge: and afterward
> shall they come out with great substance."

So the four hundred years must be fulfilled before Israel comes
out of Egypt. And Exodus 12:40,41 tells us:

> "Now the sojourning of the children of Israel, who
> dwelt in Egypt, was four hundred and thirty years. And
> it came to pass at the end of the four hundred and thirty
> years, even the selfsame day it came to to pass, that all
> the hosts of the Lord went out from the land of Egypt."

We believe that the 430 years began with the wanderings of
Abraham as a sojourner in the land of promise. Then the promise
to Abraham was made thirty years later, that the affliction of the
Israelites would last for 400 years. So God had a timetable and
Moses could not deliver the people until forty years more had
passed.

II. FAMILY OF MOSES

He was of the tribe of Levi and descended from Kohath and
Amram. It appears from Exodus 1 that Kohath was a son and
Amram a grandson and Moses was simply a great grandson of
Levi. We take that literally. Some think that "son of Levi" here

simply means a man of the tribe of Levi, a descendant of Levi, even as Jesus is called "son of David," though many generations removed. But in Genesis 15:16 God had promised that "in the fourth generation" Israel would come out of Egypt, so that means Kohath was literally a son of Levi.

Moses grew up in luxury in the royal family and was counted the son of Pharaoh's daughter. He was a great man in Egypt. But up until he was forty years old he had not married. We can imagine that he felt so different from the riches and royal family of Egypt and so out of touch with his own race of Jews, that it was not convenient for him to fall in love and marry. At any rate, not until he ran for his life into the desert was he given Zipporah, the daughter of Jethro, priest of Midian, as a wife. There are four names given for Moses' father-in-law—Jethro, Hobab, Ruel and Raguel—but we suppose it was the same man with different names.

Moses and Zipporah had two children, Gershom and Eliezer. Zipporah seemed to have been out of sympathy with the requirement that Moses' two boys must be circumcised (Exod. 4:24-26). We suppose Moses had insisted and she had refused until finally God brought the thing to a head, and to save his life, she had the boys-circumcised, though she did not like it.

She did not go with Moses in the exodus, but later in Exodus 18 we find that Jethro brought the wife and the two boys to meet Moses in the wilderness.

Nothing important is ever mentioned about these boys, except their names are given and then later they are mentioned in the genealogy in Chronicles. Isn't it strange that the greatest man of the age, Moses, did not have a son who would serve God with vigor and have great usefulness?

We do not know what became of Zipporah. Later, "Miriam and Aaron spake against Moses because of the Ethiopian woman whom he had married . . ." (Num. 12:1). Moses had married an Ethiopian woman! She is evidently not the same as Zipporah, for Zipporah was of the Midianites, descended from Midian, son of Abraham, by his wife Keturah. An Ethiopian would be descended, we suppose from Ham and not from the Semites, as was Abraham. It may be that Zipporah died or that she went back with her father again. Or it is possible that Moses took another wife at the same time.

You remember that Jacob had two full wives and two wives of lesser official standing. Abraham had at the same time Sarah and Hagar as his wives. Moses may have taken an Ethiopian wife alongside Zipporah. At any rate, he was criticised for it. She may have been black, we do not know, but she was a Cushite or descended from Ham, no doubt.

We get the impression that Moses did not spend a great deal of time with his family. He was so absorbed in God's work. And he would be with God forty days at a time. The rest of the time he was so wrapped up in serving God and in ruling the people that we suppose he had not much of a home life. And so it is not surprising that his boys did not turn out to be greatly used men of God.

We remember that Jesus said, "If any man come to me, and hate not his father, and mother, and wife, and children, and brethren, and sisters, yea, and his own life also, he cannot be my disciple" (Luke 14:26). There is a sense in which the more attention a man gives to God in full-time service, the less attention he may give to his family.

It is not surprising that Daniel was not married. We suppose he was a eunuch, either voluntarily or made so because he was a captive and brought to serve the king of Babylon. It seems that Paul the apostle never chose marriage. He was wrapped up in God's business.

I have often felt that one who gives himself wholly to God is thus less occupied with marriage and family; and while he may be a good man and do his duty by his family, he is not likely to give as much time to it as other good men might.

I started out as an evangelist, but I soon found that I was so absorbed in God's work and had to be away from home much of the time. It has turned out that thirty or thirty-five years of my married life I have been away from wife and children. Oh, I did what I could. I wrote letters. I loved them and taught them, and God wonderfully helped. But I felt then and I feel now that since I could not be at home to give the attention that a boy would need to make him a great, good man, God chose to give me six girls, and I was reconciled and happy with His plan.

III. MOSES, GREAT MAN OF CHARACTER

1. Moses Is Called the Meekest Man Who Ever Lived (Num. 12:3)

He did not feel capable of leading the children of Israel out of bondage. He complained to God that he could not speak well. Although, as God's mighty prophet and judge, he had the power of life and death over perhaps 600,000 people, there was a singular compassion, justice and unselfishness in the way he ruled. He was a meek man. Considering the enormous pressure on him continually in serving the Lord, in teaching God's people and rebuking their sins and interceding for them, it is not surprising that once he lost his temper. And when God had told him to speak to the rock, he smote it violently in anger and called the people rebels. For that he missed going into the land of Canaan. Despite this error, God's estimate of him was right. It is clearly given—he was a man of great meekness of character.

2. His Love for Israel Was Great

We can be sure that as the young prince of the house of Pharaoh went among the people and saw one man wrong another, he interceded in lovingkindness. When he saw an Egyptian oppressing a Jew, he killed the Egyptian and hid his body in the sand. He wanted to deliver his people then.

And what an intercessor he was for Israel! One of the most moving things in all the Bible is that time when he came down from Mount Sinai with the tables of law in his hand and found the people naked and dancing around a golden calf as an idol, worshiping in their drunkenness and revelry. His heart was so broken that he cast the tables of stone to the ground. And those commandments, so broken spiritually, now had the stone broken on which they were written.

When God told Moses that he should step aside and let Him

destroy these rebellious, wicked people, Moses pleaded. God offered to take Moses and his family and start again to make a great nation from whom the Messiah would come through them, but Moses refused.

Moses brought judgment on those rebels and called the sons of Levi to his side and they went each man with his sword through the camp to slay each their brother, companion and neighbor and "there fell of the people that day about three thousand men." Then Moses spoke to the people and went to make intercession. In Exodus 32:30-33 we find the plea of Moses:

"And it came to pass on the morrow, that Moses said unto the people, Ye have sinned a great sin: and now I will go up unto the Lord; peradventure I shall make an atonement for your sin. And Moses returned unto the Lord, and said, Oh, this people have sinned a great sin, and have made them gods of gold. Yet now, if thou wilt forgive their sin—; and if not, blot me, I pray thee, out of thy book which thou hast written. And the Lord said unto Moses, Whosoever hath sinned against me, him will I blot out of my book."

What loving intercession! And yet with what holy boldness and rigor did he lead the people, punish and then intercede for them!

3. Moses, a Type of Jesus Christ

It is strange that the Lord said Moses was inspired to write in Deuteronomy 18:15, "The Lord thy God will raise up unto thee a Prophet from the midst of thee, of thy brethren, like unto me; unto him ye shall hearken." Again verse 18 says, "I will raise them up a Prophet from among their brethren, like unto thee, and will put my words in his mouth; and he shall speak unto them all that I shall command him." So Moses was a likeness, a prefigure of the Saviour in some wonderful sense. When they came to ask John the Baptist if he was not the Messiah, if he was not Elias, if he was not "that prophet," they must have referred to this great prophecy that the Messiah would be like Moses.

IV. MOSES, A GREAT CHRISTIAN

I mean he was a born-again child of God, he knew about the Saviour who was to come and trusted Him. Moses was a great Christian.

1. All the Types God Gave Moses Were Surely Understood

All the types that God gave through Moses would surely be understood somewhat by such a spiritual man. Jesus spoke to people in parables, and spiritually-minded people were to get the meaning of the parables while they would be meaningless to the careless, the indifferent and the cold-hearted. We may be sure that Moses was not cold-hearted nor careless.

How could he hear and give the teaching about the passover supper and the blood on the door without knowing that that passover lamb was to be a picture of the Saviour? A male lamb of the first year, roasted with fire, without water, and eaten with bitter herbs and all at one time on the passover night—what a picture of the Saviour! Surely no one can doubt that Moses understood that. If Abraham, with so little of type and picture, saw Christ's day and was glad as Jesus said he was, how much more Moses must have known about Christ!

When Moses lifted up the serpent on the pole, he was picturing the crucified Saviour hanging on a cross. He must have noticed that. And whoever looked to that brazen serpent on the pole thus by faith was healed of his snakebite, and so the sinner who looks to Christ in the heart, as bearing our sins, has forgiveness and salvation—I am sure Moses knew that. I am sure Moses was as spiritually-minded and as well informed as any New Testament saint.

When Moses found the people complaining and starving for water in the wilderness, God had him smite a certain rock, a great stone cliff, and out of it gushed a river of water, enough for all these 600,000 people and their cattle—Moses knew that that rock was Christ, the smitten Christ. And we learn in I Corinthians 10:4 that "that spiritual Rock that followed them . . . was Christ." And Moses was impatient and seemed not to have followed the teaching of the Spirit of God that surely must have revealed it to his heart, when in anger he had the rock smitten again instead of speaking to it. Christ needed to die but once.

And then the manna from Heaven—what a miraculous manifestation for forty years! Jesus said that He is the "manna from Heaven," the bread from Heaven! Do you think Moses didn't know that?

Oh, I am sure that Moses was, in these matters, an enlightened Christian, one who understood the Gospel well and trusted himself to the Saviour he preached so well with types and shadows.

2. He Gladly Forsook Egypt to Suffer With the People of God

Moses is held up as one of the great heroes of the faith. "By faith Moses, when he was come to years, refused to be called the son of Pharaoh's daughter; Choosing rather to suffer affliction with the people of God, than to enjoy the pleasures of sin for a season" (Heb. 11:24,25).

Oh, then, no one need think Moses was expelled from Egypt. He went away gladly by his own choice. He who could possibly have had the throne or a place next to the throne, he who was learned in all the learning of the Egyptians—he left it gladly to go into the desert and live with the race of slaves God had chosen and to teach them about God. Notice that Hebrews 11:26-29, speaking of the choice of Moses, says that he was

". . . esteeming the reproach of Christ greater riches than the treasures in Egypt: for he had respect unto the recompence of the reward. By faith he forsook Egypt, not fearing the wrath of the king: for he endured, as seeing him who is invisible. Through faith he kept the passover, and the sprinkling of blood, lest he that destroyed the firstborn should touch them. By faith they passed through the Red sea as by dry land: which the Egyptians assaying to do were drowned."

Oh, he was a man of great faith! But remember, it was the reproach of Christ which he counted great riches. So he knew about Christ and loved and trusted this Saviour yet to come. Moses was a great Christian.

3. The Intimacy That Moses Had With God
Was Wonderful

But it is illustrated much more when Moses came to die. God has preserved him. His eye was not dim, his natural force not abated. But God told him to come up into Mount Nebo and there look across the land of Canaan and see the great land which he could not enter into, and Moses saw it. Then Moses died and God Himself had the angels bury him so no one could ever find the place. We see in Jude 9 that Michael the archangel had to contend with the Devil about the body of Moses. We suppose that Satan wanted to bring the people to see the place. Oh, they would have worshiped that place as an idol, no doubt.

Yes, what a mighty man of God was Moses!

4

The Prophet Samuel

God's Answer to a Barren Woman's Prayer

About eight miles north of Jerusalem at Ramah, the highest mountain or hill in the Jerusalem area, is the tomb of the Prophet Samuel. Samuel was the last of the judges, and was used of God to anoint Saul, the first king, head and shoulders above his people. But Saul failed and then Samuel was sent to anoint David to be king, although he could not ascend the throne until Saul's death.

The character of Samuel shines out with a pureness and steadfast .devotion and continued blessing of God in a most remarkable way. In many ways in his dealings with God, he approached the intimacy that God granted Moses to talk with Him when He spoke to Moses face to face. He was dealt with from his birth in answer to prayer. Even when a little child, he was called by the Lord and given a message of rebuke to Eli over his sons. Of course, the Lord told him ahead of time about Saul, who should come and he would be anointed king. He had revealed from God the manner of the kingdom and warned the people seriously that they should not turn away from the theocracy. He told how Saul would have a new heart, would go out and, strangely, the timid, tall young man would prophecy with the prophets. He had a miraculous sign of thunder and rain in the time of harvest.

Now, this is written in Jerusalem, and no rain is expected here after the first of May until December—but it, as a special sign, was given to Samuel. God told Samuel of Saul's failure and sin and how God had selected another man after His own heart to be king.

Samuel, a Child of Prayer

It is a moving story about Hannah, one of two wives of

Elkanah. The other wife sneered at her because she was barren. With a broken heart she wept and would not eat. And when they went down to the Tabernacle to offer the yearly sacrifice, she was found praying in great distress of soul. The old Prophet Eli thought she was drunken, but she told him that she was a woman of a sorrowful spirit and begging God about a matter. Eli told her that God would grant the request. She went home and conceived and the boy Samuel was born in due time.

How delicately, how earnestly the mother prepared him to serve the Lord! She would not at first take him, with her husband and others, to the sacrifice. She said she would keep him at home until he was weaned. That may have been until he was three or four or six years old or more. (The Hebrew word here means literally "to complete, ripen, wean," says Young's *Concordance.*) At any rate, he was kept at home until the time that he could be taken to the Tabernacle and left there in the care of Eli and the other priests. She said, "I have lent him to the Lord; as long as he liveth. . . ."

We are reminded that John the Baptist came from such a wonderful background of a praying mother. After thirty or forty years of prayer, Elisabeth and Zacharias were told by the angel of God that they would have a son named John, "great in the sight of the Lord . . . filled with the Holy Ghost, even from his mother's womb. And many of the children of Israel shall he turn to the Lord their God" (Luke 1:15,16). He would be the forerunner of the Saviour. And John the Baptist, so set apart and standing out from all people of his age, surely is a monument to that mother's loving prayer.

You remember the angel had said to Zacharias, "He shall drink neither wine nor strong drink," and "he shall be great in the sight of the Lord." I would imagine that old Elisabeth, who wouldn't quit praying, kept saying to God, "Lord, I don't want a son like some of these drunken priests. I want the man wholly given to the Lord."

How often in the Bible women with barren wombs pleaded with God that He would give them a child! Sarah's prayer was not answered until she was ninety years old, then Isaac was born.

Isaac couldn't have gone very far wrong after the prayers of such a mother and father.

We remember that Rebekah was barren for many years, but Isaac prayed for her and God gave the twin sons, Jacob and Esau.

Leah and Rachel were each for a season barren, but God answered their prayers for a child.

We ought to have the attitude that Bible Christians had—that children are a blessing. "Lo, children are an heritage of the Lord: and the fruit of the womb is his reward. As arrows are in the hand of a mighty man; so are children of the youth. Happy is the man that hath his quiver full of them" (Ps. 127:3-5).

It seems a little strange and, perhaps, sad that the little boy Samuel should grow up in the Tabernacle away from his mother who loved him so much. Every year she would bring little garments she had made with loving hands for the boy she had lent to the Lord! But whatever he missed in the fellowship with others, he had in the fellowship with God.

We think it rather remarkable that in the corrupt atmosphere of Eli's godless and adulterous sons, the boy Samuel should stay pure, good and near to God. I think the influence of his mother was so much greater than the wickedness about him that he stayed pure and, of course, the hand of God was on him.

Samuel, a Spirit-Filled Prophet of God

One could surely discern that God had picked out this little boy to be a mighty prophet, and God spoke to him even as a little child and gave him a rebuke even for the older and greatly respected high priest Eli. First Samuel 3:19-21 says:

> "And Samuel grew, and the Lord was with him, and did let none of his words fall to the ground. And all Israel from Dan even to Beer-sheba knew that Samuel was established to be a prophet of the Lord. And the Lord appeared again in Shiloh: for the Lord revealed himself to Samuel in Shiloh by the word of the Lord."

Again we read in I Samuel 7:15-17:

> "And Samuel judged Israel all the days of his life. And

> *he went from year to year in circuit to Beth-el, and*
> *Gilgal, and Mizpeh, and judged Israel in all those places.*
> *And his return was to Ramah; for there was his house;*
> *and there he judged Israel; and there he built an altar*
> *unto the Lord."*

He was a man of such obvious righteousness and of such Spirit-led judgment that the people could trust him. They brought to him their problems. When Saul and his servant were seeking his father's lost asses, they came to Samuel whom they did not know, whom they had not seen personally, but of whom they had heard, and asked him where the asses were. He was called "the Seer." And all his days he went in circuit to three great centers—there to meet the people and judge them. We might say he held a court and decided questions of right and wrong among the people. He gave people instruction from the Lord.

In the Bible to "prophesy" means to speak in the power of the Holy Spirit, as you can see from Acts 2:17,18. There we are told that the Holy Spirit was poured out upon old men, young men, servants, handmaids and sons and daughters "and they shall prophesy." So a prophet was one who could speak for God, with the authority of God and with the power of God. Samuel was such a mighty prophet.

Samuel Was a Go-Between, a Mediator Between Israel and God

Samuel was a spokesman for God to the people. When God would have Saul to be king, he had Samuel lead in the matter and told Samuel the man who had been selected. Later he told Samuel to go and anoint David to be king, although it must be done secretly for fear of Saul's vengeance at the present.

When the people wanted a king, it was Samuel who must tell them that they were rejecting God's direct rule and they would rue it. And Samuel must tell them the manner of the kingdom and the costs of the kingdom.

The people stubbornly insisted they must have a king, and God said that Samuel should go ahead and let them have a king. Then they pleaded with him: "Pray for thy servants unto the Lord thy God, that we die not: for we have added unto all our sins this evil, to ask us a king" (I Sam. 12:19). But he answered them, "Moreover as for me, God forbid that I should sin against the Lord in ceasing to pray for you: but I will teach you the good and the right way" (I Sam. 12:23).

So, when the people rejected Samuel as judge, they rejected God as their direct ruler. And in I Samuel 8:7 we read, "And the Lord said unto Samuel, Hearken unto the voice of the people in all that they say unto thee: for they have not rejected thee, but they have rejected me, that I should not reign over them."

We are reminded that when the people of Israel complained about the food and said, "For our soul loatheth this light bread," and complained that Moses had led them out of Egypt to starve them in the wilderness; the Scripture says "the people spake against God and against Moses" (Num. 21:5).

In some sense, every Christian should stand for God and, like Paul, we ought to be able to say, "I beseech you in Christ's stead . . . ."

Samuel Had Intimate Touch With God

As God spoke openly to the little boy in the night, so He spoke with Samuel again and again all his life. Isn't this a direct and intimate way for God to speak to Samuel? In I Samuel 9:15,16 we are told: "Now the Lord had told Samuel in his ear a day before Saul came, saying, To morrow about this time I will send thee a man out of the land of Benjamin, and thou shalt anoint him to be captain over my people Israel, that he may save my people out of the hand of the Philistines: for I have looked upon my people, because their cry is come unto me." And then again in verse 17, "And when Samuel saw Saul, the Lord said unto him, Behold the man whom I spake to thee of! this same shall reign over my people."

When the Philistines won a great victory over Israel and the ark was stolen and was in the hands of the Philistines, the Hebrews were in great distress. Samuel called the people together at Mizpeh and prayed for them. He drew water and poured it out before the Lord and fasted and had the people confess their sins. Then Samuel took a sucking lamb and offered it for a burnt-offering—a type of their helplessness, giving themselves to God. As the Philistines drew near to attack the Israelites there was great thunder upon the Philistines and they were discomfited and so Israel pursued the Philistines and smote them until they came to Beth-car.

Samuel was the intercessor between God and Israel and a go-between, speaking for God to his people. How quickly God answered his prayers! In I Samuel 12:18 we are told, "So Samuel called unto the Lord; and the Lord sent thunder and rain that day: and all the people greatly feared the Lord and Samuel."

Was Samuel inspired to write part of the Bible? In I Samuel 10:25 we are told, "Then Samuel told the people the manner of the kingdom, and wrote it in a book, and laid it up before the Lord. And Samuel sent all the people away, every man to his house." Was this part of First Samuel or Second Samuel? If not, I do not believe that what Samuel wrote was part of the Bible, but it was inspired of God for that particular time and place and, no doubt, was not meant for the rest of us and not included in the Bible.

Holy Integrity and Righteousness of Samuel

There is a fragrance of righteousness and innocence about this man of God. We are not told that Samuel was of the tribe of Levi and of Aaron's priesthood, yet it seemed that he took the place of a priest. First Samuel 2:18 says, "But Samuel ministered before the Lord, being a child, girded with a linen ephod." We suppose he was counted in Eli's family and so allowed to be a priest. In I Samuel 7:9, we see Samuel offering sacrifice of a sucking lamb, which would generally be the work of a priest. When Saul, in I Samuel 13:9,10, had offered a burnt offering as if he were a priest, it was counted a sin. But Samuel seems to have been more in the office of a prophet and he had an independent approach to God, even as did Abraham, Isaac, Jacob and Moses, before the Levitical priesthood was established.

And he never claimed the prerogatives of the priest's office. We do not hear of him demanding certain parts of the sacrifices as was done by the sons of Eli. Rather, he seemed to have lived on what offerings the people brought him voluntarily and not through the Levitical sacrifices promised to the priests. When Saul and his servant wanted to come to Samuel to inquire about the lost asses, "Then said Saul to his servant, But, behold, if we go, what shall we bring the man? for the bread is spent in our vessels, and there is not a present to bring to the man of God: what have we? And the servant answered Saul again, and said, Behold, I have here at hand the fourth part of a shekel of silver: that will I give to the man of God, to tell us our way" (I Sam. 9:7,8).

Would to God that every preacher, every man who serves God, could have as clean a slate as Samuel had when it came time to turn the leadership of the nation over to a king. In I Samuel 12:1-5 we see how Samuel presented the matter to the people, and there was not one man to blame him for taking anything from the people except what people voluntarily brought to this prophet of God.

> "And Samuel said unto all Israel, Behold, I have hearkened unto your voice in all that ye said unto me, and have made a king over you. And now, behold, the king walketh before you: and I am old and grayheaded; and, behold, my sons are with you: and I have walked before you from my childhood unto this day. Behold, here I am: witness against me before the Lord, and before his anointed: whose ox have I taken? or whose ass have I taken? or whom have I defrauded? whom have I oppressed? or of whose hand have I received any bribe to blind mine eyes therewith? and I will restore it you. And they said, Thou hast not defrauded us, nor oppressed us, neither hast thou taken ought of any man's hand. And he said unto them, The Lord is witness against you, and his anointed is witness this day, that ye have not found ought in my hand. And they answered, He is witness."— I Sam. 12:1-5.

He could have been like the sons of Eli, who demanded a certain part of all the offerings brought to the Tabernacle, the

Levitical sacrifices, but he did not. He was accepted as a man of authority for God and actually ruled the people, yet made no demands for himself.

How different that is from Gehazi, the servant of Elisha who followed Naaman the Syrian to insist on silver and changes of raiment after Naaman had been healed (II Kings 5:20-27). No, Samuel, like Elisha, did not make merchandise of his ministry.

Samuel could have been like many preachers today who demand that all of the Lord's tithe must be put in that pastor's program. He could have insisted that since he was God's prophet, all this ought to come into his hand, just as many a preacher insists today. He really believes he is exalting the local church when actually he is exalting the program he has established, and out of which he gets his salary, and out of which grows his influence and prestige. No, Samuel made no such requirements but presented himself blameless to the people and they acknowledged that his hands were clean.

Samuel Never Servile Before Saul and Other Mighty Men

There is a refreshing independence and boldness in this good man Samuel, this prophet of God who did not fear nor set out to please man. He was gentle, like a spiritual father, in supporting young King Saul and teaching him the right way. When Saul, distressed because he thought Samuel was slow in coming and he feared the Philistines were about to attack, offered burnt offerings and went ahead of God's plan, then Samuel rebuked him plainly.

"And Samuel said to Saul, Thou hast done foolishly: thou hast not kept the commandment of the Lord thy God, which he commanded thee: for now would the Lord have established thy kingdom upon Israel for ever. But now thy kingdom shall not continue: the Lord hath sought him a man after his own heart, and the Lord hath commanded him to be captain over his people, because thou hast not kept that which the Lord commanded thee."—I Sam. 13:13,14.

Samuel was not deceived when Saul returned from the slaughter of the Amalekites and had saved King Agag alive and brought him as a prisoner, and had saved many of the flocks and herds and brought them back with him, and pretended that he had fulfilled the will of the Lord. Saul said, "I have performed the commandment of the Lord." Samuel said, "What meaneth then this bleating of the sheep in mine ears, and the lowing of the oxen which I hear?" (I Sam. 15:14).

Saul made excuses that these were all for sacrifices for the Lord.

> "Then Samuel said unto Saul, Stay, and I will tell thee what the Lord hath said to me this night. And he said unto him, Say on. And Samuel said, When thou wast little in thine own sight, wast thou not made the head of the tribes of Israel, and the Lord anointed thee king over Israel? And the Lord sent thee on a journey, and said, Go and utterly destroy the sinners the Amalekites, and fight against them until they be consumed. Wherefore then didst thou not obey the voice of the Lord, but didst fly upon the spoil, and didst evil in the sight of the Lord?"—I Sam. 15:16-19.

Saul still insisted and gave other excuses. Then Samuel made that wonderful statement in verses 22 and 23:

> "And Samuel said, Hath the Lord as great delight in burnt-offerings and sacrifices, as in obeying the voice of the Lord? Behold, to obey is better than sacrifice, and to hearken than the fat of rams. For rebellion is as the sin of witchcraft, and stubbornness is as iniquity and idolatry. Because thou hast rejected the word of the Lord, he hath also rejected thee from being king."

Samuel refused to return with Saul and plainly said to him, "The Lord hath rent the kingdom of Israel from thee this day, and hath given it to a neighbour of thine, that is better than thou." Even so, Samuel loved Saul and mourned over him.

We are reminded of how Paul the apostle faced Peter in Galatians, chapter 2, and rebuked him openly and boldly for his compromise in refusing to eat with Gentile converts.

We are reminded of John the Baptist who preached so plainly in the wilderness of Judaea, who called the Pharisees and Sadducees "a generation of vipers" (snakes). He refused to baptize them until they showed evidence of repentance.

We are reminded of Elijah, the mighty prophet of God, who, although they sought to kill him, went boldly on with his prophecy, hiding out until God's time had come, but never compromising.

I have always felt badly about the Prophet Obadiah who "feared the Lord greatly" (I Kings 18:3) but played up to wicked King Ahab and Jezebel and did not fight the four hundred and fifty prophets of Baal. Yes, and I feel sorry for those prophets hiding by fifties and hundreds in caves, feeding on bread and water, instead of fighting for God or dying for God.

Oh, Samuel, gentle, godly, unselfish Samuel, had character and was wholly independent and would not be cowed by human authorities.

Samuel Paid the Price of a Broken Heart, Alienation From Saul and Others Because of Godly Stand

It was a sad day when Samuel boldly announced to Saul that he was rejected from being king and that sooner or later God would raise up another to take his place. At first Samuel would not even appear at the sacrifices with Saul. Then, in sympathy and kindness, he went with the man whom he himself had rejected, as God had rejected him. And he went away. First Samuel 15:35 tells us, "Samuel came no more to see Saul until the day of his death: nevertheless Samuel mourned for Saul: and the Lord repented that he had made Saul king over Israel."

The enmity now of Saul toward Samuel is not very clearly stated, but we can understand it from Samuel's statement when God told him to go and anoint David to be king: "How can I go? if Saul hear it, he will kill me. And the Lord said, Take an heifer with thee, and say, I am come to sacrifice to the Lord" (I Sam. 16:2). The Lord told him not to announce publicly that he was anointing David. But Samuel knew the hatred of Saul, and Samuel never saw him again.

Is that strange that Saul should hate the man who had been used of God to rear him to the place of kingship? No, that is not strange, for Jesus said, "I came not to send peace, but a sword." He said, "For I am come to set a man at variance against his father, and the daughter against her mother, and the daughter in law against her mother in law" (Matt. 10:35). He said that "the time cometh, that whosoever killeth you will think that he doeth God service" (John 16:2). And Paul wrote to young Timothy, "Yea, and all that will live godly in Christ Jesus shall suffer persecution" (II Tim. 3:12).

And in the Beatitudes, it is given so beautifully by the Saviour. Notice that these great "Blesseds" are stated in an ascending scale. It takes nine words—up to fifteen words for some of them. But when Jesus came to the climax of blessing in persecution, He said far more: "Blessed are ye, when men shall revile you, and persecute you, and shall say all manner of evil against you falsely, for my sake. Rejoice, and be exceeding glad: for great is your reward in heaven: for so persecuted they the prophets which were before you" (Matt. 5:11,12).

All who would be faithful to Christ Jesus must remember that this is a way of sorrow as well as a way of joy. This is a way of lost friendships, a way often misunderstood, a way often slandered. But one who would follow Christ must "hate . . . his father, and mother, and wife, and children, and brethren, and sisters, yea, and his own life also . . ." (Luke 14:26).

I suppose there is only one sad thing about the life of the Prophet Samuel and that is his sons did not follow his steps. In I Samuel 8:1-5 we read about this story. His sons, no doubt influenced by the corruption of the priests around them who should have been examples, were not worthy to be judges. They took bribes and perverted judgment.

I do not know how Samuel failed. He was human. In this case we must believe that, good man though he was, he neglected the discipline and rearing of his sons, for Proverbs 22:6 tells us, "Train up a child in the way he should go: and when he is old, he will not depart from it." But, let us remember that every man God ever uses has his frailties, and that God "hath chosen the weak. . .to confound the. . .mighty."

Let us rejoice in the ministry of this great, godly man, prophet and priest and judge, Samuel.

5

Prince Jonathan

Son of Saul, Beloved Friend of David

Beautiful lilies grow in the mud, and every now and then some wonderfully sweet and beautiful character arises in the midst of bad backgrounds.

Although Jonathan was the son of a king who was proud and haughty and finally insanely jealous and murderous, yet he himself was the very acme of loyalty, devotion and honor.

Jonathan was overshadowed by his father and even more by the wonderful, glamorous David. But Jonathan was a wonderful character and ought to be mentioned with those particularly attractive men in the Old Testament.

I. JONATHAN, A BRILLIANT YOUNG SOLDIER

The first mention we have of Jonathan is in I Samuel 13:1-3:

> "Saul reigned one year; and when he had reigned two years over Israel, Saul chose him three thousand men of Israel; whereof two thousand were with Saul in Michmash and in mount Beth-el, and a thousand were with Jonathan in Gibeah of Benjamin: and the rest of the people he sent every man to his tent.   And Jonathan smote the garrison of the Philistines that was in Geba, and the Philistines heard of it. And Saul blew the trumpet throughout all the land, saying, Let the Hebrews hear."

Jonathan, the young prince and so first assistant to his father, King Saul, had a garrison of a thousand soldiers under his control while two thousand were directly with King Saul at Michmash.

Jonathan was a man of initiative and so he "smote the garrison of the Philistines that was in Geba." There he caused the sim-

mering hatred between Israel and the Philistines to flame into
new war. He must have greatly hurt the pride of the Philistines,
and so they gathered great multitudes to attack the Israelites
again with "thirty thousand chariots, and six thousand horsemen,
and people as the sand which is on the sea shore in multitude."

The Philistines had long been overlords over the Israelites. In
the days of Eli, the old high priest, the Israelites were smitten in
battle by the Philistines and the Israelites foolishly took the ark
of God to the next battle. The ark of God was taken and the two
sons of Eli, Hophni and Phinehas, were slain (I Sam. 4:11). As
time went on, they had made it so the Israelites could have no
weapons and no way to make weapons of war. Only Saul and
Jonathan had swords. And they had files for their mattocks and
hoes.

Things looked bad now, for the Philistines gathered against
God's people. Saul's army seemed to begin to disintegrate until
only six hundred men were left of the three thousand who had
made up his army. "Spoilers came out of the camp of the
Philistines in three companies" to ravish the land.

But in this situation, God put it in the heart of eager, brilliant
young Jonathan to make a personal attack on the Philistines. It
seemed venturesome, almost folly, for Jonathan and his armorbearer to go alone, climbing the steep hill where the
Philistines were encamped across the valley from the Israelites'
army.

> *"Now it came to pass upon a day, that Jonathan the
> son of Saul said unto the young man that bare his ar-
> mour, Come, and let us go over to the Philistines' gar-
> rison, that is on the other side. But he told not his father.
> And Saul tarried in the uttermost part of Gibeah under a
> pomegranate tree which is in Migron: and the people
> that were with him were about six hundred men; And
> Ahiah, the son of Ahitub, I-chabod's brother, the son of
> Phinehas, the son of Eli, the Lord's priest in Shiloh,
> wearing an ephod. And the people knew not that
> Jonathan was gone. And between the passages, by which
> Jonathan sought to go over unto the Philistines' garrison,*

*there was a sharp rock on the one side, and a sharp rock
on the other side: and the name of the one was Bozez,
and the name of the other Seneh. The forefront of the one
was situate northward over against Michmash, and the
other southward over against Gibeah. And Jonathan said
to the young man that bare his armour, Come, and let us
go over unto the garrison of these uncircumcised: it may
be that the Lord will work for us: for there is no restraint
to the Lord to save by many or by few."*—I Sam. 14:1-6.

He looked to God to help. He told a great truth that only a
spiritual man of faith could understand. "There is no restraint to
the Lord to save by many or by few." This is the same kind of
boldness that young David will show later when he goes to meet
Goliath and when he will say to the giant:

*"Thou comest to me with a sword, and with a spear,
and with a shield: but I come to thee in the name of the
Lord of hosts, the God of the armies of Israel, whom thou
hast defied. This day will the Lord deliver thee into mine
hand; and I will smite thee, and take thine head from
thee; and I will give the carcases of the host of the
Philistines this day unto the fowls of the air, and to the
wild beasts of the earth; that all the earth may know that
there is a God in Israel. And all this assembly shall know
that the Lord saveth not with sword and spear: for the
battle is the Lord's, and he will give you into our
hands."*—I Sam. 17:45-47.

We've given so much attention to the marvelous feat of David,
but who knows, it may well be that this heroic and glamorous
deed of Jonathan may have inspired David to trust the same
Lord to work the same kind of a miracle when David went out
against the giant.

Now continue the story in I Samuel 14. To this brave statement of Jonathan, we read:

*"And his armourbearer said unto him, Do all that is in
thine heart: turn thee; behold, I am with thee according
to thy heart. Then said Jonathan, Behold, we will pass
over unto these men, and we will discover ourselves unto*

them. If they say thus unto us, Tarry until we come to you; then we will stand still in our place, and will not go up unto them. But if they say thus, Come up unto us; then we will go up: for the Lord hath delivered them into our hand: and this shall be a sign unto us. And both of them discovered themselves unto the garrison of the Philistines: and the Philistines said, Behold, the Hebrews come forth out of the holes where they had hid themselves. And the men of the garrison answered Jonathan and his armourbearer, and said, Come up to us, and we will shew you a thing. And Jonathan said unto his armourbearer, Come up after me: for the Lord hath delivered them into the hand of Israel. And Jonathan climbed up upon his hands and upon his feet, and his armourbearer after him: and they fell before Jonathan; and his armourbearer slew after him. And that first slaughter, which Jonathan and his armourbearer made, was about twenty men, within as it were a half acre of land, which a yoke of oxen might plow. And there was trembling in the host, in the field, and among all the people: the garrison, and the spoilers, they also trembled, and the earth quaked: so it was a very great trembling. And the watchmen of Saul in Gibeah of Benjamin looked; and, behold, the multitude melted away, and they went on beating down one another."—I Sam. 14:7-16.

The audacity of the attack was unexpected. One would think that two or three men, secure in their uphill position, could have attacked and killed the two men climbing on hands and feet up the steep hillside. But they wanted to see what would happen. They had no fear of these despised Israelites! And suddenly, as he stood among them, Jonathan thrust with his spear or sword and a man went down, and his armorbearer immediately struck him through the heart. Then another man was down and slain, the armorbearer slaying, as Jonathan, with a fury that was of God, struck men down right and left. About twenty men were killed there and God Himself began to move mightily.

"There was a trembling in the host, in the field, and among all the people: the garrison, and the spoilers, they also trembled, and the earth quaked: so it was a very great trembling." And suddenly, strangely, and frightened out of their wits and certain that God was intervening, trying to get away and striking everybody before them, the Philistines fought each other.

And the Scripture tells us how the Israelites followed and came to the battle.

And Hebrews, who had been hidden and had been over with the Philistines, now joined in the battle, and it was a wonderful victory for God's people.

Oh, what a blessed evidence that God can use two to chase a thousand, and ten to put ten thousand to flight!

I lift up a proud hand to salute young Jonathan for his faith in God, for his holy zeal.

It is a sidelight on the character of the unspiritual Saul that he made a foolish demand of the people—that no one should eat a bite until the day was gone and the battle over. Jonathan, who had already been out in battle and winning the victory before his father knew about it, had found a honeycomb and eaten a bit of the honey and renewed his strength with the food. And with a silly kind of legalism, King Saul had determined that anybody who had eaten a bite should die for it. God did not answer Saul when he appealed to God, so Saul blamed Jonathan and would have put his own son to death but the people would not have it.

II. JONATHAN'S LOVE-COVENANT WITH DAVID

In another heroic and glorious deed, the shepherd boy David, perhaps younger than Jonathan, had come down to the army camp to bring food for his brothers and to get a report for his father Jesse. And here was the giant Goliath striding out before the people and boasting that he could kill any man among the Israelites and challenging any man to fight him. No one would. Even King Saul, head and shoulders above all the men of his army, dared not go out against Goliath.

Although people scoffed at him because he was only a lad, David remembered that God had helped him when a lion had taken a lamb from the flock and he had gone out against the lion and caught him by his beard and killed him. And again when he had fought a bear. And he believed that God would deliver him for His own great name's sake.

Can you imagine what a scene it was when, with his slingshot, he had hurled a stone that crushed the forehead of the boasting giant, perhaps ten feet tall, and he had fallen prostrate? Then when David drew the giant's own great sword and cut off his head and carried that dripping weight before King Saul?

Now there came a great crisis, a conflict of interest, in the life of the young Prince Jonathan.

"And Saul spake to Jonathan his son, and to all his servants, that they should kill David. But Jonathan Saul's son delighted much in David: and Jonathan told David, saying, Saul my father seeketh to kill thee: now therefore, I pray thee, take heed to thyself until the morning, and abide in a secret place, and hide thyself: And I will go out and stand beside my father in the field where thou art, and I will commune with my father of thee; and what I see, that I will tell thee. And Jonathan spake good of David unto Saul his father, and said unto him, Let not the king sin against his servant, against David; because he hath not sinned against thee, and because his works have been to thee-ward very good: For he did put his life in his hand, and slew the Philistine, and the Lord wrought a great salvation for all Israel: thou sawest it, and didst rejoice: wherefore then wilt thou sin against innocent blood, to slay David without a cause? And Saul hearkened unto the voice of Jonathan: and Saul sware, As the Lord liveth, he shall not be slain. And Jonathan called David, and Jonathan shewed him all those things. And Jonathan brought David to Saul, and he was in his presence, as in times past."—I Sam. 19:1-7.

How loyally Jonathan stood by his friend! His irascible and flighty father, with the poison of jealousy in his veins, would have had David killed, but Jonathan would have none of that and he so valiantly interceded that Saul, for the time being, put aside his hatred and his plan to kill David.

However, that evil spirit that was in Saul mounted up again, so he tried to kill David with a javelin but David slipped away and the javelin smashed into the wall. Saul sent messengers to David's home to kill him there, but he again slipped away.

In chapter 20 we find the renewed danger to David in Saul's burning jealousy. The women had sung, "Saul hath slain his thousands, and David his ten thousands." Saul has already been told that God would put him aside and surely he must have understood that the man after God's own heart, to whom the kingdom would go, would be David. So he tried to fight against God to kill David and to keep for himself the throne, which he thought was endangered.

God had worked over Saul and he had unwillingly gone among the prophets and, beside himself, had prophesied and had lain naked a day and a night. Now, somewhat humbled, he allowed David to come back to the palace. David kept in touch with Jonathan but dared not be in the presence of King Saul. Jonathan promised faithfully to counsel with his father and bring David word of any danger.

Jonathan and David went out to the fields together and again young Prince Jonathan lovingly renounced his own right to the kingdom. And Jonathan, pledging himself to David, said:

> *"And thou shalt not only while yet I live shew me the kindness of the Lord, that I die not: But also thou shalt not cut off thy kindness from my house for ever: no, not when the Lord hath cut off the enemies of David every one from the face of the earth. So Jonathan made a covenant with the house of David, saying, Let the Lord even require it at the hand of David's enemies. And Jonathan caused David to swear again, because he loved him: for he loved him as he loved his own soul."*—I Sam. 20:14-17.

Jonathan warned David of the dangerous hatred and

murderous plans of King Saul, so David fled away into the wilderness.

We must remember that Jonathan was the greatly-honored son of the king, would be called a general in the army, second only to Saul. Yet he gave up every hope of the kingdom to sponsor and to protect David. In fact, Saul almost killed his son Jonathan in a mad fit because Jonathan had defended David.

III. JONATHAN DIED WITH HIS FATHER SAUL

The Scripture has little more to say about Jonathan, since he and David were now separated—the one a fugitive from the angry king and the other in the palace with the army of Saul. But the Philistine army, persistently attacking Israel, at last killed Saul and his sons. First Samuel 31:2 says, "And the Philistines followed hard upon Saul and upon his sons; and the Philistines slew Jonathan, and Abinadab, and Melchi-shua, Saul's sons." Saul himself was wounded and fell upon his sword and was almost dead, then a strange Amalekite came along to finish the death of the king.

The Philistines came to strip the bodies and found Saul and his three sons fallen in Mount Gilboa, cut off Saul's head (no doubt, in remembrance of what David had done to Goliath) and fastened the body of Saul to the wall of Beth-shan. But the men of Jabesh-gilead went at night and took the bodies of Saul and his sons from the wall of Beth-shan and came to Jabesh and burned them there (I Sam. 31:10-12).

What a lament young King David made for his beloved friend Jonathan and over the dead father, King Saul! Read it in II Samuel 1:17-27.

Officially David, a loyal citizen, must give reverence to the king whom God had put over them. Even when Saul tried to kill David, David would not lift his hand against God's anointed king. Now the king was dead and David gave him honor. But there is a tender lament particularly about Jonathan. "I am distressed for thee, my brother Jonathan: very pleasant hast thou been unto me: thy love to me was wonderful, passing the love of women" (vs. 26).

Handicapped by a father out of the will of God, and whose kingdom could not continue, Jonathan had no envy, no jealousy of David who would succeed and supersede King Saul. He who was a prince and would have been expected to rule after his father Saul, was a godly man, a man surrendered to the will of God and loyal to David even to the death. His love "passed the love of women."

And always, the thing most remembered about Jonathan was that loving loyalty to his friend.

6

Gideon: Judge and Deliverer of Israel

There is a sad series of cycles in the life of the nation Israel as pictured in the book of Judges.

Thirteen times they fell away into sin, backsliding, worldliness and idolatry; and thirteen times God brought judgment on them through the heathen people around them. They were beaten in battle, they were enslaved, defrauded and overcome because of their sin. Thus was fulfilled again and again the solemn warnings in Deuteronomy 28 of the trouble that was to come to them if they turned into idolatry and neglected to keep the Word of God and do the will of God.

After hundreds of years, that kind of backsliding at last led to the captivity of the northern nation under Assyria, then to Judah under Babylonian Nebuchadnezzar.

But again and again the tender mercy of God blossomed and He relented in the punishment of the people He loved and raised up a mighty man to lead them to victory again. These fourteen judges included Gideon and Jephthah and Samson and the last, Samuel.

Sometimes the brightest picture needs a black background for it to reveal best the beauty of the subject. So the apostasy and wickedness of Israel give such a background for the mercy of God. And again He raised up Gideon to be a deliverer of the people He loved.

I. AWFUL OPPRESSION BY MIDIANITES AND AMALEKITES

The Midianites and the Amalekites were two of the most awesome and continual enemies of Israel. It was the Midianites, along with the people of Moab, who had led Israel into whoredom with their women, then into idolatry.

The Moabites and the Midianites saw how God blessed Israel when they were in the wilderness, and so Balak hired Balaam the prophet to bring a curse on Israel. He could not do it, but his heart was with the Midianites and the Moabites and he was counted guilty with them and later died with them.

In Numbers 25:1-6 we are told:

> "And Israel abode in Shittim, and the people began to commit whoredom with the daughters of Moab. And they called the people unto the sacrifices of their gods: and the people did eat, and bowed down to their gods. And Israel joined himself unto Baal-peor: and the anger of the Lord was kindled against Israel. And the Lord said unto Moses, Take all the heads of the people, and hang them up before the Lord against the sun, that the fierce anger of the Lord may be turned away from Israel. And Moses said unto the judges of Israel, Slay ye every one his men that were joined unto Baal-peor. And, behold, one of the children of Israel came and brought unto his brethren a Midianitish woman in the sight of Moses, and in the sight of all the congregation of the children of Israel, who were weeping before the door of the tabernacle of the congregation."

One prince of Israel brought a Midianitish woman, a princess, into his tent for adultery, and Phinehas the priest took a spear and went into the tent and thrust them both through and killed them, then God stopped His awful anger against the people. But the Lord spake unto Moses, saying:

> "Vex the Midianites, and smite them: For they vex you with their wiles, wherewith they have beguiled you in the matter of Peor, and in the matter of Cozbi, the daughter of a prince of Midian, their sister, which was slain in the day of the plague for Peor's sake."—Num. 25:17,18.

The Moabites lived south of the Dead Sea and the Midianites in the great desert region further south and back toward Sinai.

And now they came, along with the Amalekites, to overrun Israel.

The Amalekites had come to fight Israel in the wilderness, and with Aaron and Hur holding up the hands of Moses, the Israelites prevailed in the battle.

"And the Lord said unto Moses, Write this for a memorial in a book, and rehearse it in the ears of Joshua: for I will utterly put out the remembrance of Amalek from under heaven. And Moses built an altar, and called the name of it Jehovah-nissi: For he said, Because the Lord hath sworn that the Lord will have war with Amalek from generation to generation."—Exod. 17:14-16.

God remembered this curse on the Amalekites and it is expressed again in the Lord's word to Moses in Deuteronomy 25:17-19:

"Remember what Amalek did unto thee by the way, when ye were come forth out of Egypt; How he met thee by the way, and smote the hindmost of thee, even all that were feeble behind thee, when thou wast faint and weary; and he feared not God. Therefore it shall be, when the Lord thy God hath given thee rest from all thine enemies round about, in the land which the Lord thy God giveth thee for an inheritance to possess it, that thou shalt blot out the remembrance of Amalek from under heaven; thou shalt not forget it."

Later King Saul was sent against them to utterly destroy the nation.

Now here in Judges we find the Midianites and Amalekites coming against the children of Israel. The Israelites made them dens in the mountains and caves and strongholds in which to hide.

"And so it was, when Israel had sown, that the Midianites came up, and the Amalekites, and the children of the east, even they came up against them; And they encamped against them, and destroyed the increase of the earth, till thou come unto Gaza, and left no

sustenance for Israel, neither sheep, nor ox, nor ass. For they came up with their cattle and their tents, and they came as grasshoppers for multitude; for both they and their camels were without number: and they entered into the land to destroy it. And Israel was greatly impoverished because of the Midianites; and the children of Israel cried unto the Lord."—Judges 6:3-6.

The children of Israel had gone after the gods of the Amorites and had forgotten the mercy of God. Now they were paying for it by the awful oppression by the Midianites and Amalekites.

II. GOD'S MERCY MUST PROVIDE A DELIVERER!

How often God had heard the cry of His people when they were oppressed, when they were beaten and suffering for their sins! Again and again He sent judges to deliver them. Now He looks on the unworthy people with pity and with mercy. They did not deserve His help. Oh, but that is the way with all this poor, wicked race of men. "He came unto his own, and his own received him not. But as many as received him, to them gave he power to become the sons of God, even to them that believe on his name" (John 1:11,12). Jesus wept over Jerusalem and said, ". . . how often would I have gathered thy children together, as a hen doth gather her brood under her wings, and ye would not" (Luke 13:34). So with each judge that God raised up. Mercy came to undeserving people.

Oh, that is the story of this whole world! The Lord Jesus came to the world which He made and which was against God, a race fallen and wicked and unconcerned, came and died to save sinners.

Let us take comfort and encouragement in the fact that God in due season and in great time of trouble, sent a judge. He sent Gideon. He sent Samson. He sent Samuel. And He sent Jesus. So let any poor sinner who reads this know God is a God of mercy who gives sinners, who ought to go to Hell, a free pass to Heaven.

The other day I talked to a man. With tears and in awful earnestness he said, "Dr. Rice, I had no right to be saved! I ought to have gone to Hell!" Oh, yes, that is true about every one of us.

At a country church near Decatur, Texas, a wicked man, a chicken thief, a bootlegger, one who had led a great crowd of young men into sin, was in the service. When I spoke to him about turning to Christ for mercy and forgiveness, he said, "Do you think God would take a wicked old sinner such as I?" Yes, He would, and He did!

Now God called Gideon. I think He had had Gideon in mind for a long time. It was not a sudden decision on God's part. Surely He knew the hearts of men, and just as He knew the heart of David ahead of time and would not have anybody else to be anointed king when He sent for David, so He now chose Gideon.

Joash and Gideon, his son, were threshing wheat by the winepress, hidden, we suppose, among the trees to keep the grain from the thieving, marauding Midianites and Amalekites. And there the angel came and called Gideon to come and serve the Lord and deliver the people Israel.

III. "WHERE ARE ALL THE MIRACLES?"

The angel approached Gideon and said, "The Lord is with thee, thou mighty man of valour." Gideon said unto him, "Oh my Lord, if the Lord be with us, why then is all this befallen us? and where be all his miracles which our fathers told us of, saying, Did not the Lord bring us up from Egypt? but now the Lord hath forsaken us, and delivered us into the hands of the Midianites."

How keen was the spiritual understanding of this young man! He knew that in the past God had cared for His people with mighty miracles. The Bible is a Book of miracles. The Christian religion is a religion of miracles: a miracle of direct creation by the hand of God; a miraculous flood; the miraculous leading of the children of Israel out of Egypt with mighty plagues and wonders. Miracles had followed the mighty men of God before; now, very sensibly and in deep earnestness, Gideon asked, "Why then is all this befallen us? and where be all his miracles which our fathers told us of?"

Anyone who is going to seek great things done for God must have a miracle of God.

I heard an evangelist say who came to a church for an extensive revival campaign, "I did not bring a revival with me in my suitcase." He meant that people must pay the price for revival and that real revival does not automatically come just because some good man comes to preach.

But the evangelist was not entirely right, for no man can hold great revivals and win many souls unless he has a miracle-working God along with him.

Yes, a man must carry a revival either in his suitcase or in his heart, and it must be expressed in his tears, his prayers, his fasting, his bold denunciation of sin, his confident offering of mercy. There is no revival unless the moving of God's Spirit comes mightily on His people.

When I was a lad they used to sing an old song:

> **Brethren, we have met to worship**
> **And adore the Lord our God;**
> **Will you pray with all your power,**
> **While we try to preach the Word?**
> **All is vain unless the Spirit**
> **Of the Holy One comes down;**
> **Brethren, pray, and holy manna**
> **Will be showered all around.**

Oh, every man who is called to serve God ought to say, "Lord, where are the miracles?"

Moses said about going into the land of Canaan, "If You will not go with us, then I will not go." God relented from His withdrawal of the cloud and pillar of fire and set them again over the camp so they could move when the cloud and pillar of fire moved and camp when they stopped.

I have no sympathy with the idea that "the age of miracles is passed." As Dr. Charles Blanchard, one-time president of Wheaton College, said, "If there be a God, He must act like a God."

If God controls things, that means divine, miraculous intervention in the affairs of men continually. Whether or not God's dealings obviously break what we know as the laws of nature (and sometimes certainly they do supersede those laws), yet it is Christ who keeps every heart beating; it is Christ who gives the signal for death, or raises up the sick, or controls the weather, or moves the hearts of men, or answers prayers.

I am saying, this is a miracle religion. Nobody can build a great church, no one can be a fruitful soul winner, nobody can preach with power except as God miraculously moves upon him so that it is more than human wisdom, more than human persuasion, more than human personality, that reaches the hearts of men.

Jesus said that with the prayer of faith "nothing shall be impossible unto you" (Matt. 17:20). He said, "Verily, verily, I say unto you, He that believeth on me, the works that I do shall he do also; and greater works than these shall he do; because I go unto my Father" (John 14:12). He said, "Therefore I say unto you, What things soever ye desire, when ye pray, believe that ye receive them, and ye shall have them" (Mark 11:24). Anybody who takes those sweet promises at their awesome intent must know that the God of miracles is offering His blessings, power and wonders today to the believing heart who claims Him.

Gideon called for miracles and he got them. He prayed that the fleece, left overnight, would be filled with dew and the ground dry. That prayer was answered. Then he prayed that the fleece would be dry and the ground would be wet. And that too was answered. And when Gideon would have trembled to take his little band of three hundred against the mighty host of the Midianites, God miraculously gave a Midianite man a dream that Gideon was coming to destroy their whole army, and He let Gideon overhear the man tell it!

IV. BUT GIDEON MUST FIRST PROVE
HIS FAITHFULNESS

But Gideon is not ready for the mighty power of God. He must prove himself. The Lord Jesus had a very strict standard of discipleship. "If any man come to me, and hate not his father, and mother, and wife, and children, and brethren, and sisters, yea, and his own life also, he cannot be my disciple" (Luke 14:26).

To the disciples, Jesus insisted they must count the cost. To one would-be disciple, Jesus reminded, "The foxes have holes, and the birds of the air have nests; but the Son of man hath not where to lay his head" (Matt. 8:20). To another who said, "I will follow thee" but first he must go back until he could bury his aging father, then when other duties were fulfilled he would follow Jesus, Jesus said sharply, "Follow me; and let the dead bury their dead."

I think God lets every preacher who sets out to preach and means business come to a time of poverty and, it may be, abuse and misunderstanding, a testing. He doesn't want preachers and prophets who do not mean business.

Now Gideon, will you be the man of God to deliver Israel? Then you will take a stand against idolatry. It must be open and bold. You must risk the anger of your father, the hatred of the Baalites who would want to kill you. God gave him a plain command.

An angel came and blessed him, and he built an altar.

"And it came to pass the same night, that the Lord said unto him, Take thy father's young bullock, even the second bullock of seven years old, and throw down the altar of Baal that thy father hath, and cut down the grove that is by it: And build an altar unto the Lord thy God upon the top of this rock, in the ordered place, and take the second bullock, and offer a burnt-sacrifice with the wood of the grove which thou shalt cut down."— Judges 6:25,26.

He must take, without the father's permission we suppose, the father's second bullock and offer it as a sacrifice on the altar. He did. Then he must cut down the grove about the altar of Baal and break it down. So he took ten men of his servants (we suppose it was a wealthy family) and in the night they cut down the trees that they would not then be hidden from the prophets of Baal. That sacred grove surrounding the altar was cut to the ground. The altar itself was thrown down.

"Then the men of the city said unto Joash, Bring out thy son, that he may die: because he hath cast down the

altar of Baal, and because he hath cut down the grove that was by it. And Joash said unto all that stood against him, Will ye plead for Baal? will ye save him? he that will plead for him, let him be put to death whilst it is yet morning: if he be a god, let him plead for himself, because one hath cast down his altar. Therefore on that day he called him Jerubbaal, saying, Let Baal plead against him, because he hath thrown down his altar."— Judges 6:30-32.

I have often rejoiced in the sweet promises in the first Psalm, but I remind you that that blessed promise to the man who meditates day and night in the Word of God, ". . . whatsoever he doeth shall prosper," comes only after the sharp, distinct command, "Blessed is the man that walketh not in the counsel of the ungodly, nor standeth in the way of sinners, nor sitteth in the seat of the scornful."

One who is a friend to the world is the enemy of God. You can't please both wicked men and God. If Gideon would have God's power, then he must take sides against Baal and wicked worshipers of Baal. So he did. And God wonderfully turned the heart of the father to his son, and they did not kill Gideon as they intended.

Meantime, the Midianites, Amalekites and children of the east were gathered together and they pitched in the valley of Jezreel. They had come from far south of the Dead Sea even and overrun the land; now they gathered in that great garden spot, the rich valley of Jezreel.

Gideon, you have been tested. The time comes near for a showdown with the enemies of God.

V. SPIRIT OF GOD UPON GIDEON

"But the Spirit of the Lord came upon Gideon, and he blew a trumpet; and Abiezer was gathered after him."— Judges 6:34.

The beloved D. L. Moody loved to preach that the Holy Spirit is "in" all Christians, but His coming "upon" Christians to endue them with power is an entirely different matter.

The indwelling of the blessed Spirit in every Christian's body began, we believe, on the day Jesus rose from the dead when He came into the Upper Room where the disciples were assembled for fear of the Jews and breathed on them and said, "Peace be unto you: as my Father hath sent me, even so send I you. And when he had said this, he breathed on them, and said unto them, Receive ye the Holy Ghost" (John 20:21,22). Now, "Know ye not that your body is the temple of the Holy Ghost which is in you, which ye have of God, and ye are not your own? For ye are bought with a price" (I Cor. 6:19,20). And, "If any man have not the Spirit of Christ, he is none of his" (Rom. 8:9).

But the coming of the Holy Spirit upon Christians was that same enduement of power in the Old Testament as in the New Testament. Now the Spirit of God came upon Gideon to endue and anoint him, to empower him for the work.

You remember it was said about Jesus, "The Spirit of the Lord is upon me, because he hath anointed me to preach the gospel to the poor . . ." (Isa. 61:1; Luke 4:18). The Holy Spirit of God came upon Jesus, our perfect Pattern, to endue Him for His ministry.

Joel had prophesied and that wonderful prophecy was fulfilled at Pentecost and on down through this age: "But this is that which was spoken by the prophet Joel; And it shall come to pass in the last days, saith God, I will pour out of my Spirit upon all flesh: and your sons and your daughters shall prophesy, and your young men shall see visions, and your old men shall dream dreams" (Acts 2:16,17).

And the promise of Jesus in Acts 1:8 was very plain, "But ye shall receive power, after that the Holy Ghost is come upon you: and ye shall be witnesses unto me both in Jerusalem, and in all Judaea, and in Samaria, and unto the uttermost part of the earth."

When the Prophet Samuel symbolically poured the horn of oil upon the head of the lad David, we are told, ". . . and the Spirit of the Lord came upon David from that day forward" (I Sam. 16:13).

Even of King Saul, when he began his work as king, it is said,

". . . and the Spirit of God came upon him, and he prophesied among them" (I Sam. 10:10).

We are told that the Spirit of God came upon Samson again and again: "And the Spirit of the Lord began to move him at times in the camp of Dan between Zorah and Eshtaol" (Judges 13:25).

"And the Spirit of the Lord came mightily upon him" when a lion roared against him (Judges 14:6). "And the Spirit of the Lord came upon him" when he went down to Ashkelon and killed thirty Philistines and took their garments. When the distraught Jewish leaders bound Samson and delivered him to the Philistines, ". . . the Philistines shouted against him: and the Spirit of the Lord came mightily upon him," and he broke the bonds and with the jawbone of an ass killed a thousand Philistines (Judges 15:14,15). The mighty works of Samson, like those of Gideon, were done in the power of the Holy Spirit.

VI. GIDEON'S THREE HUNDRED USED TO DEFEAT AN UNCOUNTED MULTITUDE OF MIDIANITES

"Then all the Midianites and the Amalekites and the children of the east were gathered together, and went over, and pitched in the valley of Jezreel."—Judges 6:33.

And how many!

"And the Midianites and the Amalekites and all the children of the east lay along in the valley like grasshoppers for multitude; and their camels were without number, as the sand by the sea side for multitude."—Judges 7:12.

But Gideon blew a trumpet mightily and the people were gathered to him—thousands of Israelites.

I think we must say that when God mightily anoints some man, the people will hear him. The crowds that gathered to hear Spurgeon, and the humble D. L. Moody, and Sam Jones, and Gipsy Smith and Torrey, and Bob Jones, Sr., and John Wesley, and George Truett and L. R. Scarborough—they were drawn by

the great need of the human heart and the pull of the Spirit of
God who led them to hear. So the crowd came to the young man
God had anointed with the Spirit to deliver Israel.

Gideon sent messengers through the tribes of Asher, Zebulun
and Naphtali, and they came. Some 32,000 men came to follow
Gideon and they camped opposite the Midianites. But they were
too many!

> *"And the Lord said unto Gideon, The people that are
> with thee are too many for me to give the Midianites into
> their hands, lest Israel vaunt themselves against me,
> saying, Mine own hand hath saved me. Now therefore go
> to, proclaim in the ears of the people, saying, Whosoever
> is fearful and afraid, let him return and depart early
> from mount Gilead. And there returned of the people
> twenty and two thousand; and there remained ten
> thousand."*—Judges 7:2,3.

Now he has only 10,000 left of the 32,000, but that is too many.
This victory must be not a victory of men but of God. It must be
a victory not only of superior numbers or of trained human skill
and strength, but it must be obviously using the weak to confound the mighty so God can get the glory. So the 10,000 were too
many.

They were brought down to the water and Gideon was instructed that every man who dipped the water and lapped it up
as a dog does was to be set aside, and they were especially
chosen. The others were allowed to go home.

> *"And the Lord said unto Gideon, By the three hundred
> men that lapped will I save you, and deliver the
> Midianites into thine hand: and let all the other people
> go every man unto his place."*

But if three hundred men and one intrepid leader are to face
the tens of thousands of the heathen in a battle, God must show
His hand. So the Lord instructed Gideon to take Phurah his servant and go down, slip near to the host of the Midianites and
listen to their talk.

> *"And when Gideon was come, behold, there was a man*

that told a dream unto his fellow, and said, Behold, I dreamed a dream, and, lo, a cake of barley bread tumbled into the host of Midian, and came unto a tent, and smote it that it fell, and overturned it, that the tent lay along. And his fellow answered and said, This is nothing else save the sword of Gideon the son of Joash, a man of Israel: for into his hand hath God delivered Midian, and all the host.''—Judges 7:13,14.

Ah, what a comfort that must have been! What an encouragement to the trembling heart of the young man! If God would bring enough unease, distress and fear to the hearts of the Midianites, God could win a victory that Gideon and his three hundred could not possibly have done alone.

So spectacular plans were made—foolish plans it seemed. Each one of the three hundred was to take a trumpet in his hand, each with an empty pitcher and a lamp within the pitcher. They were divided into three groups, and they came at that great camp of uneasy Midianites from three sides. Gideon blew a trumpet and every man of the three hundred blew his trumpet, broke the pitchers and shouted, "The sword of the Lord, and of Gideon."

It was "the beginning of the middle watch," that is, just after midnight. God had so put such unrest, such troubled fear in the hearts of the Midianites that when the crashing pitchers were broken, the lights revealed, the trumpets everywhere were sounding and on every side of them the men were shouting, "The sword of the Lord, and of Gideon," they broke into a crazy rout. "The Lord set every man's sword against his fellow, even throughout all the host: and the host fled to Beth-shittah in Zererath, and to the border of Abelmeholah, unto Tabbath" (Judges 7:22).

Now the time has come to mop up and destroy thoroughly the enemy. So messengers are sent throughout all Mount Ephraim and from Ephraim now new helpers came to head off the fleeing enemy at the fords of Jordan. They must not get away. The two princes of the Midianites, Oreb and Zeeb, were taken and slain.

Now the men of Ephraim were jealous. Why had they not been called in to have part in such a wonderful victory ahead of time? But very wisely Gideon praised them for the great part they had done at the end, and they were appeased.

VII. GIDEON'S STRONG CHARACTER, HIS FAITHFUL PURSUIT, HIS COMPLETE VICTORY

God had shown that the victory must be from God. "God hath chosen the foolish things of the world to confound the wise; and God hath chosen the weak things of the world to confound the things which are mighty" (I Cor. 1:27). Paul had a thorn in the flesh "lest I should be exalted above measure," he said (II Cor. 12:7). David went out against a giant, but he came in the name and in the power of Jehovah, expecting God's wisdom, protection and power, and God gave the victory and got the glory. Jonathan was right when he said that God could win the victory by many or by few (I Sam. 14:6). God always wants men to be small in their own eyes, and give God the glory. But now that God has wonderfully shown His hand, it is blessed for all of God's people to get in and share in doing the will of God.

So Gideon followed up his victory. He passed over Jordan and pleaded with the men of Succoth to give loaves of bread for the people that followed, faint after great exertion and abstinence. They scoffed at him. They did not believe the princes Zebah and Zalmunna could be defeated. Gideon promised to come back and tear their flesh with thorns of the wilderness when he had victory. At Penuel likewise the men mocked him, so he said, "When I come again in peace, I will break down this tower."

The fleeing Midianites had grouped themselves and camped, thinking that they were now across the Jordan and had escaped the vengeance of Gideon and his army. But, weary and unfed as they were, the pursuing army slipped upon the camp and "smote the host: for the host was secure." Zebah and Zalmunna fled, and he pursued and took those two kings of Midian, Zebah and Zalmunna. Then he returned to visit the promised judgment on the men of Penuel and Succoth.

He challenged Zebah and Zalmunna: "What manner of men

were they whom ye slew at Tabor?" They answered, "As thou art, so were they; each one resembled the children of a king." Ah, they were his brothers, the sons of his mother! A distinguished family, attractive, sensible, strong! But these kings must die. And when Gideon's son Jether feared to attack the kings personally and kill them, Gideon himself fell upon them and killed them.

It is said that at one time General Lee, after a great battle in the early days of the Civil War, could have taken Washington and brought the Civil War to a quick end. But he missed his opportunity. He did not know it, but doubtless God did not want two separate nations in America—Confederate States and the United States.

Elisha instructed Joash, king of Israel, that he should take bow and arrows and shoot an arrow of the Lord's deliverance from Syria. And he said, "Thou shalt smite the Syrians in Aphek till thou have consumed them" (II Kings 13:17). But again he said, "Take the arrows. And he took them. And he said unto the king of Israel, Smite upon the ground. And he smote thrice, and stayed. And the man of God was wroth with him, and said, Thou shouldest have smitten five or six times; then hadst thou smitten Syria till thou hadst consumed it: whereas now thou shalt smite Syria but thrice" (II Kings 13:18,19). He could have had victory after victory until he consumed the Syrians, but he only anticipated and claimed the blessing for three battles. But Gideon pushed his work to mighty victory.

When King Saul had brought back alive Agag, king of the Amalekites, although God had commanded he be destroyed, Samuel took a sword and hewed the king in pieces publicly! And, after the great victory and prayer at Mount Carmel in I Kings 18, ". . . Elijah said unto them, Take the prophets of Baal; let not one of them escape. And they took them: and Elijah brought them down to the brook Kishon, and slew them there" (I Kings 18:40).

Wise is the man who takes the complete blessing God has and follows through the command of God fully. Oh, there were wisdom and persistent, faithful obedience in young Gideon!

VIII. GIDEON'S ERROR—SYMBOL OF HIS VICTORY —WAS TURNED TO IDOLATRY

The victory of Gideon and Israel over the traditional enemies must be celebrated, must be remembered.

> *"And Gideon said unto them, I would desire a request of you, that ye would give me every man the earrings of his prey. (For they had golden earrings, because they were Ishmaelites.) And they answered, We will willingly give them. And they spread a garment, and did cast therein every man the earrings of his prey. And the weight of the golden earrings that he requested was a thousand and seven hundred shekels of gold; beside ornaments, and collars, and purple raiment that was on the kings of Midian, and beside the chains that were about their camels' necks. And Gideon made an ephod thereof, and put it in his city, even in Ophrah: and all Israel went thither a whoring after it: which thing became a snare unto Gideon, and to his house."*—Judges 8:24-27.

I think Gideon meant well and the people surely wanted to honor Gideon and they gladly gave the prey that they had found—earrings and other gold. But it turned out to be an idol. Instead of a reminder of God's blessing, it became like a god to Israel. And "all Israel went thither a whoring after it: which thing became a snare unto Gideon, and to his house."

It is a remarkable fact, and there is both grief and joy in it, that the best men in the world have their frailties. God has no perfect man. In a fit of temper, Moses forsook his meekness and smote the rock when God said to speak to it. David fell into adultery and murder. Peter cursed and swore and quit the ministry. Noah got drunk. Good Christians at Corinth put up with adultery and had divisions and strife that needed to be rebuked. Samuel did not securely train his sons to follow his footsteps.

So Gideon failed in this matter, and what may have been innocent in his intentions, turned out to be an object of idolatry.

We are reminded even that the brass snake upon a pole, which was used as a picture of Jesus Christ bearing our sin on the cross (Num. 21:9; John 3:14), became an idol, and Hezekiah had it destroyed. "He removed the high places, and brake the images, and cut down the groves, and brake in pieces the brasen serpent that Moses had made: for unto those days the children of Israel did burn incense to it: and he called it Nehushtan" (II Kings 18:4).

No doubt one reason God did not let men know what happened to the tables of stone where the Ten Commandments were written by the hand of God, or Aaron's rod that budded, or the safely kept pot of manna, or the golden candlestick or lampstand, is that these things would have been objects of worship. So God had them disappear.

In the Holy Land it is sad that the people who have made the most of sacred places and built churches and grown up traditions about them, seem to know less of the Gospel, and are less moved by the Spirit of God than others. Perhaps that is why no one can be sure of the place where Jesus was born. I do not think it was that cave in Bethlehem but it was in a stable. Perhaps that is why God left it intentionally doubtful between the Church of the Holy Sepulchre and the garden tomb and Gordon's Calvary in Jerusalem. God does not want men worshiping places. He is not concerned that men worship at Jerusalem, or Mount Gerizim with the Samaritans, but only "in Spirit and in truth."

But the life and the career of Gideon ought to stir the heart of every Christian and teach us to expect great things from God and give us a holy devotion to do the will of God at any cost, and completely.

7

Eli, the Preacher Whose Boys Went to Hell

He Was High Priest, a Judge in Israel, Yet His Sons, Though Priests, Were Unconverted, Irreverent, Adulterers; Were Slain for Their Sins, and Brought a Curse on Family Forever. God Said Father Was to Blame

Eli was the high priest in Israel, and judge, and could probably be called a prophet. His sons were so wicked that both were killed in God's anger and a curse was put on the whole family line forever. God held the father Eli responsible.

It is a sad story when the sons of a man of God go wrong, shame their father and mother, disgrace the name of God, and curse their own children.

Preachers' children get many a jibe; most of them are not deserved. Actually a larger proportion of ministers' sons go on to college and to striking usefulness in professions and the pulpit and business than from other homes. The godly influence of a really Christian home shows up wonderfully in the children.

But a preacher's family is so closely and critically watched that this family, in an exceptional case where children go wrong, gets more blame and is more noted by worldly people. They are anxious to criticise the preacher and his family.

It is only fair to consider that the children of very prominent families in any community have more temptations than others. They are more subject to criticism, are oftentimes more favored and spoiled. Any man in prominent leadership has to be extra careful to rear his children well.

But let all of us learn burning lessons, preachers and others, of how parents are responsible for their children and can always bring them up well and successfully for God. And if they fail, they must answer to God for their failure.

I. ELI, THE PRIEST AND JUDGE

The time of the judges was a time of confusion and disorganization in Israel. Judges 21:25 says, "In those days there was no king in Israel: every man did that which was right in his own eyes." In these two or three hundred years God had raised up Samson, Gideon and other judges to deliver Israel or to act as judges, settling matters between the people. The judges were also, in some sense, prophets of God.

1. Eli, Priest of God

We might call him "high priest" because he seems to have been in charge at the tabernacle where worship was carried on and offerings were brought. He was a very old man. When he died a little later, he was ninety-eight and had judged Israel forty years (I Sam. 4:15,18). His sons, Hophni and Phinehas, were active as priests, though Eli was in charge.

There is much evidence that Eli was a godly, good man. He rebuked Hannah when he thought she was drunken though she was not. He was greatly concerned about the ark of God when it was sent to battle, though he ought not to have allowed it to go. He was so brokenhearted when he heard the sad news that the ark was taken that he fell over backward from the bench where he sat waiting, and died. He was grieved over the sins of his boys, though not enough to discipline them or put them out of the priesthood.

He had the confidence of the people, as illustrated in Elkanah and Hannah who were glad to commit the child Samuel, given in answer to prayer, to his care and rearing.

He instructed Samuel, who heard a voice in the night, to answer back, "Speak, Lord; for thy servant heareth." There is much evidence that he was a good man but without much strength of character, a man who loved his boys more than he loved God, who was not insulted as he should have been by their irreverence. Yet when God's judgment was pronounced, he took it with resignation. He was a good man who yet let his boys go to ruin and so was responsible to God for it.

2. He Had a Place of Authority as a Judge in Israel

Since Eli judged Israel forty years, he was the one outstanding authority in all the nation. We remember how other judges took leadership of armies, executed the death penalty when necessary, and acted with all the authority of God.

So Eli had the authority to see that things went right in the priesthood and with his sons. He did not. Besides that, he was in such a place of prominence that all would look to his family for an example. He was all the more accountable because of God's blessings. The more God blesses, the more He holds people to account. The more authority He gives, the more responsibility He requires.

And Eli had the authority which all fathers had in the Jewish state. According to Deuteronomy 21:18-21 a father and mother could bring a drunken or rebellious son to the elders of the city, could declare him stubborn and rebellious, a glutton and a drunkard "and all the men of his city shall stone him with stones, that he die: so shalt thou put evil away from among you; and all Israel shall hear, and fear." So Eli had all the authority necessary to control his sons even when they were old.

It is a sad thing when a man of God lets his children go wrong. If a man is not a good Christian at home, he is not a good Christian. If a man is not a successful Christian in the rearing of his family, he is not a successful Christian, no matter if he preach great sermons, if he write important books, if he pastor a great church. The man who does not control his family and rear his children for God is a poor example for God's people and must suffer the judgment of God on himself and on his family.

3. Eli's Wicked Sons

The two sons of Eli mentioned here are Hophni and Phinehas, "the priests of the Lord," as you see from I Samuel 1:3. And we learn several things about their sinfulness.

First, they were unsaved.

First Samuel 2:12 says, "Now the sons of Eli were sons of Belial; they knew not the Lord."

In the Old Testament as in the New, no one could be right with God without being born again. Did you think that in Old Testament times people were saved through sacrifices, through ceremonial law? No! For in Acts 10:43 Peter said with authority, "To him [Jesus] give all the prophets witness, that through his name whosoever believeth in him shall receive remission of sins."

Romans 4 holds up Abraham's conversion as a type for all of us: "Abraham believed God, and it was counted unto him for righteousness" (Rom. 4:3; Gen. 15:6).

Nicodemus was surprised when Jesus said to him, "Ye must be born again." But he ought not have been, and Jesus rebuked him saying, "Art thou a master of Israel, and knowest not these things?" (John 3:10).

We remember that Psalm 19:7 says, "The law of the Lord is perfect, converting the soul." And in Psalm 51 David promised, "Restore unto me the joy of thy salvation; and uphold me with thy free spirit. Then will I teach transgressors thy ways; and sinners shall be converted unto thee" (vss. 12,13).

Proverbs 11:30 says, "The fruit of the righteous is a tree of life; and he that winneth souls is wise."

Eli should have won his children to the Lord. These boys were unconverted, even though they were priests. And they are typical of thousands of unconverted preachers—liberal, unbelievers, actually more followers of Ingersoll and Tom Paine than they are of godly preachers. They have on sheep's clothing but are ravening wolves. They are false prophets, claiming to be prophets of God. Eli's sons were unconverted.

Second, they were irreverent and sacrilegious.

In I Samuel 2:13-17 we read about how little regard these unsaved priests had for spiritual matters and for the office they served:

> "And the priests' custom with the people was, that,
> when any man offered sacrifice, the priest's servant

came, while the flesh was in seething, with a fleshhook of three teeth in his hand; And he struck it into the pan, or kettle, or caldron, or pot; all that the fleshhook brought up the priest took for himself. So they did in Shiloh unto all the Israelites that came thither. Also before they burnt the fat, the priest's servant came, and said to the man that sacrificed, Give flesh to roast for the priest; for he will not have sodden flesh of thee, but raw. And if any man said unto him, Let them not fail to burn the fat presently, and then take as much as thy soul desireth; then he would answer him, Nay; but thou shalt give it me now: and if not, I will take it by force. Wherefore the sin of the young men was very great before the Lord: for men abhorred the offering of the Lord."

I entered the ministry with fear and trembling. I remember how in my ordination I told my father I wanted godly, spiritual, soul-winning preachers to lay hands on my head, not men who were ordained but powerless.

I remember in my first full-time pastorate at Shamrock, Texas, how I pleaded with God, "Lord, if I cannot do it now in the first full-time pastorate, how can I ever be a success in the ministry!" I felt then as I feel now, I must have the blessing of God. No one is fit to be a minister who does not tremble at the responsibility laid upon him. I do not wonder that Paul the Apostle said, "I magnify mine office."

These sons of Eli had no reverence for the office of the priesthood nor for the sacrifices which were symbols and pictures of the coming Messiah. They thought of the priesthood as a good way to live richly on the offerings of the people.

We are reminded of the prophecy about false prophets in II Peter 2:3, "And through covetousness shall they with feigned words make merchandise of you . . . ." To these priests, Hophni and Phinehas, the priesthood was simply a way to live high. And their blasphemous hearts did not please God.

Third, these priests were openly adulterers.

In I Samuel 2:22-25 the Scripture says:

> *"Now Eli was very old, and heard all that his sons did
> unto all Israel; and how they lay with the women that as-
> sembled at the door of the tabernacle of the congrega-
> tion. And he said unto them, Why do ye such things? for
> I hear of your evil dealings by all this people. Nay, my
> sons; for it is no good report that I hear: ye make the
> Lord's people to transgress. If one man sin against
> another, the judge shall judge him: but if a man sin
> against the Lord, who shall intreat for him?
> Notwithstanding they hearkened not unto the voice of
> their father, because the Lord would slay them."*

Are you shocked? You should be and I should be. For anybody
who claims to serve God and then leads the people into sin, there
must be an awful punishment. For anyone to act as God's
representative and yet condone or excuse lewdness and im-
morality is a wicked business.

In the midst of a great independent revival campaign in Wax-
ahachie, Texas, a man, just returned from serving five years in
the state penitentiary as a bootlegger, sent for me. I had
preached plainly against sin. My wife was frightened and urged
me not to go. There had been many threats because of my
preaching on the liquor traffic, but I knew God was in it.

I found the man in a wheel chair. He had heart trouble. The
doctor told him that he probably wouldn't live but a few months.

He started to complain, telling how he had provided a car for
the man who ran for the sheriff's office, had put $200 cash into
his support, then he said, "Then he was elected, and then he sent
me to five years in hell in the penitentiary!"

I told him frankly, "I am glad to help you any way I can, and I
will be glad to pray for you, but let's have it understood from the
beginning: I am against the dirty liquor business and everybody
who takes part in it, and I am for the law enforcement and the
men in authority."

The man looked up to me and very pitifully said, "That is why

I sent for you. There are many preachers in this town, but you can't tell what side they are on. You can't trust what they tell you. I have only a few months to live, and I have to get right with God. I want somebody true to God to tell me how." The man soon forgave those he hated and he trusted the Lord and was wonderfully saved. Every week young people would go to his home to sing and pray with him until he died. But he wanted somebody who spoke plainly against sin. He could trust such a man of God.

Oh, how can anybody trust any man of God who doesn't take a plain, sharp stand against sin and wickedness!

I do not wonder that God was insulted and His anger burned hot against the sons of Eli and the family that produced them.

II. GOD'S CURSE ON THESE SINFUL MEN

The judgment of God on such sin was inevitable.

1. The Whole Family to Die Before Old Age

So in I Samuel 2:30-34 a prophet of God foretold what God would do:

> "Wherefore the Lord God of Israel saith, I said indeed that thy house, and the house of thy father, should walk before me for ever: but now the Lord saith, Be it far from me; for them that honour me I will honour, and they that despise me shall be lightly esteemed. Behold, the days come, that I will cut off thine arm, and the arm of thy father's house, that there shall not be an old man in thine house. And thou shalt see an enemy in my habitation, in all the wealth which God shall give Israel: and there shall not be an old man in thine house for ever. And the man of thine, whom I shall not cut off from mine altar, shall be to consume thine eyes, and to grieve thine heart: and all the increase of thine house shall die in the flower of their age. And this shall be a sign unto thee, that shall come upon thy two sons, on Hophni and Phinehas; in one day they shall die both of them."

2. The Family's Iniquity Not to Be Purged
by Sacrifice

And again the Lord spake to the little boy, Samuel:

"And the Lord came, and stood, and called as at other times, Samuel, Samuel. Then Samuel answered, Speak; for thy servant heareth. And the Lord said to Samuel, Behold, I will do a thing in Israel, at which both the ears of every one that heareth it shall tingle. In that day I will perform against Eli all things which I have spoken concerning his house: when I begin, I will also make an end. For I have told him that I will judge his house for ever for the iniquity which he knoweth; because his sons made themselves vile, and he restrained them not. And therefore I have sworn unto the house of Eli, that the iniquity of Eli's house shall not be purged with sacrifice nor offering for ever."—I Sam. 3:10-14.

And so it came to pass that these sons of Eli took the ark of God in battle against the Philistines. They were both slain, the ark was taken, and when the messenger brought the word to Eli, he fell off the seat backward and broke his neck.

That judgment of God was to continue to other generations. In I Kings 1:7 we find Abiathar the priest was one who followed Adonijah, trying to take the kingdom that should have gone to Solomon. And in I Kings 2:27 we read, "So Solomon thrust out Abiathar from being priest unto the Lord; that he might fulfil the word of the Lord, which he spake concerning the house of Eli in Shiloh."

An age-long curse came on the family because of the sins of these priests.

III. ELI WAS RESPONSIBLE FOR HIS SONS AND THEIR SINS

Does it seem shocking to you that Eli, the godly father, must suffer for the sins of his sons? Yes, but he was to blame for them, the Bible plainly says.

1. Scriptures Expressly Teach One Can Raise Children in Fear of the Lord and They Will Turn Out Good

Proverbs 22:6 says, "Train up a child in the way he should go: and when he is old, he will not depart from it."

Children who are reared for God can be turned out to be noble Christians and honor God.

A mother in Texas wrote me about her forty-year-old son, married and with a wife and five children. He was a drunkard, a whoremonger, but the brokenhearted mother who wrote asking me to pray said, "But I know I raised him right and when he is old he will come back to it, the Scripture said."

I found it necessary to write her that the Bible says nothing of the kind. It says if she had reared the boy right, he would not, right now, be a drunkard and an adulterer. The Bible doesn't say when a child gets old he will go back to his rearing, but when he is old, independent and grown, he will still live for God as he was reared.

Again Proverbs 22:15 says, "Foolishness is bound in the heart of a child; but the rod of correction shall drive it far from him." And the promise is enlarged in Proverbs 23:13,14, "Withhold not correction from the child: for if thou beatest him with the rod, he shall not die. Thou shalt beat him with the rod, and shalt deliver his soul from hell."

2. Many Scriptures Promise Success, Prosperity, Sure Blessing to Those Who Follow the Lord and Obey Him

What a rich blessing is promised in Psalm 1. For the man who turns away from the fellowship and counsel of the ungodly, the wicked, the scorner but who meditates day and night in the Word of God is the promise, ". . . whatsoever he doeth shall prosper." That promise leaves no room for a son to turn out to be a drunkard and a rebel, an adulterer, unsaved, godless and wicked. No, one can be prospered in rearing his family for God.

And do not all those great promises about God's answering prayer apply to the matter of rearing children, too? God hears those who seek Him with all their heart, as Jeremiah 29:12,13 tells us, and if God shows great and mighty things to those who call unto Him, as Jeremiah 33:3 says, could not one ask God's help about rearing children and get it?

If one lacks wisdom about rearing his family, could he not claim the promise of James 1:5, "If any of you lack wisdom, let him ask of God, that giveth to all men liberally, and upbraideth not"?

And wouldn't John 15:7 apply? "If ye abide in me, and my words abide in you, ye shall ask what ye will, and it shall be done unto you." Surely that means that one who is wholly committed to the Word of God and to Christ can have whatever his enlightened and dedicated heart wants.

3. Blessed, Divine Law of Sowing and Reaping Applies to Children

If Galatians 6:7-9 is true, then it will be true about rearing a family:

> *"Be not deceived; God is not mocked: for whatsoever a man soweth, that shall he also reap. For he that soweth to his flesh shall of the flesh reap corruption; but he that soweth to the Spirit shall of the Spirit reap life everlasting. And let us not be weary in well doing: for in due season we shall reap, if we faint not."*

Evidently those who sow righteously will reap righteously. One cannot be excused for letting his children grow up rebels, unconverted, disobedient, irreverent and wicked.

IV. HOW ELI FAILED WITH HIS SONS

Since God plainly teaches that Eli was responsible for his sons, and that all of us must give an account for our families, let us carefully consider how Eli failed.

1. He Failed to Get Them Converted

We are told that "the sons of Eli were sons of Belial; they knew not the Lord." They were unconverted.

A father can make sure his children are saved. Joshua said, "As for me and my house, we will serve the Lord" (Josh. 24:15).

Of Abraham, God said, "For I know him, that he will command his children and his household after him, and they shall keep the way of the Lord, to do justice and judgment" (Gen. 18:19).

I remember in a revival campaign a lovely, bright ten-year-old girl who was unconverted. I spoke to her mother about it. The bright child was in the fifth grade. But the mother said, "I want her to make up her mind for herself. She thinks everything I do is wonderful. She would do anything to please me, so I do not want to over-influence her about this."

I asked her, "If she were a thief, would you not do anything to see that she learned to be honest? If she wanted to drink whiskey, would you let her make up her own mind about that? If she decided to be a harlot, a prostitute, would you leave it to her to make up her own mind? Why does God give a mother influence over a child if not to use it to get the child to Heaven? You must answer to God for your daughter."

The next service the mother and daughter both came weeping, the girl trusting Christ at her mother's insistence.

In Tabernacle Baptist Church in Cooke County, Texas, a fine country church, I was pastor during my student days in Southwestern Seminary, at Fort Worth. I remember one morning I preached on the Christian home and said that Mother and Dad should be responsible for the children and that they should "train up a child in the way he should go: and when he is old, he will not depart from it." An agitated father insisted I go home with him. He must talk to me. When the mother went into the house, the man, standing in the yard, said, "What you preached this morning is not so; I know I did raise my boy right." Since he had challenged what I said, I told him very plainly, "You are not arguing with me but with God. It is He who says, 'Train up a child in the way he should go: and when he is old, he will not depart from it.' What is wrong with your boy?" He didn't want to tell me. I insisted, "Either you tell me now or I will go in the house and ask your wife. You have said that the Bible isn't true; now we are going to settle this matter. Where is your boy?"

Sadly he said, "He is in the state penitentiary being punished for a major crime. But I know I raised him right. I am not to blame."

I asked him, "Since you insist you have done right about it, let me ask you, Did you have a family altar and take time to read the Bible and pray with your family every day?"

He had not. Indignantly he said, "You city people may have time for that kind of foolishness, but here on the farm we work hard, and we don't have time for it."

I asked him, "Did you ever try to win that boy to Christ? Did you ever say to him, 'Son, we are starting revival services at our church, and I want you to come to Christ and be saved'?"

He said, "No, I never did believe in this Methodist way of dragging children into the church when they don't know what it is all about."

So I said, "You never had a family altar; you never taught the child the Bible; you never tried to get him saved. Now he is in the penitentiary and you think you are not to blame! Let me ask another question. Did you whip that boy and make him mind? Did you make him say, 'Yes, Sir!' and 'Yes, Ma'am!' and did you whip him and make him obey?"

He answered back, "Dr. Rice, my boy was different. He was nervous and high-strung and you couldn't use those methods on him."

I explained that I was nervous and high-strung also but that my dad just got a little more nervous than I did, so we early got that settled.

The boy had gone to the state penitentiary a criminal and the father tried to evade the blame. He was wrong. He could have won that boy to Christ and could have disciplined him and made him into a good character, but he did not.

Eli did not get his boys saved.

I went to a home where a fifteen-year-old girl had suddenly died. The girl had been in my home and she had told me when she trusted Christ as Saviour. In the home the mother lay weeping. I told her, "You must not weep as if you had no hope. Goldie was a Christian. You can see her again."

Suddenly she sat up in the bed and said, "How do you know

she was a Christian? How do you know she went to Heaven?"

I answered, "Because she told me." And some women in the room spoke up to remind the mother that in a Methodist revival campaign Goldie had trusted the Lord and claimed Him openly.

The mother sobbed, "Oh, I thought she had gone to Hell! I didn't know that she was saved!"

But that mother would have been to blame had the child gone to Hell, and had nobody else cared any more than she did, the girl would have been lost.

I am saying that God holds parents responsible to win their children to Christ. Eli did not win his sons.

3. Eli Did Not Chasten His Sons, Nor Discipline Them

The Scripture says in I Samuel 3:13, "For I have told him that I will judge his house for ever for the iniquity which he knoweth; because his sons made themselves vile, and he restrained them not."

He did not restrain these wicked sons. He did not chastise them. Now that they are grown men with families and official priests, they have no fear of God because they were not taught to fear their father when they were younger.

In many a home the wife is a rebel against her husband and the parents turn out rebellious, criminal-minded children. They do not respect their father nor obey the rules at home. So, then, they do not respect the teacher nor obey the rules at school. Then on the street they do not respect the policeman and the laws of the land. From that kind of people come the dope-heads, the draft-card burners, the hippies, the rebellious youth. The so-called "generation gap" is settled very early in homes where there is godly, strict discipline.

Someone may say, "Oh, I love my boy too much to whip him." No, you love your own lazy self and do not have the character and the integrity to make the boy do right; so you take your easy, lazy way and let the boy go to Hell! Proverbs 13:24 says, "He that spareth his rod hateth his son: but he that loveth him chasteneth him betimes." It is a fake kind of love that does not punish the child and make him do right.

You may say, "I do not think it is right to always be beating on a child." No, you don't have to do that. There is a way of whipping children that gets things settled. There is a way of whipping children that lasts for a long time.

Years ago a woman columnist in the newspaper wrote, "If my father had beaten me, I would have hated him as long as I lived." My brother, Dr. Bill Rice, said, "If it had been our father, by the time he got through, she wouldn't hate anybody; she would love him to death for stopping."

God chastens every son whom He receives; why should a human father think he is a better father than God? Those wicked priests could have been converted when they were young, could have been taught reverence for God and for Dad and Mother and could have had all that rebellion taken out long ago had Eli chastened them as he should have done.

And even after they were grown, Eli was wrong to let them go on in their sin. For in Deuteronomy 21:18-21 he was given the plain instructions how a father and mother could take a rebellious son before the elders of the city and charge him with being stubborn, rebellious and drunken and have him stoned to death. Eli was the high priest and could have put his boys out of the priesthood, but he did not do so. His sons "made themselves vile, and he restrained them not."

That was part of David's great sin, too. He was a great man of God, but he did not restrain and discipline his children. In I Kings 1:5,6 we read how, after the rebellion of Absalom, Adonijah planned to take the kingdom and be king instead of Solomon whom David had appointed:

> *"Then Adonijah the son of Haggith exalted himself, saying, I will be king: and he prepared him chariots and horsemen, and fifty men to run before him. And his father had not displeased him at any time in saying, Why hast thou done so? and he also was a very goodly man; and his mother bare him after Absalom."*

Ah, there is the secret—"his father had not displeased him at any time in saying, Why hast thou done so?" That, too, no doubt was the trouble with Absalom. He had not been disciplined nor taught strict obedience.

How the Rechabites obeyed Jonadab, the son of Rechab, their father! They are held up as a holy example to the rebellious Jews. In Jeremiah 35:2 God commanded Jeremiah, "Go unto the house of the Rechabites, and speak unto them, and bring them into the house of the Lord, into one of the chambers, and give them wine to drink." So, Jeremiah brought these Rechabites into the house of the Lord and put pots full of wine and cups and asked them to drink. And in Jeremiah 35:5-10 we read:

> *"And I set before the sons of the house of the Rechabites pots full of wine, and cups, and I said unto them, Drink ye wine. But they said, We will drink no wine: for Jonadab the son of Rechab our father commanded us, saying, Ye shall drink no wine, neither ye, nor your sons for ever: Neither shall ye build house, nor sow seed, nor plant vineyard, nor have any: but all your days ye shall dwell in tents; that ye may live many days in the land where ye be strangers. Thus have we obeyed the voice of Jonadab the son of Rechab our father in all that he hath charged us, to drink no wine all our days, we, our wives, our sons, nor our daughters; Nor to build houses for us to dwell in: neither have we vineyard, nor field, nor seed: But we have dwelt in tents, and have obeyed, and done according to all that Jonadab our father commanded us."*

No, they would not drink wine. Their father taught them better. And they would dwell in tents, following the pattern of Abraham, Isaac and Jacob in remembering that they are strangers and sojourners in this world for they look for a heavenly home later. Ah, had Eli reared his children like that! But he did not.

We can be sure that two elements are absolutely necessary in raising godly children. Those elements are by earnestly teaching them the Word of God and so teaching them to be saved and live for God, with family altar and Bible teaching; and second, by discipline and correction so that they must grow habits of godly living and respect for law and order and right and God.

4. Eli Put Sons Before God!

In I Samuel 2:29 God charged Eli, "Wherefore kick ye at my sacrifice and at mine offering, which I have commanded in my habitation; and honourest thy sons above me, to make yourselves fat with the chiefest of all the offerings of Israel my people?"

Eli honored his sons above God. He did not care about the careful regulations God had made concerning these sacrifices, nor did his rebellious, unbelieving sons.

Did Eli love his sons too much? Well, he did not love God and righteousness enough to make his sons do right.

Many, many good Christians put their children ahead of God in their plans.

I am thinking about a greatly-used man of God, an out-and-out fundamental, Bible-believing preacher. But his daughter went to a denominational college where she was very popular and had leadership among students. The father was greatly influenced, and so he went into the denomination and let up for the time on his protest against modernism.

I am thinking about another man greatly used of God but whose wife did not like the reproaches that came on hard-preaching, out-and-out fundamentalists. She did not want her children to suffer the reproach that the father had. The pressure increased until the father went back into the denomination and sacrificed the great blessing of God on his evangelistic ministry.

I know another family with a brilliant son, a gifted speaker and musician. They sent him to a fine Bible-believing Christian college, but wanting him to have favor with the denomination, they sent him to Louisville to the Southern Baptist Seminary. There his strict standards of life and doctrine were scoffed at. Soon he was smoking cigarettes and attending movies. Later Christian workers found him in a great city and when they talked to him about the Lord, he told them plainly that he had once believed all that, too, but he had now laid it aside; he did not now believe the Bible, did not now try to live a clean, Christian life. He was ruined by the compromising position that sent him to the denominational seminary in order to get prestige and standing.

God is a jealous God. It is true that a man is to love his wife, even as himself, but he is not to love her before God. It is true that a man must love his children, provide for them, teach them, but they are not to be before God. Jesus said plainly, "If any man come to me, and hate not his father, and mother, and wife, and children, and brethren, and sisters, yea, and his own life also, he cannot be my disciple" (Luke 14:26).

If a man loves God as much as he ought, his love for others will take a far lesser part in his life. A man will not love his children nor his wife less, but they cease to be the dominating part of his life, if he really puts Christ first. Ah, too bad, Eli, that you honored your sons above God.

5. Religious Impact of Eli on Sons Was for a Formal Religion

Eli was high priest. He was a good man, a judge of Israel, but he took a rather formal attitude toward his duties as a priest and the duties of his sons. Isn't it strange that he would think anyone could do the work of a priest without being converted, and without living a holy life? And when war came with the Philistines, he permitted his two ungodly sons to take the ark of the covenant with them into battle. No doubt they thought that in some rather mysterious way the ark itself would help win the battle. They thought of God in rather general, ceremonial terms. No doubt Eli had felt the same way or he would not have allowed the ark of the covenant to be taken into battle. They thought there must be some efficacy in carrying the ark of God itself out into the battle.

Even today people think that sprinkling and catechism and confirmation make a Christian and they think that going to church and going through Christian ceremonies are enough service for God.

And today the formal worship services in the churches are the enemy of evangelism and hinder soul winning. Many men would like to have Billy Sunday results from an Episcopalian-type format of the services. But it doesn't work that way. Robed choirs, services starting with, "Holy, Holy, Holy," and the Doxology and where it is counted a sin to greet people happily when they come into the church building, and where the religion is largely a matter of form and people must know when to rise and when to sit— that kind of formality is the enemy of Bible Christianity. No formal worship services come in the Bible. The terms are not used nor the practice approved in the Bible.

I held services in a large Reformed church on two different occasions. The pastor, a noble, good man, earnestly urged me to return for a revival campaign. He said plainly that many of his church officers were unconverted. He wanted me to come and help win them. But I felt I must turn it down. I told him that as long as he kept on teaching young people the catechism and confirming them and taking them into church membership without their definitely committing themselves to trust Christ and be saved, I felt I could not come to try to get them saved.

Formality is the enemy of heartfelt Bible religion.

CONCLUSION—OUR LESSON!

Let every father and mother who reads this take seriously to heart this truth: You must answer to God for your children. If you do not see that they are saved, if you do not punish them and teach them to obey, if you do not have family altar and teach them the Word of God, then you must answer to God for the ruin that will come on your children.

I earnestly suggest that every family set aside a certain period daily, and plan that with the whole family assembled you will read, usually, a full chapter in the Bible and then have a circle of prayer. There is no way to have a Christian home without having a time of Bible reading and prayer together.

In our home, one read two verses, then the next would read two verses, so each one would know when his time came. He must follow the reading carefully and keep up. We read around and around the breakfast table after we had our meal, until the whole chapter was read. The next day we took the next chapter.

Oh, set out to read the Bible. Teach it diligently to your children, and get them saved, and make them into good Christians. You must answer to God for your children.

8

King Solomon

Great King of Israel Who Fell Into Idolatry

The Lord Jesus spoke of "Solomon in all his glory" (Matt. 6:29; Luke 12:27). Solomon ruled over Israel in its widest sweep of territory and population. He built the mighty Temple of God in Jerusalem. He asked for and had the greatest spiritual wisdom of any man of his time. He was used of God to assemble the book of Proverbs, largely his own; to write the books of Ecclesiastes and The Song of Solomon, and perhaps two Psalms, 72 and 127.

It is a beautiful story but with a sad ending. Here was a great and admirable character, one who turned away into ruin and sin. He was a great king. He married hundreds of wives, including daughters of the greatest kings in the world. He had a regular income of millions in gold. His court was the most lavish and beautiful and sophisticated in the world. Yet the power, the riches, and the heathen wives led to decay in his character and finally into open idolatry. This beautiful story has a sad ending. And where he ruled over all the twelve tribes of Israel, ten tribes split away from his son Rehoboam and Israel will never have the same greatness until Christ the Son of David comes to reign.

I. SOLOMON HAD A GREAT START

Some men climb from abject poverty to riches, and from obscurity to fame. Not so Solomon. He had a great start: born to a king, accustomed to riches, seated on a great throne which he did not earn by labor or war.

1. Was Beloved of God

Solomon was born to David and Bathsheba after the pitiful story of their sin and the curse it brought. When David took Bathsheba the wife of Uriah the Hittite and led her into sin, and had her husband killed, Nathan the prophet pronounced the judgment of God upon him. He must restore fourfold. The baby died despite David's fasting and prayer. David's daughter Tamar was raped by her half-brother Amnon. Amnon was slain then by the hand of Absalom, Tamar's brother. Then Absalom, neglected and held at a distance by David, rebelled and sought the kingdom, resulting in the death of thousands. David and Bathsheba suffered greatly for their sin.

But how pitiful and forgiving is God! "He will not always chide: neither will he keep his anger for ever. He hath not dealt with us after our sins; nor rewarded us according to our iniquities" (Ps. 103:9,10). It is wonderful that when God forgives He forgets and God has promised to forgive sins, "And their sins and and iniquities will I remember no more" (Heb. 10:17).

Some time ago a preacher friend prayed saying, "Lord, I am so sorry for all my sins," and the Lord seemed to answer, "What sins?"

And so God, with such a tender heart, smiled on the second baby of David and Bathsheba. Second Samuel 12:24,25 says: "And David comforted Bath-sheba his wife, and went in unto her, and lay with her: and she bare a son, and he called his name Solomon: and the Lord loved him. And he sent by the hand of Nathan the prophet; and he called his name Jedidiah, because of the Lord."

Ah, that baby! "The Lord loved him." And God seemed some way to comfort David and Bathsheba in this son. It is just as if a father, after chastising sorely a son for his disobedience, takes the penitent child into his arms and loves him. So God gave Solomon, ". . . and the Lord loved him."

I am sure this is part of the reason why David felt Solomon should be king. And God seemed to have ordained it so, too. Even Adonijah, who sought to seize the kingdom, later came to Bathsheba and said about Solomon, ". . . howbeit the kingdom is turned about, and is become my brother's: for it was his from the Lord" (I Kings 2:15).

God, by drastic action, showed King Nebuchadnezzar ". . . that the most high God ruled in the kingdom of men, and that he appointeth over it whomsoever he will" (Dan. 5:21). So God had a part in preparing Solomon, whom He loved, and putting him on the throne of Israel, and all Israel rejoiced.

The older brothers were passed by and the young son was given the great honor to follow David as king.

2. Sought Spiritual Wisdom to Rule Aright

When Solomon took the throne, we read in II Chronicles 1:1, "And Solomon the son of David was strengthened in his kingdom, and the Lord his God was with him, and magnified him exceedingly." Then verses 7 to 12 tell us how Solomon sought the greatest wisdom from God and found it:

> "In that night did God appear unto Solomon, and said unto him, Ask what I shall give thee. And Solomon said unto God, Thou hast shewed great mercy unto David my father, and hast made me to reign in his stead. Now, O Lord God, let thy promise unto David my father be established: for thou hast made me king over a people like the dust of the earth in multitude. Give me now wisdom and knowledge, that I may go out and come in before this people: for who can judge this thy people, that is so great? And God said to Solomon, Because this was in thine heart, and thou hast not asked riches, wealth, or honour, nor the life of thine enemies, neither yet hast asked long life; but hast asked wisdom and knowledge for thyself, that thou mayest judge my people, over whom I have made thee king: Wisdom and knowledge is granted unto thee; and I will give thee riches, and wealth, and honour, such as none of the kings have had that have been before thee, neither shall there any after thee have the like."

And besides the wisdom which God gave Solomon and promised him for the future, he was promised also wealth and honor and long life, "such as none of the kings have had that have been before thee, neither shall there any after thee have the like."

3. Set Out Boldly to Build a Great Temple for the Lord and to Lead People in Faithful Service to God

Second Chronicles 2:1 says, "And Solomon determined to build an house for the name of the Lord, and an house for his kingdom." David had saved up much gold, silver and brass. In I Chronicles 29:2-5 David said:

"Now I have prepared with all my might for the house of my God the gold for things to be made of gold, and the silver for things of silver, and the brass for things of brass, the iron for things of iron, and wood for things of wood; onyx stones, and stones to be set, glistering stones, and of divers colours, and all manner of precious stones, and marble stones in abundance. Moreover, because I have set my affection to the house of my God, I have of mine own proper good, of gold and silver, which I have given to the house of my God, over and above all that I have prepared for the holy house, Even three thousand talents of gold, of the gold of Ophir, and seven thousand talents of refined silver, to overlay the walls of the houses withal: The gold for things of gold, and the silver for things of silver, and for all manner of work to be made by the hands of artificers. And who then is willing to consecrate his service this day unto the Lord?"

David is giving a solemn charge to Solomon, saying,

"I go the way of all the earth: be thou strong therefore, and shew thyself a man; And keep the charge of the Lord thy God, to walk in his ways, to keep his statutes, and his commandments, and his judgments, and his testimonies, as it is written in the law of Moses, that thou mayest prosper in all that thou doest, and whithersoever thou turnest thyself: That the Lord may continue his word which he spake concerning me, saying, If thy children take heed to their way, to walk before me in truth with all their heart and with all their soul, there shall not fail thee (said he) a man on the throne of Israel."—I Kings 2:2-4.

So Solomon set out to conscript thousands of men to prepare material for the Temple and he set out to offer sacrifices and judge the people righteously. It was a good start Solomon had.

II. THE GRANDEUR OF SOLOMON'S REIGN

God had promised Solomon, ". . . and I will give thee riches, and wealth, and honour, such as none of the kings have had that have been before thee, neither shall there any after thee have the like." That indicates that neither the courts of the Pharaohs of Egypt, nor the Babylonian palaces, nor the emperors at Rome had the impressive grandeur of the reign of Solomon.

The Lord Jesus, speaking of the lilies of the field, compared them favorably with "even Solomon in all his glory." How sad that such a glorious reign should lead away from God, but Solomon's reign was rich and glorious!

1. Built the Grandest Temple Ever Built

David had already laid aside three thousand talents of gold (about 90 million dollars) and some 20 million dollars' worth of silver, to overlay all the walls of the Temple (I Chron. 29:3,4). So Solomon made no small plans. He made a levy of 30,000 Israelites to spend each one month in Lebanon and two months at home. Besides these of the remnants of the Gentile nations who were under tribute, Solomon drafted 70,000 common laborers and 80,000 woodsmen in the mountains to prepare the cedars of Lebanon and bring them to the coast and down by sea to the coast of Israel and over land. These were helped by many of King Hiram's builders. The stonework was of costly cut stones. All the walls and the floors were covered with solid gold. The tremendous building was seven years in building (I Kings 6:38). What a glorious building!

The great church buildings—St. Peter's at Rome, St. Paul's in London, St. Sophia in Istanbul—may be larger, though probably the Temple with the courts and porches was larger, but none is so magnificent and rich as was Solomon's Temple.

2. Kingdom of Israel Was at Its Largest and
Strongest Under Solomon

We learn that David had conquered the Syrians and the Moabites and Edom and had garrisons in Damascus, Amman and at Edom (II Sam. 8:2,5,6,12). So Solomon's reign included not only Palestine on the left bank but what is now Jordan and Syria. Solomon had conquered and occupied Hamath-Zobah, had built Tadmor in the wilderness and the store cities. The remnants of the Hittites, Amorites, Perizzites, Hivites and Jebusites were made to pay tribute, as we see in II Chronicles 8. First Kings 4:21 tells us, "And Solomon reigned over all kingdoms from the river unto the land of the Philistines, and unto the border of Egypt: they brought presents, and served Solomon all the days of his life."

Unfortunately Solomon patterned after the Pharaoh in Egypt and the Hittites and Syrians, for "Solomon gathered together chariots and horsemen: and he had a thousand and four hundred chariots, and twelve thousand horsemen, whom he bestowed in the cities for chariots, and with the king at Jerusalem" (I Kings 10:26). And verse 27, "And the king made silver to be in Jerusalem as stones, and cedars made he to be as the sycamore trees that are in the vale, for abundance."

The riches of Solomon were astonishing. One year's income was 666 talents of gold (about 19 million dollars), besides his support in food and other provisions from the people (II Chron. 9:13). "And all the kings of Arabia and governors of the country brought gold and silver to Solomon" (II Chron. 9:14).

"And king Solomon passed all the kings of the earth in riches and wisdom. And all the kings of the earth sought the presence of Solomon, to hear his wisdom, that God had put in his heart. And they brought every man his present, vessels of silver, and vessels of gold, and raiment, harness, and spices, horses, and mules, a rate year by year. And Solomon had four thousand stalls for horses and chariots, and twelve thousand horsemen; whom he bestowed in the chariot cities, and with the king at Jerusalem."—II Chron. 9:22-25.

3. Solomon's Fame Reached Throughout the
Then Known World

The magnificent Temple of Jehovah which Solomon built at Jerusalem, taking seven years and employing nearly 200,000 men, must have become famous worldwide. Solomon built a palace for himself and for the queen, Pharaoh's daughter, of like grandeur.

And the wisdom of Solomon, a gift of God, became the talk of all the kingdoms.

> "And God gave Solomon wisdom and understanding exceeding much, and largeness of heart, even as the sand that is on the sea shore. And Solomon's wisdom excelled the wisdom of all the children of the east country, and all the wisdom of Egypt. For he was wiser than all men; than Ethan the Ezrahite, and Heman, and Chalcol, and Darda, the sons of Mahol: and his fame was in all nations round about. And he spake three thousand proverbs: and his songs were a thousand and five. And he spake of trees, from the cedar tree that is in Lebanon even unto the hyssop that springeth out of the wall: he spake also of beasts, and of fowl, and of creeping things, and of fishes. And there came of all people to hear the wisdom of Solomon, from all kings of the earth, which had heard of his wisdom."—I Kings 4:29-34.

Solomon married one of Pharaoh's daughters and that great Pharaoh conquered a city and gave it to his daughter as a dowry. Hiram, king of Tyre, loved David and sent him sixscore talents of gold.

The Queen of Sheba heard afar of the wisdom and glory of Solomon and came to see. She brought gold and spices and treasured things. But she was overwhelmed with the magnificence which she found.

> "And when the queen of Sheba heard of the fame of Solomon concerning the name of the Lord, she came to prove him with hard questions. And she came to Jerusalem with a very great train, with camels that bare

spices, and very much gold, and precious stones: and when she was come to Solomon, she communed with him of all that was in her heart. And Solomon told her all her questions: there was not any thing hid from the king, which he told her not. And when the queen of Sheba had seen all Solomon's wisdom, and the house that he had built, And the meat of his table, and the sitting of his servants, and the attendance of his ministers, and their apparel, and his cupbearers, and his ascent by which he went up unto the house of the Lord; there was no more spirit in her. And she said to the king, It was a true report that I heard in mine own land of thy acts and of thy wisdom. Howbeit I believed not the words, until I came, and mine eyes had seen it: and, behold, the half was not told me: thy wisdom and prosperity exceedeth the fame which I heard. Happy are thy men, happy are these thy servants, which stand continually before thee, and that hear thy wisdom. Blessed be the Lord thy God, which delighted in thee, to set thee on the throne of Israel: because the Lord loved Israel for ever, therefore made he thee king, to do judgment and justice. And she gave the king an hundred and twenty talents of gold, and of spices very great store, and precious stones: there came no more such abundance of spices as these which the queen of Sheba gave to king Solomon."—I Kings 10:1-10.

Was the Queen of Sheba converted? I hope so, though we do not know. But the fame of the wisdom of Solomon was worldwide.

Meantime, God used him to write The Song of Solomon, Ecclesiastes and perhaps most of the Proverbs in the book of Proverbs. The book is entitled "The Proverbs of Solomon the son of David King of Israel." Dr. Scofield says,

"That the Proverbs were Solomon's (1.1) implies no more than that he gathered into orderly arrangement sayings already current amongst the people, the wisdom of the Spirit, perhaps through many centuries (Eccl. 12.9) Chapters 25-29 were current in Hezekiah's time (25.1).

Chapter 30 and 31 are by Agur and Lemuel."

At least a thousand of the proverbs belong to Solomon and he, no doubt, collected most of the others.

Solomon, son of David, with the grandest reign any king of Israel ever had, did not end well.

III. DECLINE AND RUIN OF SOLOMON

We know that when a strong, good man falls into sin, bad habits, bad company and wickedness, it is a result of a progressive course of compromise, of letting down the bars, of giving way more and more to surrounding influences. So it was with Solomon.

1. His Riches and Success Provided Sore Temptation

We do not wonder that Jesus said, "How hardly shall they that have riches enter into the kingdom of God!" (Mark 10:23). If a man has a mansion here, he is not so much attracted to the mansion in Heaven. When a man has fame and popularity in this world, he does not feel the need for the comfort of salvation. It is hard to convince the man who has a fine moral character and a great reputation for spiritual wisdom that he is a sinner, that he needs forgiveness and salvation. Solomon's riches were a hindrance. God had clearly commanded that a king "neither shall he greatly multiply to himself silver and gold" (Deut. 17:17).

Solomon was put on a great throne which he did not earn. He did not earn the place as had David his father. Riches and prosperity were a snare.

2. There Is Evidence That Solomon Was Not
Very Strictly Reared

David was a man after God's heart, we are told, and he followed God with all his heart. But he did have difficulty with his children. That is partly because he had a number of wives and there could not be a close family relationship of a father with all his children. So it turns out that one son, Amnon, raped his sister Tamar; Absalom, Tamar's brother, killed Amnon and then rebelled against David and tried to take the kingdom.

Adonijah, another son, tried to take the kingdom when it was intended for Solomon. Thus we find David's children seemed to be undisciplined.

That is indicated particularly in the case of Adonijah. In explanation of why he tried to seize the kingdom, I Kings 1:6 says, "And his father had not displeased him at any time in saying, Why hast thou done so?"

We may be sure, then, that while Solomon was greatly loved and was straitly charged by David in spiritual matters and no doubt had good intentions and an honest ambition to please God, and have His wisdom and power, yet he had not grown the character that comes from a well-disciplined home. It is likely that Solomon himself was inspired to write that Scripture, "Train up a child in the way he should go: and when he is old, he will not depart from it" (Prov. 22:6). And Proverbs 29:15 gives us God's solemn word, "The rod and reproof give wisdom: but a child left to himself bringeth his mother to shame."

It is no accident when a child, trained up in the way he should go, stays with his godly life and heritage. It is not surprising when a child, undisciplined, no matter how sincere his intentions, does not have the character to stay straight after he comes to great temptation. Solomon missed, we think, the proper discipline in childhood.

3. Solomon Was Too Much Influenced by Heathen World About Him

We know that Solomon was on very friendly terms with many foreign kings and princes. He patterned after Egypt and had fourteen hundred chariots and thousands of horsemen. His mind was overmuch on riches. He oppressed the people so that when he died they came to beg his son Rehoboam to lighten their burdens, but he would not.

And Solomon's contact with the outside world and his anxiety to please the great crowds that fawned upon him and the kings and great people who came to see him, was, no doubt, a part of the attitude that led him to marry many wives and heathen women who led him into sin.

4. His Fatal Mistake Was Marrying Heathen Women Who Led Him Into Idolatry

Think for a moment how far wrong Solomon went in his marriages.

The Lord had plainly commanded Israel that when they came into the land of promise that they should smite and destroy the heathen idolaters there:

> *"Neither shalt thou make marriages with them; thy daughter thou shalt not give unto his son, nor his daughter shalt thou take unto thy son. For they will turn away thy son from following me, that they may serve other gods: so will the anger of the Lord be kindled against you, and destroy thee suddenly."*—Deut. 7:3,4.

And in Exodus 34 Israel was strictly charged not to make any covenant or tie with the Amorites, Canaanites, Hittites, Perizzites, Hivites or the Jebusites, but they should be destroyed and their altars and images and groves cut down:

> *"For thou shalt worship no other god: for the Lord, whose name is Jealous, is a jealous God: Lest thou make a covenant with the inhabitants of the land, and they go a whoring after their gods, and do sacrifice unto their gods, and one call thee, and thou eat of his sacrifice; And thou take of their daughters unto thy sons, and their daughters go a whoring after their gods, and make thy sons go a whoring after their gods."*—Exod. 34:14-16.

Marriage to a heathen woman was strictly forbidden, yet Solomon married Pharaoh's daughter and princesses of other kings far and near. We are told:

> *"But king Solomon loved many strange women* [foreign women], *together with the daughter of Pharaoh, women of the Moabites, Ammonites, Edomites, Zidonians, and Hittites; Of the nations concerning which the Lord said unto the children of Israel, Ye shall not go in to them, neither shall they come in unto you: for surely they will turn away your heart after their gods: Solomon clave unto these in love."*—I Kings 11:1,2.

Oh, Solomon, bad company is the way to ruin! It led to the captivity and blinding and death of Samson. Heathen marriages before the flood, when the sons of God took the daughters of men, as many as they chose and the whole world became violent and wicked, led to a violent, wicked race. So when Peter sat by the fire with soldiers who would crucify Jesus, he lost all his courage and cursed and swore and denied the Saviour.

King Asa was a good man, but he made a treaty for help in war with the king of Syria, and God rebuked him (II Chron. 16:7-9).

Jehoshaphat the son of Asa was also a good man, but he made a bargain with ungodly Ahab of the Northern Kingdom and helped him in the battle in which Ahab was killed. And God sent a prophet to censure Jehoshaphat:

> *"And Jehu the son of Hanani the seer went out to meet him, and said to king Jehoshaphat, Shouldest thou help the ungodly, and love them that hate the Lord? therefore is wrath upon thee from before the Lord."*—II Chron. 19:2.

No king is great enough to avoid the ruin that comes from bad influences, bad company. The unequal yoke is forbidden for Christians today, as it was then (Eph. 5:11; II John 9-11; II Cor. 6:14-18).

But Solomon sinned more in that he took so many wives. That was a special temptation to kings who had money and influence to pick out the women they might choose. David had had too many wives, but except possibly for the mother of Absalom and Adonijah they were Hebrew women and generally good women. So, certainly, was Abigail, and so, no doubt, was Bathsheba who had been the wife of Uriah the Hittite and sinned with David. Even so David had too many wives.

But Solomon went far beyond that, marrying many wives, heathen, wicked women. Yet there had been plain instructions on this matter from God. In Deuteronomy 17 God had plainly told them that when Israel should seek a king, then:

> *". . . he shall not multiply horses to himself, nor cause the people to return to Egypt, to the end that he*

*should multiply horses: forasmuch as the Lord hath said
unto you, Ye shall henceforth return no more that way.
Neither shall he multiply wives to himself, that his heart
turn not away: neither shall he greatly multiply to
himself silver and gold."*—Deut. 17:16,17.

Kings were forbidden to multiply horses and chariots and thus
depend on human strength. But they were also plainly commanded, "Neither shall he multiply wives to himself, that his
heart turn not away: neither shall he greatly multiply to himself
silver and gold." So with a love for money and following the nations about him in multiplying horses and chariots, Solomon did
worse yet in that he married many, many heathen women who
turned his heart away from God.

So in I Kings 11:3-8 we read how Solomon became an idolater
through the influence of his heathen wives:

*"And he had seven hundred wives, princesses, and
three hundred concubines: and his wives turned away
his heart. For it came to pass, when Solomon was old,
that his wives turned away his heart after other gods:
and his heart was not perfect with the Lord his God, as
was the heart of David his father. For Solomon went
after Ashtoreth the goddess of the Zidonians, and after
Milcom the abomination of the Ammonites. And
Solomon did evil in the sight of the Lord, and went not
fully after the Lord, as did David his father. Then did
Solomon build an high place for Chemosh, the abomination of Moab, in the hill that is before Jerusalem, and for
Molech, the abomination of the children of Ammon. And
likewise did he for all his strange wives, which burnt incense and sacrificed unto their gods."*

The Lord was angry and plainly told Solomon that because of
his sin the kingdom should be rent from the hand of his son
Rehoboam and he would be left only two tribes to govern.

When a remnant of Israel returned from Babylon under
Nehemiah, some of them married heathen wives and brought
trouble. Nehemiah contended with them and said, "Did not

Solomon king of Israel sin by these things? yet among many nations was there no king like him, who was beloved of his God, and
God made him king over all Israel: nevertheless even him did
outlandish women cause to sin."

In the city of Jerusalem, adjoining the Mount of Olives on the
south is the place still called "The hill of scandal," because there
Solomon built temples to idol gods and worshiped, influenced by
his heathen wives.

And now the great kingdom is to be torn asunder. Ten of the
tribes will go away unto another king. The arrogant son, raised
by a sinning, compromising father, will lose most of the
kingdom.

IV. LESSONS FROM LIFE AND FALL OF
KING SOLOMON

The psalmist said, "Thy word have I hid in mine heart, that I
might not sin against thee" (Ps. 119:11). Blessed indeed is the
man who reads and hides in his heart the Bible truths about
Solomon and other men of the past as revealed in the Bible. For
concerning Israel and God's dealing with them, the Scripture
says, "These things happened unto them for ensamples: and
they are written for our admonition, upon whom the ends of the
world are come" (I Cor. 10:11). Several lessons crowd upon us as
we review the wonderful story that ends so sadly.

1. To Turn Out Well, Children Must Have Discipline
and Christian Training

We suppose that Solomon, like Adonijah, was not reproved
and disciplined in the home. David had so many wives and so
many children he did not adequately train his children.
Although Solomon was a better man than Absalom or Adonijah,
there was a weakness in his character, so he gave way to the love
of wealth, the love of fame, and military might and married
heathen princesses. The right kind of character needs to be built
in in childhood, with discipline, restraint and holy teaching.

Two things, then, every Christian parent should decide now:

First, the children must be taught obedience. They must be disciplined. Sin must be punished. "He that spareth his rod hateth his son: but he that loveth him chasteneth him betimes" (Prov. 13:24).

Then every home ought to have a family altar, a daily time of Bible reading and prayer, with the whole family together. In Deuteronomy 6:6-9 the Scripture gave these emphatic commands:

> "And these words, which I command thee this day, shall be in thine heart: And thou shalt teach them diligently unto thy children, and shalt talk of them when thou sittest in thine house, and when thou walkest by the way, and when thou liest down, and when thou risest up. And thou shalt bind them for a sign upon thine hand, and they shall be as frontlets between thine eyes. And thou shalt write them upon the posts of thy house, and on thy gates."

I do not know any way that one can diligently teach his children the Word of God except by taking time every day for a session of Bible reading and prayer together with whatever comments and applications are necessary.

I think we may say that the home that does not have a daily time of Bible reading and prayer together is not in any real sense a Christian home. The people may be Christians, but Solomon was a Christian, too, no doubt. David was a Christian, too. The fact that the father and mother are Christians and even that the children are won to Christ does not guarantee they will turn out well unless they are brought up with rigorous attention. "Train up a child in the way he should go: and when he is old, he will not depart from it." Since Solomon departed from the worship of the true God and went into idolatry, that is certainly evidence he was not trained up in the way he should go or he would not have departed from it.

Parents are accountable for their children! I beg every father who reads, if you do not have a time of daily Bible reading and prayer with the whole family, by all means begin at once.

2. Let the Failure of Solomon Show the Temptation and Emptiness of Riches

The Scripture says, "For the love of money is the root of all evil" (I Tim. 6:10). That is literally of every kind of evil. Thrift is good, hard work to earn a competent living is admirable, but too much thought to money and anxiety to lay by riches is sinful and leads to compromise and sin.

We are commanded to beware of "covetousness, which is idolatry" (Col. 3:5). Riches are a great temptation. When the rich young ruler turned away, having great possessions and loving them, Jesus said, "Verily I say unto you, That a rich man shall hardly enter into the kingdom of heaven. And again I say unto you, It is easier for a camel to go through the eye of a needle, than for a rich man to enter into the kingdom of God." Then Jesus added, ". . . but with God all things are possible" (Matt. 19:23-26).

First Timothy 6:17 tells us, "Charge them that are rich in this world, that they be not high-minded, nor trust in uncertain riches, but in the living God, who giveth us richly all things to enjoy." Money is a good servant but a bad master. It is far better to be poor and content, with ordinary comforts and without much luxury, than to be rich and tempted and worldly, as was Solomon.

3. Let Us Cling to the Sanctity of Marriage

Solomon had "seven hundred wives, princesses, and three hundred concubines" (I Kings 11:3). Then marriage could not have been much of a holy and blessed matter of permanent love with Solomon. To marry seven hundred princesses would mean he must have a wedding every week for fourteen years! And three hundred concubines besides would mean usually some beautiful girl taken without love for a night of lust and then probably ignored in the palace of women.

Those seven hundred wives, princesses, were probably taken to make a political tie with other nations and thus it may be that Solomon bought some peace for his country by these alliances. I do not know. At any rate, marriage was not a holy business with the blessing of God, and Solomon, with none of his wives, ever really "became one flesh," with a daily sharing of joys and ideals and sorrows and the problems of the family in serving God.

None who read this will expect to have seven hundred wives and three hundred concubines, but you may be tempted to take marriage lightly. One of every three marriages in America ends in divorce. Everywhere I go I find the shocking example of Christian people, who are born again, who believe the Bible, who go to fundamental churches, yet they break up their marriage. Good Christians ought to set out to make marriage a lifetime business and they ought to mean it with all their hearts and live or die by their pledge to "love, honor and cherish [or obey] 'til death do us part." Christian people should stay together.

Let no foolish man and woman make the excuse that "I don't love him any more." What people are commanded to do, they can do. And the Bible commands, "Husbands, love your wives, even as Christ also loved the church, and gave himself for it" (Eph. 5:25). And elder women are plainly commanded "that they may teach the young women to be sober, to love their husbands, to love their children" (Titus 2:4). Let good women dress themselves modestly and reserve their love and beauty and charm of their bodies and their caresses for one man alone for a lifetime. And let every man set out to be to his wife as Christ was to the church; love his own by grace, and to be the head and high priest, protector and provider for the wife.

Oh, Solomon came out of too scanty a home environment and his own home made nothing sacred of marriage.

4. Close Company With Unsaved and Ungodly Is Way to Ruin

The first Psalm says, "Blessed is the man that walketh not in the counsel of the ungodly, nor standeth in the way of sinners, nor sitteth in the seat of the scornful." When Solomon married unsaved, heathen, idolatrous women, he went against the plain command of God. And any Christian who marries an unsaved mate thus goes in violation of the plain command, "Be ye not unequally yoked together with unbelievers: for what fellowship hath righteousness with unrighteousness? and what communion hath light with darkness? And what concord hath Christ with Belial? or what part hath he that believeth with an infidel? And what agreement hath the temple of God with idols?" (II Cor. 6:14-16).

A Christian who has his closest friends in a lodge fellowship, tied with bloody oaths, to some who are saved and some who are unsaved, thus puts himself under influences that are certain to be bad.

Let every student take to heart this fact before he ties himself up to get his education in a heathen, atheistic atmosphere and to take as his teachers and thus his examples ungodly scientists and wicked unbelievers.

Bad company is the way to ruin. It ruined Solomon, with his wicked, heathen wives. It ruined Samson, with his head in the lap of Delilah. It ruined Peter, sitting at the fire with the enemies of Christ. It has ruined many a preacher who stayed in a denomination where he had fellowship with wicked, unbelieving infidels who were enemies of Christ and the Bible, wolves in sheep's clothing. Christians ought not yoke up with unbelievers, ought not support the things they know are wrong, ought not be mildly complacent and tolerant toward the enemies of Christ and the Bible.

Solomon was greatly loved of God. He made a wonderful start, seeking the wisdom of God and God's blessing. He built a great Temple for God, but he grew more worldly, more rich, married more heathen women and finally turned into idolatry himself. And his son Rehoboam had left only two tribes of the kingdom because of Solomon's compromise and his own weak character which resulted.

V. SOLOMON LEFT OUT OF ANCESTRAL LINE OF CHRIST

In closing, here is a strange thought. David was in the ancestral line of Jesus Christ and God had promised that the throne of David would be restored. To the Virgin Mary the angel said about Jesus, "The Lord God shall give unto him the throne of his father David: And he shall reign over the house of Jacob for ever; and of his kingdom there shall be no end" (Luke 1:32,33).

But would this kingly line of David down through Jesus come through Solomon? We would have thought so, but, no!

The descendants of David through Solomon stayed on the throne until the time of the captivity. But of Jehoiakim, son of Josiah, king of Judah, Jeremiah was inspired to write, "Thus saith the Lord, Write ye this man childless, a man that shall not prosper in his days: for no man of his seed shall prosper, sitting upon the throne of David, and ruling any more in Judah" (Jer. 22:30). So no descendant of that line of kings through Jehoiakim can sit on the throne of David. Hence Christ could not come from that line.

How, then, did Christ come as Son of David? He came through Nathan, another son of David, not from Solomon. The genealogy of Jesus through Mary is given in Luke 3:23-38. Verse 23 says Jesus was supposed to be "the son of Joseph, which was the son of Heli." But the words "the son" are not in the Greek and so they are in italics in the King James Bible. Joseph was "of Heli," that is, evidently son-in-law of Heli. And verse 31 routes that genealogy through "Nathan, which was the son of David." In Matthew 1 we have the literal genealogy of Joseph, foster father and legally, according to Jewish law, counted the father of Jesus. Joseph's lineage was through King Solomon, as you see in verse 6. But Jesus was born of a virgin mother without a human father and came through the line of Nathan and of David and thus He will sit on the throne of David, though Solomon and his descendants are all omitted from the ancestral line of Jesus.

Who knows? It may be that God would have let the Messiah come through Solomon's own line if Solomon had stayed true.

Several great lessons pound at the door of attention about Solomon:

1. Riches, fame, power do not bring happiness, but may lead to ruin.

2. Evil companions or an unequal marriage tend to compromise and ruin. Poor Solomon!

3. Solomon's son, without godly rearing and without

character, used to luxury and his own way, came to failure and disgrace.

O Christian, remember humility, sacrifice, godly family and faithful obedience are essential to happiness and blessing.

9

Elisha

The Man Who Determined to Be God's Prophet

Elijah, the mighty prophet of God, drawing near the end of his ministry in Israel, was discouraged and depressed. He was one of the greatest men in the Old Testament, standing with Abraham and David, if not quite the same stature as Moses. He was transfigured, taken to Heaven alive, without death, even as was Enoch before the flood. He appeared with Moses, meeting Jesus and Peter, James and John on the Mount of Transfiguration. It is promised in Malachi 4:5, "Behold, I will send you Elijah the prophet before the coming of the great and dreadful day of the Lord." John the Baptist probably typified Elijah, for we are told, "And he shall go before him in the spirit and power of Elias [Elijah]."

Elijah is held up in James 5:13-16 as our model in prayer.

But now Elijah has grown discouraged. After amazing answers to prayer, when God shut up Heaven without rain or dew for three and a half years at his word, and then gave a wonderful fire from Heaven in answer to prayer on Mount Carmel, and after he had killed the 450 prophets of Baal who ate at Jezebel's table, yet Jezebel threatens to kill him, and he does not know that the people were really turning back to serve the true God as they said they would.

So, running for his life from wicked Queen Jezebel, he went into the wilderness, tired, worn out with his exertion and his fasting and he asked God that he might die. He is nearly alone of the prophets left alive. There seems to be no hope of great blessing on Israel.

But God had an angel prepare food for him, God encouraged him, and God said, "Yet I have left me seven thousand in Israel, all the knees which have not bowed unto Baal, and every mouth which hath not kissed him" (I Kings 19:18). He was told that he had work yet to do. He must anoint Hazael to be king of Syria, anoint Jehu to be king of Israel, and Elisha, the son of Shaphat, to be a prophet.

Oh, God must have someone prepared to represent Him when Elijah goes to Heaven. And he has in mind this Elisha.

I. GOD CALLS A MAN TO BE HIS PROPHET WHO GLADLY ANSWERS

The call of Elisha is told with charming language.

> "So he departed thence, and found Elisha the son of Shaphat, who was plowing with twelve yoke of oxen before him, and he with the twelfth: and Elijah passed by him, and cast his mantle upon him. And he left the oxen, and ran after Elijah, and said, Let me, I pray thee, kiss my father and my mother, and then I will follow thee. And he said unto him, Go back again: for what have I done to thee? And he returned back from him, and took a yoke of oxen, and slew them, and boiled their flesh with the instruments of the oxen, and gave unto the people, and they did eat. Then he arose, and went after Elijah, and ministered unto him."—I Kings 19:19-21.

What a strangely simple way Elijah used to let the young man know that he should be a prophet! Elijah passed by and simply threw his mantle upon the man at the plow! I do not know that he said a word. But Elisha understood that he was to be a prophet of God.

1. God Must Have Given the Man Some Indication, Some Call in His Heart

God had already planned to call Elisha and had told Elijah to anoint him. I am sure that God had put some sweet tugging at his heartstrings, some hunger for God, some concern about the people who ought to be warned and called back to God! Already there was a readiness and willingness. The call of God was not some sudden climactic surprise to him.

Often I am embarrassed when people ask me to tell about my

call to preach. The simple truth is that years ago, when God had put a yearning in my heart that I did not know was a call of God, I more or less volunteered to serve Him. But now I know how God had been dealing with me from childhood.

I learned that when I was born, my father and mother had given me to God to be a preacher. I did not know that until I was twenty-four years old and read a letter from my mother long gone to Heaven twenty years before! Then I remembered that she called me her "preacher boy." I remembered I had been taught to answer, when people asked me my name, "I am John the Baptist preacher." I remembered also when I was ten years old that I had dreamed dreams of preaching to great crowds and speaking for God. I remembered how, as a fifteen-year-old boy, my heart was so stirred when I found the amazing story of Pentecost and three thousand people saved in a day, and when I won my first soul.

I wanted to sing gospel songs, so I became a song leader for revival services. I began to win souls and earnestly pray for sinners. When I was in college, I volunteered to go with preacher boys to preach in jails and have services on the street. In Baylor University I was greatly distressed when the sociology professor taught evolution. And when doing graduate work in the University of Chicago, after college teaching and planning a college-teaching career, I won some poor lost sinners to the Lord from Skid Row, and I had the greatest joy I had ever known in soul winning, I rather pressed upon the Lord to let me preach.

I am saying, I had some intimation ahead of time that God was dealing with me to make me a preacher, although I did not recognize it as a call.

It was a shocking but pleasant surprise when I told dear Dr. Ward, president of Decatur College where I had graduated, that I was going to preach. He said, "Yes, Mrs. Ward and I have known for a long time that you were going to be a preacher."

Then in Baylor University, in a Bible class in which my sweetheart attended, Dr. J. B. Tidwell said, "If any of you girls don't want to marry a preacher, don't marry John Rice."

So Elisha surely, surely found his heart leaping for joy when Elijah placed his mantle upon him, and he had some sweet evidence God would make a prophet of him and he could wear a prophet's mantle!

When did the anointing take place, that is, oil upon his head? I do not know whether it was this time or later.

2. Elisha Had No Resistance but a Glad Surrendering of Self to Call of God

I think all Elisha needed was simply to know that God was willing to use him. It has often seemed to me that Elijah must have been surprised at Elisha's reaction.

When he laid his mantle on the shoulders of Elisha, the young man suddenly called a halt to the twelve teams of oxen and said, "Let me, I pray thee, kiss my father and my mother, and then I will follow thee." Elijah, the old prophet, seemed startled and said, "Go back again: for what have I done to thee?" No doubt Elijah was surprised at the joyful acceptance of the first intimation to Elisha that God would use him. Elisha was a volunteer. All he needed to know was that God was willing and he was ready to go.

In Romans 12:1,2 we read, "I beseech you therefore, brethren, by the mercies of God, that ye present your bodies a living sacrifice, holy, acceptable unto God, which is your reasonable service. And be not conformed to this world: but be ye transformed by the renewing of your mind, that ye may prove what is that good, and acceptable, and perfect, will of God."

God wants people to volunteer for His service. He doesn't want to whip men into preaching the Gospel. It is true that Jonah resisted the call of God and was punished. But I think what God wants most of all is a glad surrender, a willing offering of ourselves, a volunteering to serve the Lord. In His business God likes volunteers, not draftees.

We remember the same glad surrender of Isaiah. When King Uzziah died, the Lord made Himself known in the Temple and the seraphims cried out, "Holy, holy, holy, is the Lord of hosts: the whole earth is full of his glory. And the posts of the door moved at the voice of him that cried, and the house was filled with smoke" (Isa. 6:3).

Isaiah was deeply convicted of his sinfulness: "Then said I, Woe is me! for I am undone; because I am a man of unclean lips, and I dwell in the midst of a people of unclean lips: for mine eyes have seen the King, the Lord of hosts. Then flew one of the seraphims unto me, having a live coal in his hand, which he had taken with the tongs from off the altar: And he laid it upon my mouth, and said, Lo, this hath touched thy lips; and thine iniquity is taken away, and thy sin purged. Also I heard the voice of the Lord, saying, Whom shall I send, and who will go for us? Then said I, Here am I; send me" (Isa. 6:5-8).

As soon as he was conscious of forgiven sins and as soon as he heard the voice of God calling, Isaiah said, "Here am I; send me." You will note that God wanted him to volunteer and Isaiah did gladly.

A simple man of God, a converted stone mason, preached at the Pacific Garden Mission, using these Scriptures. With only a fifth-grade education and stumbling words, this man showed how God was glad when someone would offer himself.

That day I offered myself to God. I said, "Lord, I do not have the dramatic instinct and the moving voice of Dr. George W. Truett, and I do not have the gifts some men have, but I will be faithful. I will not be bribed nor bluffed nor bought nor scared. I will preach the Gospel straight." And I began to preach.

Oh, I know God is glad to have people volunteer. He wants willing service.

3. To Serve God, Elisha Gladly Forsook Way of Ease, Riches and Security

In Palestine a farm plowing with twelve teams of oxen in one field would be a large farm, requiring at least eleven servants, either hired men or slaves. And since no brother is mentioned, it may be that Elisha was the only son of the man Shaphat and his wife. At any rate, Elisha was in a prosperous family. He was well-to-do. He would have a good inheritance, far above the average. If he was the only son, we can suppose he was the dearest and possibly only support of his old father and mother.

But Elisha was glad to leave it in a moment. He called all the servants to stop the plows. He took one yoke of oxen and killed them as a sacrifice to God and a feast for the people. It was a joyful, exuberant spirit he showed in leaving all for the Lord Jesus.

Did he shirk from the career of a simple servant waiting on the man of God? I think not. Did he stop to consider that he would be often poor, sometimes hungry, and no doubt sometimes he would be recipient of part of the rebellion people had against the prophet he served? No, he gladly left all for Jesus.

I think he knew now what Jesus would later say in Luke 14:26,27:

> "If any man come to me, and hate not his father, and mother, and wife, and children, and brethren, and sisters, yea, and his own life also, he cannot be my disciple. And whosoever doth not bear his cross, and come after me, cannot be my disciple."

So he left the farm, left his security, left his inheritance, left his father and mother, to serve the Lord.

I wonder what they said. The Bible does not tell us. Neither does it tell us what the father and mother of James and John said when they left father and nets to follow Jesus. The Bible does not say what the wife of Levi the publican said when he gave up his rich job to become a poor preacher and follow Jesus.

But it seems that every time God calls somebody to preach, He must put them through a certain mill of trial. He must rub their noses in the dirt of poverty. If a man does not want to serve God enough to be poor for God, then He would rather get somebody else.

As Moses left Egypt and perhaps gave up the possibility of the throne, "Choosing rather to suffer affliction with the people of God," so Elisha gladly accepted the call to be a prophet.

II. ELISHA WAS GLAD TO BE A SERVANT TO GOD'S PROPHET

He was simply known as "Elisha the son of Shaphat, which poured water on the hands of Elijah" (II Kings 3:11).

Elijah had had a servant before, but when he ran for his life from Jezebel down to Beersheba, he "left his servant there" (I Kings 19:3). We hear no more of that servant. So it is only fair to suppose that Elisha was simply a servant for Elijah. He poured water for the man when he would wash his hands and face. No doubt he carried baggage, ran errands, and doubtless cared for the clothes of the prophet, perhaps secured or prepared the food.

But he entered into that work gladly.

1. He Must Serve an Apprenticeship if He Would Be a Prophet of God

One who would be greatly used of God must get ready for it. Paul took young Timothy with him and taught him, treated him as a son, and at last Timothy could be trusted to supervise as a pastor the work of the great church of Ephesus (I Tim. 1:3).

When Paul and Barnabas started on the first missionary journey, they took with them Mark to be their minister or servant. People traveling on long journeys would have to have somebody carry baggage, arrange for food, carry messages, leaving godly men time for prayer, preaching and rest.

But, Mark did not like that hard work. Perhaps he was lonely. Perhaps he was afraid of the opposition they began to face. So he did not go with them again on the next missionary journey. Paul was not pleased with that. But Barnabas took him and trained him, and at long last Paul in jail could say to Timothy, "Take Mark, and bring him with thee: for he is profitable to me for the ministry."

People need to serve an apprenticeship in order to learn the work of God.

R. A. Torrey attached himself to D. L. Moody. Though a graduate of Yale University and with a doctorate from German universities, yet he was willing to be a servant, a messenger, a helper to D. L. Moody who had only a grade-school education! Torrey knew the hand of God was on that earnest, powerful evangelist, so he was willing to be his helper.

Torrey took over Moody's school, now Moody Bible Institute, and was the first superintendent. He set up conferences for Moody. He made dates for him. He even looked after his laundry on occasions. And R. A. Torrey became the mighty preacher who followed Moody in great campaigns in America, Australia, New Zealand and England.

When he was converted, Billy Sunday went to work in a YMCA with such contacts as he could make and such personal work and testimonies as he could do for Jesus. Then he had an opportunity to go with J. Wilbur Chapman, a blessed, anointed evangelist. Sunday was willing to set up chairs, willing to talk to a men's meeting, willing to run a book table. He was a helper with the great evangelist.

When Chapman felt led to accept the call to the great Bethlehem Presbyterian Church in Buffalo, hoping to lead the whole Presbyterian denomination more into soul winning and revival, what would Billy Sunday do?

When Dr. Chapman told him, "You can be an evangelist," Billy Sunday said, "I have no sermons."

Chapman said, "I will give you ten, enough for eight days' revival—two messages each Sunday and one every week night."

So Bill Sunday took the ten sermons and started out. He had blessed results and God opened more doors and he learned more sermons. But he learned as an apprentice to Chapman.

I could never tell how much I was blessed as I sat in the class of evangelism under Dr. L. R. Scarborough in Southwestern Seminary, and the work I did under supervision in driving the truck and leading the teams for personal workers in jail services, in the city rescue missions, etc.

I remember how much I learned when a godly, small-town pastor asked me to lead singing for him in country revivals. Then in more revivals. Then a student pastor in country churches, then assistant pastor to the great First Baptist Church at Plainview, Texas. Then pastor at Shamrock. Then I launched out into evangelistic work.

Those who would serve as prophets of God must get ready.

Elisha was willing to go as a servant for Elijah. Ussher's chronology indicates he was for about six years a helper to the man of God, all the time learning, dreaming, waiting on God for the time when he could be a mighty prophet also.

2. Elisha Had No Jealousy, No Distaste
for the Menial Task

It is too bad when a preacher is not willing to get his hands dirty, not willing to do whatever is necessary to learn the Word of God and how to preach.

With joy I look back to times in junior college when I worked many hours at not more than 14¢ or 15¢ an hour, and later in the seminary when sometimes I got as high as 30¢ an hour! I milked cows. I dug flower beds. I carried the mail. I worked in a bookstore. I did janitor work for churches and for the college.

The mighty Paul was not above making tents when necessary.

Was Elisha jealous of the great man he served? I think not. The man who makes good as a servant can make good as a boss. The one who can learn to obey orders can learn to give orders. The man who has loyalty of heart in following leadership, may develop the character that leaders need.

We remember that when the young Apostle Paul started out, the older man Barnabas, the mature Christian, sought him out and encouraged him in the work. When the team started out together, it was "Barnabas and Saul." But before long Saul was the principal speaker, and it became "Paul and Barnabas." We never hear a word of complaint nor a hint of jealousy in all the accounts of the good man Barnabas.

Preachers are human. Those in Christian work have the same kind of temptations others have. Oh, but be sure of this: If you do your job as well where you are, and are patient and faithful, you will have a better place to work. And if you can make it easier for somebody else to grow a great church, then in due time God will give you your opportunity, too.

III. ELISHA WAS A MAN OF DEEP CONVICTIONS AND GOOD CHARACTER

There is no substitute for character in God's man. So important is the teaching of I Timothy 3:27.

1. Elisha Was Sharp and Plain in Denunciation of Sin, in Withdrawing From Evil Men

The king of Judah was Jehoshaphat. He agreed with Jehoram,

the idolatrous and wicked son of Ahab and Jezebel of the northern kingdom, Israel, to enter into a war to subdue rebellious Moab who had been subject to the king of Israel. So Jehoshaphat, Jehoram and the king of Edom with them went a compass of seven days' journey down south below the Dead Sea to come to Moab. In the wilderness there was no water for the great host, and it looked as if there they would die. Jehoshaphat, a godly man, said, "Is there not here a prophet of the Lord, that we may enquire of the Lord by him? And one of the king of Israel's servants answered and said, Here is Elisha the son of Shaphat, which poured water on the hands of Elijah."

So the three kings went down to Elisha. "And Elisha said unto the king of Israel, What have I to do with thee? get thee to the prophets of thy father, and to the prophets of thy mother. And the king of Israel said unto him, Nay: for the Lord hath called these three kings together, to deliver them into the hand of Moab. And Elisha said, As the Lord of hosts liveth, before whom I stand, surely, were it not that I regard the presence of Jehoshaphat the king of Judah, I would not look toward thee, nor see thee" (II Kings 3:11-14).

Then he called for a minstrel, and for the sake of godly King Jehoshaphat, he found the will of God and said they should dig ditches in the valley. God filled them with with water. God delivered the people of Moab into their hands.

But Elisha spoke plainly and sharply, showing that Jehoshaphat was wrong to yoke up with such idolaters. How sharply he spoke to the wicked Jehoram and boldly against his father Ahab and his mother Jezebel.

Oh, God give us men who will not sell out, not compromise!

"Blessed is the man that walketh not in the counsel of the ungodly, nor standeth in the way of sinners, nor sitteth in the seat of the scornful."—Ps. 1:1.

Elisha would not condone a yoke with unbelievers. He did not believe in secondary separation; so he did not avoid Jehoshaphat, but he openly rebuked unbelievers and told them frankly he would not help them.

2. He Did Not Shun to Call Down Judgment
on Wicked Sinners

When Elisha had received the power of the Holy Spirit upon
him and entered into his miraculous ministry, "There came forth
little children [literally young men] out of the city, and mocked
him, and said unto him, Go up, thou bald head; go up, thou bald
head. And he turned back, and looked on them, and cursed them
in the name of the Lord. And there came forth two she bears out
of the wood, and tare forty and two children of them."

The man of God must have boldness to condemn sin and must
expect God to take his part.

3. Elisha Was Not Tempted by Money and Fame

It is a marvelous story we have about Naaman who was captain of the host of Syria, a valiant man greatly regarded and
whom God had made of great use to preserve Syria. But he was a
leper! Syrian raids over on Israel had taken captive a little
Jewish girl who loved her mistress and we suppose her master.
She said, "Would God my lord were with the prophet that is in
Samaria! for he would recover him of his leprosy" (II Kings 5:3).

The word was brought to Naaman and then to the king of
Syria. "And the king of Syria said, Go to, go, and I will send a
letter unto the king of Israel. And he departed, and took with
him ten talents of silver, and six thousand pieces of gold, and ten
changes of raiment. And he brought the letter to the king of
Israel. . ." (vss. 5,6).

You can understand the distress of the king. How could he cure
leprosy? Could he make dead people alive? Was the king of Syria
trying to start a war, to provoke a war? But Elisha the prophet
heard of it and sent word, "Wherefore hast thou rent thy clothes?
let him come now to me, and he shall know that there is a
prophet in Israel."

So Naaman came out to the house of the prophet. He had supposed Elisha would come down and make a big display over this
famous general of the armies of Syria, clap his hands over the
place and thus in some wondrous manner cure the leprosy.
Instead, the prophet sent a messenger saying, "Go and wash in

Jordan seven times." After some hesitation and argument, Naaman dipped and was wonderfully healed.

Oh, he must reward this mighty prophet of God, so he came back with all his company and said, "Behold, now I know that there is no God in all the earth, but in Israel: now therefore, I pray thee, take a blessing of thy servant. But he said, As the Lord liveth, before whom I stand, I will receive none. And he urged him to take it; but he refused." He would take none of the ten talents of silver, the six thousand pieces of gold, the ten changes of expensive raiment. No, Naaman and others must not think one could buy the favor of God nor the favor of a prophet.

And when Elisha's servant, Gehazi, ran after the man and begged of him money and clothes for two supposed sons of the prophets who had come, Elisha pronounced the curse of leprosy on Gehazi because of his sin. Oh, this man could not be bribed nor bought. He was not impressed with fame or fortune.

He had genuine character.

How we need preachers and Christians everywhere with honest character and faithfulness who will not put their job nor their own income above the work of God.

IV. ELISHA, A MAN OF GREAT COMPASSION FOR TROUBLED EVERYWHERE

Everyone seemed to bring their burdens to Elisha, and he seemed to care about everybody. He had a tender, compassionate heart for people in trouble. What a blessing that is!

Paul told of "that which cometh upon me daily, the care of all the churches." I have found that a few men—and only a few—have a great burden for the whole cause of Christ. The approximately ninety names I call in prayer every day are great men of God. May God raise up in every city great soul-winning churches! May God help the fundamental schools to stay straight and true, and defend the faith, and keep the moral standards strict and high!

I have found in these Sword of the Lord conferences on evangelism that some good men, great preachers, cannot enter into the burdens of other preachers, cannot inspire, convict and transform preachers for the ministry. Some can.

Elisha had great compassion for people everywhere.

1. There Was the Widow Whose Boys Were About to Be Sold as Slaves

This woman was the widow of one of the young prophets. He had gone in debt; now he had died and left a burden on the family. How wrong it is for people to load themselves down in monthly payments so that when there is sickness or hospital bills or unemployment, they are not able to serve the Lord. How many preachers are called of God to preach, but they can't go off to college because they are married and have a family. They have car payments and color TV payments, payments on washer and dryer, and dining room suites, and a new car every two years.

But they were about to sell this widow's two sons as bondslaves. What would she do? She must ask Elisha!

He asked her, "What hast thou in the house?" She had only a little pot of oil. He told her, "Go, borrow thee vessels abroad of all thy neighbours, even empty vessels; borrow not a few."

They were to go back and shut the door upon themselves and she and her sons were to pour out the oil. All the vessels were wondrously filled, and Elisha told her, "Go, sell the oil, and pay thy debt, and live thou and thy children of the rest." She knew where to go and the great heart of Elisha, with the power of God on him, had the answer for her need.

2. The "Great Woman" of Shunem Had No Child

It is a charming story in II Kings 4 of that "great woman" of Shunem. She told her husband that this was a man of God and they should build a little room on the wall, with a bed, table, stool and candlestick. They did, and that was the prophet's chamber where Elisha was wont to come for rest on his way.

How moved he was with their kindness! The Shunammite was called up to the room. What could he do for her? Should he speak to the king for her? No, they did not need anything. He was very kind.

But his servant reminded him, "Verily she hath no child, and

her husband is old. And he said, Call her. And when he had called her, she stood in the door. And he said, About this season, according to the time of life, thou shalt embrace a son. And she
said, Nay, my lord, thou man of God, do not lie unto thine hand-
maid. And the woman conceived, and bare a son at that season
that Elisha had said unto her, according to the time of life" (II
Kings 4:14-17).

Oh, preachers and Christian workers ought to bear the burden
of others. Who knows the hunger of that woman's heart for years;
now Elisha, the man of God, could speak for God and promise
her a child. The child was born.

We do not wonder that when her boy died, she did not even tell
her husband, but simply asked for a donkey and a servant. She
had the servant drive the donkey and run until she came to the
prophet of God. She would not leave until Elisha would come
and bring the child to life. He did.

3. When a Son of the Prophet Lost His Ax From the Handle, He Knew What to Do

Down at Jericho they were building a house for the sons of the
prophets. One man with a borrowed ax chopped away at a tree
by the bank of the Jordan. Suddenly the ax slipped from the
handle and fell into the muddy waters of the Jordan. The young
man came to Elisha and said, "Alas, master! for it was borrowed.
And the man of God said, Where fell it? And he shewed him the
place. And he cut down a stick, and cast it in thither; and the
iron did swim. Therefore said he, Take it up to thee. And he put
out his hand, and took it."

He helped the king of Israel when the king of Syria would have
waylaid him and killed him but for Elisha's warning. He cured
the poisoned pottage. He cured the water of Jericho so that
Elisha's fountain still runs clear today. I have seen it many
times. He had a compassionate heart that people could depend
on. They loved and trusted him. They came with their burdens,
and this man of God wept with those that did weep and rejoiced
with those that did rejoice.

V. ELISHA HAD GREAT VISION OF
USEFULNESS IN ISRAEL

Elisha was for six or more years a body servant, waiting on the
Prophet Elijah. We do not know if during that time he was given
any major prophet's duty or vision or anointing. But he is God's
man. God is working on his heart.

1. He Asked for a Double Portion of the Spirit
That Was on Elijah

That is an amazing request when you consider that Elijah is
one of the half dozen or more greatest men in the Bible. Oh, what
faith, what boldness, what leadership! But Elisha wants twice
that.

We sin against God with small prayers!

Psalm 81:10 tells us, "I am the Lord thy God, which brought
thee out of the land of Egypt: open thy mouth wide, and I will fill
it." The Lord is saying, "Do you remember how I opened the Red
Sea and you marched through on dry ground? That is the kind of
God I am! Do you remember the manna from Heaven for forty
years, with plenty for everybody every day? Don't you see I can
do great things? Why don't you ask Me? Do you remember that
your clothes never wore out in forty years? Do you remember the
river of water that gushed out of the rocky cliff when Moses
smote the rock, so that three and a half million people and their
cattle had all they could drink? Don't you remember how I cared
for My people? I am a great God. Ask Me great things. Open thy
mouth wide, and I will fill it."

In Jeremiah 33:3 the Lord says, "Call unto me, and I will
answer thee, and shew thee GREAT AND MIGHTY things."
God would like to do big things, mighty things. He is a great
God. We are reminded in Jeremiah 32:17,27 that there is nothing
too hard for God. In Numbers 11:23 the Lord asked doubting
Moses, "Is the Lord's hand waxed short?" Oh, Jesus plainly
promised that those who had faith without doubt could see
mountains removed and cast into the sea, for He said, "Verily I
say unto you, If ye have faith as a grain of mustard seed, ye shall
say unto this mountain, Remove hence to yonder place; and it

shall remove; and nothing shall be impossible unto you" (Matt. 17:20).

And in the matter of prayer, the Lord gives this challenge in Ephesians 3:20, "Now unto him that is able to do exceeding abundantly above all that we ask or think . . . ."

This man Elisha asked for big things.

When he told Elijah what he wanted, I do not wonder at the reply: "Thou hast asked a hard thing." But Elisha wanted it and got it. He wanted a double portion of the Spirit of God that was on Elijah, and got it.

He didn't want money. He didn't ask for a great crowd of followers. He didn't ask for financial support. He did not ask for an easy life. He did not ask for loved ones, family and friends, and we suppose he lived a lonely bachelor's life, wholly dedicated to the Lord. But he did not ask for what other men wanted—he asked for the power of God in superabundant measure!

When a Pentecostal Holiness woman preacher said to me, "Brother Rice, I am praying for you that you will be filled with the Spirit," I answered then, and I answer now, "Keep on praying for me. I pray more for the fullness of the Spirit of God than for anything else in the world." She may have expected talking in tongues or something else, but I knew that the power of God is essential to the work of God.

So Elisha asked big things, expected big things, and so big things were given.

2. "A Double Portion," That Is, Sixteen Major Miracles Compared to Eight!

With Elijah, there were probably eight major miracles recorded:

1. Three and half years of drouth without rain or dew at the word of Elijah (I Kings 17:1; James 5:17).

2. Fed by ravens (I Kings 17:6).

3. The widow of Zarephath's meal and oil multiplied (I Kings 17:14-16).

4. The widow's son raised from the dead (I Kings 17:17-23).

5. Wonderful answer by fire on Mount Carmel (I Kings 18:36-39).

6. The miraculous announcement of Ahab's doom (I Kings 21:17-26).

7. The doom of King Ahaziah (II Kings 1).

8. The miraculous crossing of Jordan (II Kings 2:8).

The sixteen major miracles coming from the hand of Elisha are:

1. Crossing the Jordan miraculously.

2. The healing of Elisha's fountain.

3. The curse on the young people who mocked him: torn by bears.

4. The miracle of water in the desert for the kings.

5. The miraculous confusion of the Moabites and their defeat.

6. The increase of the widow's oil.

7. The giving of child to the "great woman" of Shunem.

8. That boy restored to life.

9. The healing of the poisoned pottage so it was good.

10. The multiplication of the twenty loaves of barley so that a hundred men ate and were satisfied.

11. The healing of Naaman the Syrian.

12. The curse of leprosy on Gehazi.

13. The lost ax head recovered from the Jordan.

14. Elisha learned and revealed Ben-hadad's plan to capture Israel's king.

15. The angels around Dothan and the Syrian army blinded and led captive.

16. The wonderful deliverance of Samaria from the Syrian army, with Heaven-sent panic upon the Syrians who fled away and left food for everybody.

These are all found in II Kings, chapters 2 to 7.

It seems that the Scriptures hold Elijah higher and greater in God's sight than Elisha, yet surely God intended this double portion of miracles to test the answer to Elisha's prayer, his insistent, pleading prayer that a double portion of the Spirit of God might rest on him.

I would today that God would help me open my mouth wide, expect much from Him, attempt great things for Him.

VI. ELISHA WAITED IN PERSISTENT PRAYER AND SEEKING FOR GOD'S POWER

How determined was this man Elisha to have the power of God! Israel must not be left without some mighty prophet and without one who could answer for God, who could show God's power, who could prove there was a living God, even as Elijah before him had done.

No doubt Elisha had watched with loving excitement the wonderful things done by the hands of Elijah. And how poor indeed is any country without some mighty prophet of God.

Some time ago Dr. Lee Roberson was laid aside for a time with operations upon his throat. Doctors thought he would never preach again. But many of us prayed. I called Dr. Roberson's attention to the earnest prayer of the disciples in Acts 4:29,30, "And now, Lord, behold their threatenings: and grant unto thy servants, that with all boldness they may speak thy word, By stretching forth thine hand to heal; and that signs and wonders may be done by the name of thy holy child Jesus."

Every generation needs to see some evidence of the miraculous power of God, some manifestation of His willingness to do wonders.

I needed, and all of us needed, to see God work; and how happy multitudes are that Dr. Roberson has been restored and is again preaching week by week with great power.

1. How Persistent Elisha Determined to Be With Elijah When He Was Translated!

Sometimes deeds are stronger prayers than words. Sometimes the cry of our hearts is so insistent that it cannot be expressed in simple words but the pleading goes into our actions. So Elisha determined he would not leave his master, would not have him go, until he should receive that mantle which, by implication, had been promised to him when he was first called and when the mighty Prophet Elijah laid it across the young man's shoulders at the plow, on his big farm! Second Kings, chapter 2, tells the entrancing story. Elijah was to be taken to Heaven that day in a whirlwind and Elijah and Elisha went from Gilgal.

"And Elijah said unto Elisha, Tarry here, I pray thee; for the Lord hath sent me to Beth-el. And Elisha said unto him, As the Lord liveth, and as thy soul liveth, I will not leave thee. So they went down to Beth-el. And the sons of the prophets that were at Beth-el came forth to Elisha and said unto him, Knowest thou that the Lord will take away thy master from thy head to day? And he said, Yea, I know it; hold ye your peace.

"And Elijah said unto him, Elisha, tarry here, I pray thee; for the Lord hath sent me to Jericho. And he said, As the Lord liveth, and as thy soul liveth, I will not leave thee. So they came to Jericho. And the sons of the prophets that were at Jericho came to Elisha, and said unto him, Knowest thou that the Lord will take away thy master from thy head to day? And he answered, Yea, I know it; hold ye your peace.

"And Elijah said unto him, Tarry, I pray thee, here; for the Lord hath sent me to Jordan. And he said, As the Lord liveth, and as thy soul liveth, I will not leave thee. And they two went on. And fifty men of the sons of the prophets went, and stood to view afar off: and they two stood by Jordan. And Elijah took his mantle, and wrapped it together, and smote the waters, and they were divided hither and thither, so that they two went over on dry ground.

"And it came to pass, when they were gone over, that Elijah said unto Elisha, Ask what I shall do for thee, before I be taken away from thee. And Elisha said, I pray thee, let a double portion of thy spirit be upon me. And he said, Thou hast asked a hard thing: nevertheless, if thou see me when I am taken from thee, it shall be so unto thee; but if not, it shall not be so. And it came to pass, as they still went on, and talked, that, behold, there appeared a chariot of fire, and horses of fire, and parted them both asunder; and Elijah went up by a

*whirlwind into heaven. And Elisha saw it, and he cried,
My father, my father, the chariot of Israel, and the
horsemen thereof. And he saw him no more: and he took
hold of his own clothes, and rent them in two pieces.*

*"He took up also the mantle of Elijah that fell from
him, and went back, and stood by the bank of Jordan;
And he took the mantle of Elijah that fell from him, and
smote the waters, and said, Where is the Lord God of Elijah? and when he also had smitten the waters, they
parted hither and thither: and Elisha went over."*—II
Kings 2:2-14.

Oh, for an insistent heart that will not go without the power of
God! It was so when the disciples waited in that upper room in
Acts 1:14: "These all continued with one accord in prayer and
supplication, with the women, and Mary the mother of Jesus,
and with his brethren."

And the promise of the Saviour in Luke 11:13 is, "If ye then,
being evil, know how to give good gifts unto your children: how
much more shall your heavenly Father give the Holy Spirit to
them that ask him?"

And Isaiah 40:29-31 gives us this same great emphasis: "He
giveth power to the faint; and to them that have no might he in-
creaseth strength. Even the youths shall faint and be weary, and
the young men shall utterly fall: But they that wait upon the
Lord shall renew their strength; they shall mount up with wings
as eagles; they shall run, and not be weary; and they shall walk,
and not faint."

Those who wait upon the Lord shall renew their strength. God
will give the Holy Spirit power to those who plead with Him.
Elisha pleaded in his heart and determined he would not go
without the power of God. Israel must have a Spirit-filled
prophet. He would be that prophet.

Let us learn the lesson and wait on God for His anointing.

2. Note the Faith of This Man Who Must Have
the Prophet's Mantle and Power

I think there is something quaint and beautiful in verse 12,

"And Elisha saw it, and he cried, My father, my father, the chariot of Israel, and the horsemen thereof. And he saw him no more: and he took hold of his own clothes, and rent them in two pieces." And I have thought sometimes with a smile that Elisha may have seized the wheels of that chariot of fire and would not let it go until the mantle from Elijah fell! He was determined to have that prophet's mantle and the power that it implied.

The mantle of Elijah fell, and Elisha took hold of his own clothes and tore them in two pieces. He was no more "Elisha the son of Shaphat, which poured water on the hands of Elijah"; now he is the Prophet Elisha, the prophet of God; so he put on the prophet's mantle and went back to the Jordan river. And the first act he performed was to repeat the last miracle he had seen at the hands of Elijah. He cried out, "Where is the Lord God of Elijah?" and smote the waters of the River Jordan as he had seen Elijah do, and the waters parted. He had faith and claimed the promise which he had so persistently sought.

We ought to believe that God is ready to fill with power those who wait upon Him. There ought to be an expectancy, a glad surrender but a holy confidence that God will give the power we seek—power to win souls, power to witness for Him, power to do what He wants us to do. It was so with this man Elisha.

O Christians, let us learn from this man of God who was willing to be a servant, who humbled himself, who was willing to do the most menial task to help another prophet of God but who was steadfastly determined that he himself would have the power of God and be for God a spokesman or prophet in Israel.

May He teach us to seek and have the same mighty power of God.

You must remember it is promised in Acts 1:8, "But ye shall receive power, after that the Holy Ghost is come upon you: and ye shall be witnesses unto me both in Jerusalem, and in all Judaea, and in Samaria, and unto the uttermost part of the earth."

Remember Jesus has promised, "If ye then, being evil, know how to give good gifts unto your children: how much more shall your heavenly Father give the Holy Spirit to them that ask him?"

I beg you, seek the Lord's face and claim His power and witness for Him.

10

Nebuchadnezzar of Babylon

The World Emperor

Nebuchadnezzar, king of Babylon, was one of the greatest names in all history. He was in the class of Caesar, Napoleon, Hitler, and others. He was the first world emperor reigning over the people of the then known world.

His character and deeds are discussed in the last few chapters of II Kings, in II Chronicles, in Jeremiah and in Daniel.

His most important place in the Bible is that he was used of God in the captivity of Judah and the destruction of Jerusalem.

Babylon is thought to have been near the site and the city to be the outgrowth of the Tower of Babel and the people that assembled there, when languages were confused and other people scattered over the world soon after the flood.

It was a great civilization. A thousand years before Nebuchadnezzar, Hammurabi built the city of Babylon into a great city of culture.

> "The Babylon of Hammurabi also produced dictionaries, mathematical treatises, astronomical texts, and cuneiform documents dealing with a wide variety of scientific and pseudoscientific knowledge. Best known of the texts from Hammurabi's Babylon is the famed law code by Jacques de Morgan in 1901." (*The Wycliffe Historical Geography of Bible Lands,* p. 23.)

There is much evidence that the culture and civilization which prevailed before the flood, with musical instruments, use of brass and iron, with large cities, were carried over into the centers of Babylon, Nineveh, and elsewhere after the flood (Gen. 4:16-22).

The foolish idea of the stone-age culture, with savage, illiterate people, is not true of the people immediately after the flood. The races degenerated as they scattered after Babel. Romans, chapter 1, tells how God blinded the minds of wicked people and they went away into darkness intellectually as well as spiritually. They went into heathen idolatry and sexual orgies, and the blindness of heathendom came upon them around the world. Man did not climb up from animal ancestry to civilization. Many went backward from civilization to ignorance, from Noah's worship of the one true God to the animal worship and heathen perversions mentioned in Romans 1.

But ancient Babylon was a place of culture, law and literature, not a seat of world empire in the first thousand years, but a great nation.

Assyria, north of Babylon, became great and for years superseded Babylon. Shalmaneser of Assyria, and Sargon, his successor, carried away the northern kingdom, Israel, long before Nebuchadnezzar's day. Sennacherib of Assyria tried to take Jerusalem in King Hezekiah's days, but in answer to prayer and to shame his boasting, God sent the death angel one night and the next morning 185,000 of Sennacherib's army camped around Jerusalem were found slain.

Later Nebuchadnezzar's father defeated the Assyrians. The Assyrian kingdom was destroyed and Babylon then took over the whole area and began the conquest that led it to become the first of the "world empires."

I. NEBUCHADNEZZAR CAPTURED THE JEWS AND DESTROYED JERUSALEM

Usually when the name is mentioned in the Bible it is spelled Nebuchadnezzar. It is also spelled a few times Nebuchadrezzar.

A chain of events led up to the destruction of Jerusalem by Nebuchadnezzar and his taking Jewish people in a third and final great captivity over to Babylon.

1. God's Patient Dealing With Rebellious Israel Preceded Captivity

The course of Judah was downward from Hezekiah's time on. There were some ebbs and flows, but continually the rulers and the people turned more and more toward idolatry, less and less attention to God and His prophets and the true religion. The northern nation, Israel, was already carried captive by Assyria.

The northern tribes had, from the time of Jeroboam and his idolatrous calves, gone largely into idolatry. There was a big intermission in the time of Jehu, who burned the temple of Baal and killed all the avid Baal worshipers. But the people again and again went on in sin and idolatry.

God's warnings brought only temporary turning back to God. The sins of Ahab and Israel were a continual infection for Judah. Jehoram, king of Judah, the son of the good king Jehoshaphat, was with his father, we suppose, when Jehoshaphat joined in with Ahab and visited him at Samaria. We are not surprised but sad to find that Jehoram married Ahab's daughter and was greatly influenced by the idolatry of Ahab and Jezebel.

God warned by one prophet and then another and another. Jeremiah, midst persecution and abuse, warned repeatedly that captivity was coming.

God sent armies against Judah from Syria, from Edom and Assyria for a time. For a time Pharaoh of Egypt held sway in Judah and put a son of Josiah on the throne, calling him Jehoiakim.

Then Nebuchadnezzar, coming into power as a worldwide rival of Pharaoh, demanded tribute from King Jehoiachin, but Jehoiachin was on the throne as an eight-year-old child, three months and ten days. "When the year was expired King Nebuchadnezzar sent and brought him to Babylon, with the goodly vessels of the house of the Lord, and made Zedekiah, his brother, king over Judah and Jerusalem" (II Chron. 36:10).

But King Zedekiah, after reigning eleven years, had rebelled against Nebuchadnezzar, broke his solemn oath unto the king, and so Nebuchadnezzar came again and besieged the city and after a year and a half took and destroyed it.

> *"Zedekiah was one and twenty years old when he began to reign, and reigned eleven years in Jerusalem. And he did that which was evil in the sight of the Lord his God, and humbled not himself before Jeremiah the prophet speaking from the mouth of the Lord. And he also rebelled against king Nebuchadnezzar, who had*

*made him swear by God: but he stiffened his neck, and
hardened his heart from turning unto the Lord God of
Israel."*—II Chron. 36:11-13.

Nebuchadnezzar left in the country many of the poor people to
till the land. Yet Jerusalem was totally destroyed, the nation
Israel was broken and the northern nation had been carried away
by the king of Assyria. Then in two different captivities
Nebuchadnezzar had cleaned out all the ruling people, the rich
people, the principal soldiers and leaders of Judah.

We can understand the impatience and violence of
Nebuchadnezzar's sacking the city, putting out the eyes of King
Zedekiah, killing all his sons, the princes, and utterly tearing
down the wall of Jerusalem and destroying it as a city. It was not
only a place of idolatry and wickedness but of broken promises,
of disloyalty and deceit. The patience of Nebuchadnezzar was
exhausted.

2. Nebuchadnezzar Came as the Servant of God to Do God's Will in Destroying Jerusalem

Does God sometimes use heathen, wicked people to do His will
with chosen people of His own? Oh, yes. You read in the book of
Judges again and again how God brought the Philistines, the
Midianites, and others to fight Israel and to bring misery and
suffering because they did not serve the Lord.

So here God used Nebuchadnezzar to do His will in the
destruction of Jerusalem. The Bible says so more than once.

In Jeremiah 25:9 God says, "Behold, I will send and take all
the families of the north, saith the Lord, and Nebuchadrezzar
the king of Babylon, my servant, and will bring them against this
land, and against the inhabitants thereof, and against all these
nations round about, and will utterly destroy them, and make
them an astonishment, and an hissing, and perpetual
desolations." Nebuchadnezzar was the servant of the Lord.

In II Chronicles 36:15-17 God tells how, after long warning and
patient, loving pleading by prophets of God, He brought the king
of the Chaldees against them. Those verses say:

"And the Lord God of their fathers sent to them by his

messengers, rising up betimes, and sending; because he
had compassion on his people, and on his dwelling place:
But they mocked the messengers of God, and despised
his words, and misused his prophets, until the wrath of
the Lord arose against his people, till there was no
remedy. Therefore he brought upon them the king of the
Chaldees, who slew their young men with the sword in
the house of their sanctuary, and had no compassion
upon young man or maiden, old man, or him that
stooped for age: he gave them all into his hand."

And the Scripture goes on to tell that not only did God give the
people, old and young, into his hand, but the vessels of the house
of God were given him. And they burnt the house of God, broke
down the whole wall of Jerusalem, burned all the palaces and
destroyed the goodly vessels. And those who escaped the sword
were carried away into Babylon.

I say, God sent Nebuchadnezzar to destroy Jerusalem and
take captive the Jews.

Jeremiah 39 tells of the fall of Jerusalem and how Nebuzar-
adan, the captain of the guard for Nebuchadnezzar, was in
charge of taking captive the remnant of the people. Verses 13 and
14 tell how Nebuzar-adan and other princes of Babylon took
Jeremiah out of the court of the prison.

Then Jeremiah 40:2-4 tells us:

"And the captain of the guard took Jeremiah, and said
unto him, The Lord thy God hath pronounced this evil
upon this place. Now the Lord hath brought it, and done
according as he hath said: because ye have sinned
against the Lord, and have not obeyed his voice,
therefore this thing is come upon you. And now, behold, I
loose thee this day from the chains which were upon
thine hand. If it seem good unto thee to come with me
into Babylon, come; and I will look well unto thee: but if
it seem ill unto thee to come with me into Babylon,
forbear: behold, all the land is before thee: whither it
seemeth good and convenient for thee to go, thither go."

You see, not only Nebuchadnezzar but the captain of his guard and his princes evidently knew that God had sent Nebuchadnezzar to take Jerusalem. And they knew that Jeremiah was a prophet of God and that he had foretold this destruction and warned the people.

You may be sure that sometimes God uses men of the world to chastise His own people for their sins. Psalm 24:1 says, "The earth is the Lord's and the fulness thereof; the world, and they that dwell therein." God can use any people, any person, any circumstances, to bring about His will with His people.

After Ezekiel was over in Babylon and was burdened about the awful destruction that came upon the people in punishment, God took him back in a vision to show the wickedness of the city, and how, unseen, behind the Babylonian army were the angels of God, who were sent to bring destruction on the city for the idolatry and wickedness of the people. There he tells the story about how six "men" (angels of God) with slaughter weapons in their hands were sent to destroy, after one "man" (or angel) with a linen garment and an inkhorn by his side, had been sent to mark upon the forehead every one that would sigh and cry over the abominations that went on in Jerusalem! God is saying that although people could see Nebuchadnezzar and his armies, they did not see that behind all that was the hand of God.

Nebuchadnezzar was the servant of God in the destruction of Jerusalem.

3. The Most That We Know About Nebuchadnezzar Appears After Captivity

In the book of Daniel we learn that Daniel and three of his companions were taken from noble families, and in Babylon they were to be trained to help the king and the government of this great empire. And the events in the book of Daniel show how that great man of God came to be prime minister in five kingdoms and served God. These were in the days of Nebuchadnezzar, and Belshazzar and, we think, his father Nabonidus, and Darius the Mede, and then with Cyrus. Daniel lived, we suppose, most of the seventy years of the captivity, or all of them.

Then the story is taken up in Ezra and Nehemiah about their return to Jerusalem to rebuild the Temple under Ezra and to build the wall under Nehemiah. But Daniel and his friends had most touch with Nebuchadnezzar. Through these incidents in the book of Daniel, we must judge the character of Nebuchadnezzar.

II. FIRST WORLD EMPIRE ESTABLISHED

"In the third year of the reign of Jehoiakim king of Judah came Nebuchadnezzar king of Babylon unto Jerusalem, and besieged it. And the Lord gave Jehoiakim king of Judah into his hand, with part of the vessels of the house of God: which he carried into the land of Shinar to the house of his god; and he brought the vessels into the treasure house of his god."—Dan. 1:1,2.

Note this was in the third year of Jehoiakim. In II Kings 23:36 we find that Jehoiakim reigned eleven years in Jerusalem. But in the third year, probably connected with the rebellion against Nebuchadnezzar mentioned in II Kings 24:1, Nebuchadnezzar came and besieged Jerusalem, took away vessels from the house of God, and took Daniel and other fine young men of personality and family and training, that they might be taught in the ways of the Chaldeans and learn to help him rule the nations of the world in this, the first world empire (Dan. 1:1-5).

Note carefully, later, after Jehoiakim died, Jehoiachin, his son, reigned for three months or so. Nebuchadnezzar came against the city again and took it. The Scofield Reference Bible mistakenly calls this "the first deportation to Babylon." It is the second one and after the time mentioned in Daniel 1:1-5. Again he carried out the treasures of the house of God and took captive some 10,000 people and took them and Jehoiachin to Babylon.

A third captivity, the final one, was when Zedekiah had made an oath to support Nebuchadnezzar and then rebelled; so Jerusalem was besieged and then utterly destroyed, and the wall torn down and the people carried away (II Kings 25; II Chron. 36).

Daniel was already in Babylon and these young men taken

perhaps as hostages, but certainly to train them to help rule the countries being combined in the empire, and was there during the second and third captivities, when the rest of the people of Israel, except a few that were to keep the land, were brought to Babylon.

1. Nebuchadnezzar's Vision of a Great Image

Nebuchadnezzar had a dream. Perhaps he went to sleep thinking about the growth of his empire, being the first one who had ever set out to rule all the nations then known. His father had overthrown the Assyrian kingdom. The remnants of the Assyrian kingdom and Nineveh were under his control. He had taken over all that pertained to Egypt. The then known civilized nations were being combined under one man.

So he went to sleep and dreamed dreams. They must be concerning some of the things about which he was thinking he knew, but he could not remember the dreams!

"Then the king commanded to call the magicians, and the astrologers, and the sorcerers, and the Chaldeans, for to shew the king his dreams."—Dan. 2:2.

They could not do it. So Nebuchadnezzar commanded them all to be slain. They were frauds! But word came to Daniel. He and his friends were to be slain, too, but Daniel "said to Arioch the king's captain, Why is the decree so hasty from the king? Then Arioch made the thing known to Daniel. Then Daniel went in, and desired of the king that he would give him time, and that he would shew the king the interpretation" (Dan. 2:15,16). So Daniel and his three friends, Shadrach, Meshach, and Abednego, set out to pray, and God revealed the secret of the dreams. Daniel came before the king to tell him.

"Thou, O king, sawest, and behold a great image. This great image, whose brightness was excellent, stood before thee; and the form thereof was terrible. This image's head was of fine gold, his breast and his arms of silver, his belly and his thighs of brass, His legs of iron, his feet part of iron and part of clay. Thou sawest till that

a stone was cut out without hands, which smote the image upon his feet that were of iron and clay, and brake them to pieces. Then was the iron, the clay, the brass, the silver, and the gold, broken to pieces together, and became like the chaff of the summer threshingfloors; and the wind carried them away, that no place was found for them: and the stone that smote the image became a great mountain, and filled the whole earth."—Dan. 2:31-35.

2. There Were to Be Four World Empires: Nebuchadnezzar's the First

Nebuchadnezzar was "king of kings." God had given him to bear rule over every person and every beast as far as he wanted to go. He was the head of gold. Not just a king over a country but a king over other kings.

Then there was to follow another inferior kingdom, the Media-Persian kingdom, represented by the breast and arms of silver of the image.

But the belly and thighs of the image were of brass, and this pictured a third kingdom, the Grecian kingdom, which would rise under Alexander the Great.

"And the fourth kingdom should be strong as iron: forasmuch as iron breaketh in pieces and subdueth all things: and as iron that breaketh all these, shall it break in pieces and bruise."—Dan. 2:40.

So the fourth would be the Roman Empire, far stronger than these others, not as benevolent as Nebuchadnezzar, perhaps, this kingdom of iron. Here are the pictures of the world empires, the only ones that this world has ever seen: Babylon, Media-Persia, Greece and Rome.

And the feet and toes of the beast represented the kings that would come out of the Roman Empire, including, of course, Greece, Italy, France, Spain, Portugal, the Balkan countries, Palestine, etc. These four kings were pictured in Daniel, chapter 7, as the lion with eagle's wings, Babylon; the beast like a bear with three ribs in its mouth—the Media-Persian empire with

Babylon, Media and Persia, that is the three ribs, we suppose. Then there was one like a leopard with four wings and four heads—the Grecian kingdom, divided by the four generals of Alexander's army when he died. Then the fourth beast, dreadful and terrible, would be the Roman Empire.

Since that time many, many have tried to build a world empire. So did the pope at Rome. So did Charlemagne. So did Napoleon. So did Kaiser Wilhelm. So did Hitler. That was a dream also of Mussolini. But none succeeded and none will succeed until in the time of the tribulation when the Antichrist himself shall come and restore the Roman Empire.

You can understand how Nebuchadnezzar would be greatly interested and troubled until he could understand the meaning of what God had in mind.

"For the mystery of iniquity doth already work." The tendency to a world empire is always there, but it is always restrained because "he who now letteth will let, until he be taken out of the way. Then shall that Wicked be revealed" (II Thess. 2:7,8). Always someone will try to have a world empire, try to have a world market, try to have a world church. Satan works at it, but the influence of born-again Christians and the Spirit of God in them holds these things in abeyance until Christians, and thus the powerful influence of the Holy Spirit through Christians, are taken out of the way at the rapture, then the Man of Sin will be revealed.

3. Kingdoms of Earth Will Be Destroyed When Christ Returns in Glory to Set Up His Kingdom

In the great dream of Nebuchadnezzar, Daniel explained there was a stone cut out of a mountain without hands and smote the image on its feet and ground them to powder and the wind carried the dust away. So the kingdoms of this earth will one day become the kingdoms of our Lord and His Christ. The stone hit ". . . in the feet of the image." Not in the days of Babylon nor Media-Persia, nor of Greece, nor of Rome, but in the feet, that is, in the group that came out of the Roman Empire as it is today, and with the Antichrist trying to revive a world empire.

So Nebuchadnezzar knew that there was a Messiah, a Christ coming who would take over the rule and that Nebuchadnezzar himself was only a little foretype or at least an illustration of another world ruler, the Lord Jesus Himself, who would one day come.

III. NEBUCHADNEZZAR WOULD HAVE HAD A ONE-WORLD RELIGION

Daniel, chapter 3, tells how . . .

"Nebuchadnezzar the king made an image of gold, whose height was threescore cubits, and the breadth thereof six cubits: he set it up in the plain of Dura, in the province of Babylon. Then Nebuchadnezzar the king sent to gather together the princes, the governors, and the captains, the judges, the treasurers, the counsellors, the sheriffs, and all the rulers of the provinces, to come to the dedication of the image which Nebuchadnezzar the king had set up. Then the princes, the governors, and captains, the judges, the treasurers, the counsellors, the sheriffs, and all the rulers of the provinces, were gathered together unto the dedication of the image that Nebuchadnezzar the king had set up; and they stood before the image that Nebuchadnezzar had set up. Then an herald cried aloud, To you it is commanded, O people, nations, and languages, That at what time ye hear the sound of the cornet, flute, harp, sackbut, psaltery, dulcimer, and all kinds of musick, ye fall down and worship the golden image that Nebuchadnezzar the king hath set up: And whoso falleth not down and worshippeth shall the same hour be cast into the midst of a burning fiery furnace. Therefore at that time, when all the people heard the sound of the cornet, flute, harp, sackbut, psaltery, and all kinds of musick, all the people, the nations, and the languages, fell down and worshipped the golden image that Nebuchadnezzar the king had set up."—Dan. 3:1-7.

I do not think Nebuchadnezzar at this time had great religious convictions. I do not know that this image represented any special heathen religion. I think Nebuchadnezzar's intent was to unite the diverse peoples of his empire in one religion so he made a great statue and image, an idol, and he wanted to centralize and unite the hearts of the people and thus make his empire sure and strong.

So they brought the chief men of the empire together and great musicians gathered in that tremendous throng and when they were to play their instruments, everybody was to bow down to his image.

But three Hebrew young men, friends of Daniel, did not bow. And they were cast into the fiery furnace. We note the rage of Nebuchadnezzar who had these men bound and the fiery furnace was so heated that it destroyed even the strong soldiers who took the Hebrew young men to cast them into the furnace! And lo and behold, the three young Jews walked unharmed in the fire! They had said they expected to be delivered, but if not, they would still refuse to worship the image. The Lord protected them, and one like the Son of man came and walked in the fire with them.

The impression stayed on Nebuchadnezzar! Shadrach, Meshach, and Abednego were cast into the burning fiery furnace bound hand and foot.

> *"And these three men, Shadrach, Meshach, and Abed-nego, fell down bound into the midst of the burning fiery furnace. Then Nebuchadnezzar the king was astonied, and rose up in haste, and spake, and said unto his counsellors, Did not we cast three men bound into the midst of the fire? They answered and said unto the king, True, O king. He answered and said, Lo, I see four men loose, walking in the midst of the fire, and they have no hurt; and the form of the fourth is like the Son of God."*—Dan. 3:23-25.

They had no smell of smoke. The fire had no power on these men of God. There was not even the smell of smoke on their garments. Their bonds were simply burned off and they were free from harm.

"And the princes, governors, and captains, and the king's counsellors, being gathered together, saw these men, upon whose bodies the fire had no power, nor was an hair of their head singed, neither were their coats changed, nor the smell of fire had passed on them. Then Nebuchadnezzar spake, and said, Blessed be the God of Shadrach, Meshach, and Abed-nego, who hath sent his angel, and delivered his servants that trusted in him, and have changed the king's word, and yielded their bodies, that they might not serve nor worship any god, except their own God. Therefore I make a decree, That every people, nation, and language, which speak any thing amiss against the God of Shadrach, Meshach, and Abed-nego, shall be cut in pieces, and their houses shall be made a dunghill: because there is no other God that can deliver after this sort. Then the king promoted Shadrach, Meshach, and Abed-nego, in the province of Babylon."—Dan. 3:27-30.

I believe Nebuchadnezzar was sincerely convinced that the God of Shadrach, Meshach, and Abednego was the true God. Certainly he knew God had miraculously delivered these servants. And now the penalty was set against anybody who should speak anything against the God of these Hebrew people. He acknowledges, ". . . because there is no other God that can deliver after this sort."

I am sure that this great statue of Nebuchadnezzar was an effort of Satan who tries continually to bring about a one-world religion, as he does try to bring about a world empire. That effort of one-world religion is shown in the rise of a Moslem religion under Mohammed. It showed under the papacy when the Roman church tried to take control of the nations of the earth and rule the rulers. It shows in modern times in the modernism that creeps into all the denominations and tries to make an ecumenical religion for everybody, a kind of consensus of Protestants and Catholics, Christians and Jews and Buddhists, and Moslems.

And one day it will be so with the false prophet and the state religion of the Antichrist.

"For the mystery of iniquity doth already work," but the plans of the Devil cannot come to pass yet. They are restrained by the influence of the Holy Spirit in Christians until the time of the rapture.

IV. NEBUCHADNEZZAR'S TREE VISION

Daniel, chapter 4, tells the wonderful story of another dream of Nebuchadnezzar.

1. Pride Brings King's Downfall

Daniel 4:10-16 says:

> *"Thus were the visions of mine head in my bed; I saw, and behold a tree in the midst of the earth, and the height thereof was great. The tree grew, and was strong, and the height thereof reached unto heaven, and the sight thereof to the end of all the earth: The leaves thereof were fair, and the fruit thereof much, and in it was meat for all: the beasts of the field had shadow under it, and the fowls of the heaven dwelt in the boughs thereof, and all flesh was fed of it. I saw in the visions of my head upon my bed, and, behold, a watcher and an holy one came down from heaven; He cried aloud, and said thus, Hew down the tree, and cut off his branches, shake off his leaves, and scatter his fruit: let the beasts get away from under it, and the fowls from his branches: Nevertheless leave the stump of his roots in the earth, even with a band of iron and brass, in the tender grass of the field; and let it be wet with the dew of heaven, and let his portion be with the beasts in the grass of the earth: Let his heart be changed from man's, and let a beast's heart be given unto him; and let seven times pass over him."*

Nebuchadnezzar called Daniel to explain what the dream meant. It was a solemn warning from God. The tree pictured Nebuchadnezzar and the Babylonian empire under him. So his kingdom had prospered as the tree had fruit and leaves and the beasts of the field dwelt under the tree, and the fowls of the heaven sat in the branches. But Nebuchadnezzar had grown strong and with his "dominion to the end of the earth" (Dan. 4:22).

Up in Heaven God saw the coming pride and arrogance. Burke, the English statesman, said, "Power corrupts." So it did here. The meaning is, Daniel said:

> *"That they shall drive thee from men, and thy dwelling shall be with the beasts of the field, and they shall make thee to eat grass as oxen, and they shall wet thee with the dew of heaven, and seven times shall pass over thee, till thou know that the most High ruleth in the kingdom of men, and giveth it to whomsoever he will. And whereas they commanded to leave the stump of the tree roots; thy kingdom shall be sure unto thee, after that thou shalt have known that the heavens do rule. Wherefore, O king, let my counsel be acceptable unto thee, and break off thy sins by righteousness, and thine iniquities by shewing mercy to the poor; if it may be a lengthening of thy tranquility."*—Dan. 4:25-27.

2. Dream Fulfilled

Twelve months went by and mighty Nebuchadnezzar considered the great city he had built and the empire he controlled. And while his proud heart was lifted up thinking that he himself had done it, God sent a voice from Heaven saying:

> *"O king Nebuchadnezzar, to thee it is spoken; The kingdom is departed from thee. And they shall drive thee from men, and thy dwelling shall be with the beasts of the field: they shall make thee to eat grass as oxen, and seven times shall pass over thee, until thou know that the most High ruleth in the kingdom of men, and giveth it to whomsoever he will."*—Dan. 4:31,32.

That day came to pass and Nebuchadnezzar some way had the mind of a beast in his body and he went out to eat grass like an ox. His hair grew like eagle's feathers; his nails like birds' claws. And so it went for "seven times," we suppose, for seven years.

He had seen the tree cut down but with a band of iron and brass around the stump, so his kingdom had been preserved for him. His mind was restored, and his kingdom. Now he says, "I blessed the most High, and I praised and honoured him that liveth for ever, whose dominion is an everlasting dominion, and his kingdom is from generation to generation" (Dan. 4:34). Again, "Now I Nebuchadnezzar praise and extol and honour the King of heaven, all whose works are truth, and his ways judgment: and those that walk in pride he is able to abase" (Dan. 4:37).

V. WAS NEBUCHADNEZZAR SAVED?

I think that he was saved eventually. There are several reasons we should consider.

1. He Was Called the Servant of the Lord

In Jeremiah 25:8,9 the Lord says:

> *"Therefore thus saith the Lord of hosts; Because ye have not heard my words, Behold, I will send and take all the families of the north, saith the Lord, and **Nebuchadrezzar the king of Babylon, my servant,** and will bring them against this land, and against the inhabitants thereof, and against all these nations round about, and will utterly destroy them, and make them an astonishment, and an hissing, and perpetual desolations."*

God said, "Nebuchadrezzar the king of Babylon, my servant . . . ." I do not think that this indicates that Nebuchadnezzar was saved at that time, but he was an agent of God.

This matter is expressed again in II Chronicles 36:15-17:

> *"And the Lord God of their fathers sent to them by his messengers, rising up betimes, and sending; because he had compassion on his people, and on his dwelling place: But they mocked the messengers of God, and despised his words, and misused his prophets, until the wrath of*

the Lord arose against his people, till there was no remedy. Therefore he brought upon them the king of the Chaldees, who slew their young men with the sword in the house of their sanctuary, and had no compassion upon young man or maiden, old man, or him that stooped for age: he gave them all into his hand."

So God brought the king of the Chaldees, Nebuchadnezzar, to destroy Jerusalem.

Nebuzar-adan, captain of the guard of Nebuchadnezzar, knew that their coming was from the Lord and that in taking Jerusalem they served the Lord. He sent and got Jeremiah out of prison.

"And the captain of the guard took Jeremiah, and said unto him, The Lord thy God hath pronounced this evil upon this place. Now the Lord hath brought it, and done according as he hath said: because ye have sinned against the Lord, and have not obeyed his voice, therefore this thing is come upon you."—Jer. 40:2,3.

Since so much follows about God's dealing with Nebuchadnezzar we soon get the impression that He has great plans for this man and will lead him more and more to know the true God.

2. He Heard of the True God and Saw His Power

We can well believe that Nebuchadnezzar had not, before, fully surrendered to the Lord. He was convinced that the God of Daniel was a "God of gods," but are there other gods? He did not at first know so much about that, and still he wanted a national religion, and so set up the great image in the plain of Dura.

But when the three Hebrew children were delivered from the fiery furnace and when he saw one like the Son of Man walking in the fiery furnace, he was wonderfully moved.

"Then Nebuchadnezzar spake, and said, Blessed be the God of Shadrach, Meshach, and Abed-nego, who hath sent his angel, and delivered his servants that trusted in him, and have changed the king's word, and yielded their bodies, that they might not serve nor worship any god, except their own God. Therefore I make

> *a decree, That every people, nation, and language, which
> speak any thing amiss against the God of Shadrach,
> Meshach, and Abed-nego, shall be cut in pieces, and
> their houses shall be made a dunghill: because there is
> no other God that can deliver after this sort."*—Dan.
> 3:28,29.

Now the Lord God of Daniel is above other gods, and no one
will be allowed to speak anything against that God.

Then God foretold the proud and haughty way he would feel
and he would be brought down to serve as a common beast of the
field for a time until he should know that the kingdoms of the
earth were given by the hand of God and not seized by men
without His will. Now he wants to give a testimony. After this oc-
curs, he wants to tell the story and he says:

> *"Therefore I make a decree."*

And he writes a proclamation,

> *"Nebuchadnezzar the king, unto all people, nations
> and languages, that dwell in all the earth; Peace be mul-
> tiplied unto you. I thought it good to shew the signs and
> wonders that the high God hath wrought toward me.
> How great are his signs! and how mighty are his
> wonders! his kingdom is an everlasting kingdom, and his
> dominion is from generation to generation."*—Dan. 4:1-
> 3.

Thus he tells the whole story.

Will you note that there is praise and admiration and, I think,
love and worship in this proclamation of King Nebuchadnezzar?

Even in this dealing with Nebuchadnezzar, God seems to deal
with him as He deals with the Christians. As Paul had a thorn in
the flesh to keep him from being exalted above measure, so
Nebuchadnezzar is brought low to cure his pride that he may
give God the glory.

3. Nebuchadnezzar Had Surely Understood a Prophecy
About the Coming of the Saviour

You remember that in Nebuchadnezzar's dream of a great

image he saw the stone cut out of the mountain without hands that smote the kingdoms of this earth. He was told plainly in Daniel 2:44,45:

> *"And in the days of these kings shall the God of heaven set up a kingdom, which shall never be destroyed: and the kingdom shall not be left to other people, but it shall break in pieces and consume all these kingdoms, and it shall stand for ever. Forasmuch as thou sawest that the stone was cut out of the mountain without hands, and that it brake in pieces the iron, the brass, the clay, the silver, and the gold; the great God hath made known to the king what shall come to pass hereafter: and the dream is certain, and the interpretation thereof sure."*

This seems to be enough of a picture that a seeking heart could understand. It is as clear as was the promise to Abraham that through his seed all nations should be blessed, and Abraham some way saw through it that it meant the Saviour, "And he believed in the Lord: and he counted it to him for righteousness" (Gen. 15:6).

And can we doubt that as the spiritually-minded men saw the Saviour through such dealings, Nebuchadnezzar likewise saw the Saviour? We will be glad if, when we get to Heaven, we find King Nebuchadnezzar there, a humble and joyful servant of the Saviour.

11

Barnabas—a Good Man

"For he was a good man, and full of the Holy Ghost and of faith: and much people was added unto the Lord."—Acts 11:24.

In Antioch, some men of Cyprus and Cyrene came and preached the Gospel to the Greek Jews and a great many were saved. And the apostles at Jerusalem felt they must check up on this matter.

"Then tidings of these things came unto the ears of the church which was in Jerusalem: and they sent forth Barnabas, that he should go as far as Antioch. Who, when he came, and had seen the grace of God, was glad, and exhorted them all, that with purpose of heart they would cleave unto the Lord. For he was a good man, and full of the Holy Ghost and of faith: and much people was added unto the Lord."—Acts 11:22-24.

Barnabas was "a good man." He must have been a delightfully blessed Christian. Like some others, he is placed alongside such a spiritual giant that often people do not recognize the greatness of this man.

It was so with Jonathan, son of King Saul. His integrity, his spiritual insight, his boldness of faith, his loyalty and love for the man who took his appointed kingship, marked Jonathan as one of the purest, noblest characters in the Bible. But in his day and place David, the incomparable, holds the center of the stage, so few note the beautiful character of Jonathan.

Joshua was a mighty man with the anointing of God upon him. What leadership! What boldness! What devotion! What faith he had as he led the children of Israel to conquer the land of Canaan! But alongside the giant Moses, Joshua is more often remembered as the servant of Moses and in some sense the lesser successor of that giant of God.

So Barnabas is pictured alongside the spiritual giant, Paul, the apostle to the Gentiles, the one whose ministry took the Gospel not only to Asia Minor but to Greece and Rome, and the account of it dominates most of the New Testament after Acts 12. God used Paul to write thirteen or fourteen of the books of the Bible. How may Apollos or Silas or Barnabas greatly impress me when placed alongside Paul?

But here we find that the Bible has a rich picture of Barnabas, "a good man." Oh, may we learn by his example, and pattern after his goodness, his faith and his soul winning.

I. HE WAS A GOOD MAN

Of course we know that in a literal and exact sense, "there is none good, save one, that is, God." Jesus was perfectly good because He is God (Matt. 19:17; Luke 18:19). But we use the term in a relative sense; what a man may call good as compared to wicked men, men of evil motives and character. But rarely is such language of praise used in the Bible. I believe only of Joseph of Arimathaea is the term used in addition to its use about Barnabas (Luke 23:50). Joseph, the husband of Mary, was called "a just man" (Matt. 1:19). There was "a great woman" of Shunem who entertained Elisha (II Kings 4:8). Unsaved Cornelius was "a devout man"; and some men were "mighty men of valor," that is, brave. But almost alone is Barnabas called of God "a good man." Let's consider how good he was.

1. What a Generous Heart He Had!

We first learn about Barnabas when a famine is on among the believers in Jerusalem. Many have been converted, and we suppose many had lost their jobs. It was soon necessary to elect seven deacons who would carefully and systematically see after the feeding of widows who had no other support. It would soon be revealed to the Prophet Agabus that a great famine would be on in Jerusalem and they should send gifts. But people said that what they had was not their own, but they had all things common. And because of the generosity of good people, no one lacked. Some people sold their lands, or houses and brought the money, that the apostles might distribute to "every man according as he had need." And in Acts 4:36,37 we read:

> *"And Joses, who by the apostles was surnamed Barnabas (which is, being interpreted, The son of consolation,) a Levite, and of the country of Cyprus, Having land, sold it, and brought the money, and laid it at the apostles' feet."*

His real name was Joses. Ah, but he earned another name, and soon the apostles called him "Barnabas . . . the son of consolation." What a comfort to their hearts was this good man!

He had land in the far-away island of Cyprus. And he did not have local pressure as did some of these others. Though he was a Levite who had grown up in another country, yet he sold the land and brought the money to the apostles. And day by day his joyful giving and his loyal service made him so beloved of the apostles and such a comfort that they called him "Barnabas . . . the son of consolation."

Oh, he had a generous, giving heart. What shows better the generosity of a good heart than how liberally and how lovingly he gives to God's cause and to others? Stinginess and avarice and covetousness are not the marks of a good man. These were not in the heart of Barnabas.

Oh, if God would give to us such a "grace of giving," as Paul called it in relation to those Macedonian churches that gave with all their heart (II Cor. 8), then we might be more like Barnabas, the good man, the generous, giving man. He laid all he had on the altar. Perhaps he had heard—at any rate he obeyed—the implied command of Jesus, "Whosoever he be of you that forsaketh not all that he hath, he cannot be my disciple" (Luke 14:33). He was a good man, a generous man.

2. What a Loving, Trusting Heart He Had for Young Christians!

Saul the persecutor, that arrogant young agent of the Sanhedrin who went around arresting Christians and giving testimony against them, who held the garments of the men who stoned Stephen to death, now says he has been converted. He had gone to Damascus to arrest Christians. He went to persecute, but he met Jesus on the road and so was wonderfully saved. Now he is on fire for God, is filled with the Holy Spirit, and he comes back to Jerusalem and wants to meet with the other Christians.

But they are all afraid of him. No doubt they thought, "Yes, that is just a trick of these deceitful Pharisees and chief priests to get in among us and find out who is a good Christian and get people sent to jail or get them stoned like Stephen was!" But Barnabas saw the young man. He had that inner sight that comes from faith and Christian charity. He saw in the eager face and burning eyes of this young man some evidence of conversion. He believed his testimony. He believed that Saul was really saved. So he brought him before the others and vouched for him.

Acts 9:26-28 tells us:

> *"And when Saul was come to Jerusalem, he assayed to join himself to the disciples: but they were all afraid of him, and believed not that he was a disciple. But Barnabas took him, and brought him to the apostles, and declared unto them how he had seen the Lord in the way, and that he had spoken to him, and how he had preached boldly at Damascus in the name of Jesus. And he was with them coming in and going out at Jerusalem."*

Good Barnabas helped a young man get into the ministry and have fellowship with other Christians!

I can well imagine the suspicion of these Christians who were already under great persecution. They would be a little afraid, a little slow to take in one who had been such an enemy of Christians. There is a certain Pharisaism that comes so easy to good Christians. Peter would hardly go down to preach to Cornelius until God compelled him in a vision. So those Christians at Jerusalem would blame Peter and accuse him until he convinced them that God sent him and he had to go. Yes, and even Peter later would fear these other Jewish Christians and be afraid to eat meals with the Gentiles, as we learn in Galatians 2:4-11.

But Barnabas had some tenderness of heart, some openness of spirit that made him able to tune in to the work God was doing in young Saul's heart. And good Barnabas took Paul to his heart and brought him before the people. And Paul went on preaching with great power in Jerusalem.

This attitude of Barnabas—looking to help young Christians, looking to push out young preachers—was a blessed trait. We do not know that Paul the apostle would ever have amounted to anything for God but for Barnabas. He preached in Jerusalem, and Acts 9:29,30 says:

> *"And he spake boldly in the name of the Lord Jesus, and disputed against the Grecians: but they went about to slay him. Which when the brethren knew, they brought him down to Caesarea, and sent him forth to Tarsus."*

Now young Saul (called now Paul) has gone back to Tarsus, his old home, and has quit his preaching.

That is too bad.

Can you blame him? At Damascus he had started out preaching so earnestly and there he barely escaped with his life. He was inspired to tell us in II Corinthians 11:32,33:

> *"In Damascus the governor under Aretas the king kept the city of the Damascenes with a garrison, desirous to apprehend me: And through a window in a basket was I let down by the wall, and escaped his hands."*

And now Paul had come to Jerusalem and had preached again with power, and again we are told, "they went about to slay him"; and so he was sent away to Tarsus and for the moment it seems his preaching ministry has stopped.

We go right on through chapters 9, 10, 11 and we do not find Paul preaching again until Barnabas comes on the scene. Barnabas was sent by the church in Jerusalem to Antioch to check up on the blessed revival there. He came. He was glad and preached that they should cleave unto the Lord. He was such a good man. But in Acts 11:25, after the text telling us that Barnabas was such a good man, we read:

> *"Then departed Barnabas to Tarsus, for to seek Saul:*
> *And when he had found him, he brought him unto An-*
> *tioch. And it came to pass, that a whole year they as-*
> *sembled themselves with the church, and taught much*
> *people. And the disciples were called Christians first in*
> *Antioch."*—Acts 11:25,26.

It seems that for three or four years Paul had stayed at Tarsus, the place where he grew up, and we hear nothing of his preaching. But Barnabas remembers the young man. He says, "God can use him! God has His hand on him! He must not quit this preaching!" So Barnabas got him; and Paul and Barnabas preached together for a year in Antioch.

Barnabas was a good man, a maker of preachers, a promoter of others.

3. Barnabas Took Second Place Without a Murmur, Superseded by the Man He Promoted

In Acts 13 we find that in the church at Antioch, where Paul and Barnabas had been preaching a year, certain leaders came into the church for a prayer meeting: Barnabas, Simeon, Lucius, Manaen. Here are named distinguished men, leaders in the Lord's work. But Paul is not named as one of these four leaders here, though he was present, doubtless, with others at the prayer meeting.

> *"As they ministered to the Lord, and fasted, the Holy*
> *Ghost said, Separate me Barnabas and Saul for the work*
> *whereunto I have called them. And when they had fasted*
> *and prayed, and laid their hands on them, they sent*
> *them away."*—Acts 13:2,3.

Now it is Barnabas and Saul. But that would indicate Barnabas, the older man, the more mature Christian, is recognized as a leader and that young Saul goes as his helper.

They go to the island of Cyprus where Barnabas had lived. This is the first stop on the first missionary journey. There it is "Barnabas and Saul" (vs. 7). But Paul begins to preach, and then in verse 13 we find, "Now when Paul and his company loosed from Paphos, they came to Perga." It was now "Paul and his company" instead of "Barnabas and Saul." And when they get to Antioch in Pisidia, it was Paul who stood up and preached (vs. 16). And then verse 43: "Now when the congregation was broken up, many of the Jews and religious proselytes followed Paul and Barnabas." Now it is "Paul and Barnabas."

In verse 46 again it is "Paul and Barnabas," as it is the rest of the way. Paul took first place and, without a murmur, it seems, Barnabas took second place and pushed forward Paul, the more gifted man, anointed of God. No doubt Paul owed much of his ministry to the gracious kindness and unselfish help of Barnabas.

It takes real grace for a man to rejoice in another man's prosperity and usefulness. A beloved preacher friend of mine said, "It is hard for a man to say 'Amen' to another man's revival." I have sometimes felt that it takes more grace to be an assistant pastor than a pastor. How often has the assistant grown jealous, has listened to the voice of complainers, has tried to steal away the hearts of the people from the pastor! But not Barnabas. He was willing to take second place that Paul might be the great man God intended him to be. John the Baptist had said about Jesus, "He must increase, but I must decrease." So I think Barnabas delighted in the marvelous ministry of the man he had pushed along and had vouched for and had brought back into the active ministry.

4. The Charity and Patience of Barnabas With Immature Christians Was Part of His Good Character

There came a time when Paul and Barnabas broke up. I suspect that both were somewhat to blame, or it may be that God simply used this method to send out two evangelistic teams instead of one. John Mark, the nephew of Barnabas, had gone with Barnabas and Saul to the island of Cyprus to be their minister, their servant, no doubt to carry baggage, to run errands, to make the beds, or to prepare meeting places. At any rate, he soon got enough, and when they left Cyprus, "John departing from them returned to Jerusalem" (Acts 13:13).

Well, after a great missionary journey, Paul and Barnabas decided:

> *"Let us go again and visit our brethren in every city*
> *where we have preached the word of the Lord, and see*
> *how they do. And Barnabas determined to take with*
> *them John, whose surname was Mark. But Paul thought*
> *not good to take him with them, who departed from*
> *them from Pamphylia, and went not with them to the*
> *work. And the contention was so sharp between them,*
> *that they departed asunder one from the other: and so*
> *Barnabas took Mark, and sailed unto Cyprus; and Paul*
> *chose Silas, and departed, being recommended by the*
> *brethren unto the grace of God. And he went through*
> *Syria and Cilicia, confirming the churches."*—Acts
> 15:36-41.

Barnabas determined to take with him John Mark but Paul would not allow it. The impatient Paul could not abide sloppy work, indecision and perhaps cowardice and lack of devotion to the Lord. So he did not want to take John Mark along.

It may be that Paul was right. It may be that both were partly right. But even if Barnabas had made a mistake, it must be said to his credit that he had a charity of heart to want the young preacher to have a chance and to make good. He was willing to give Mark a second chance.

We remember that God called Jonah but he ran away; yet the Scripture says, "And the word of the Lord came unto Jonah the second time, saying, Arise, go unto Nineveh, that great city, and preach unto it the preaching that I bid thee" (Jonah 3:1,2). A "second time"! What a blessed thing that God doesn't quit us when we fail Him, but He gives us a second chance.

When Peter cursed and swore and denied Christ and quit the ministry, Jesus went out to get him and He called him back into the service. We remember even when David committed such awful sins of adultery and murder, yet God loved him and gave him another chance. Even Paul the apostle had gone back to Tarsus, and was out of the picture for perhaps three or four years, but God sent Barnabas to get him and bring him back into service. How good that somebody like Barnabas loved the young man who faltered and tried his best to get him back into the ministry.

I cannot forget that a godly country preacher, Brother R. H. Gipson, pastor of a village church that I attended in the cow country in West Texas, was not content to let me go on in my ambition to be a college teacher but insisted I lead singing for him in meetings. He sent me to preach when I never intended to preach and did not know that I was called of God to preach. Oh, you could hardly stay around that godly man without getting on fire to preach and win souls. God surely must be pleased when somebody loves young preachers and sees in them what others do not yet see—the plan of God.

J. Wilbur Chapman took Billy Sunday to run his book table, to give talks to meetings for men, to help set up chairs for the meeting places and do other odd jobs for the Chapman revival party. When Chapman left the evangelistic field to go back to the pastorate in Philadelphia, he insisted that Billy Sunday start out as an evangelist. But Billy had no sermons!

"I'll give you ten sermons," Chapman said, "And that will run you through one week and two Sundays."

So Billy held his first eight-day revival—that was all the sermons he had! Chapman had helped make the great evangelist Billy Sunday became.

It is a matter of joy to me that later when Paul is a prisoner at Rome and foresees he will soon be beheaded for the witness of the faith, he writes to Timothy, "Take Mark, and bring him with thee: for he is profitable to me for the ministry" (II Tim. 4:11). Paul had found other people to be unfaithful, too. Demas had forsaken him, having loved the present world; and others had left the old man, a prisoner of the Lord, in jail, and now he finds he can use the young man Mark whom Barnabas had cultivated and pushed along in the ministry.

II. BARNABAS WAS "FULL OF FAITH"

Faith must be a part of good Christian character. We are told that "without faith it is impossible to please him [God]: for he that cometh to God must believe that he is, and that he is a rewarder of them that diligently seek him" (Heb. 11:6). And again we read that "Whatsoever is not of faith is sin." So this good man Barnabas was "full of faith."

1. Faith Prompted Barnabas to Give All

Those who do not give liberally, generously, sacrificially to God do not really have faith that He will repay. They do not believe the promise of Jesus in Luke 6:38, "Give, and it shall be given unto you; good measure, pressed down, and shaken together, and running over, shall men give into your bosom. For with the same measure that ye mete withal it shall be measured to you again." They do not believe the promise of II Corinthians 9:6,7 that "he which soweth sparingly shall reap also sparingly; and he which soweth bountifully shall reap also bountifully. Every man according as he purposeth in his heart, so let him give; not grudgingly, or of necessity: for God loveth a cheerful giver." Oh, it is lack of faith that does not believe that "the liberal soul shall be made fat: and he that watereth shall be watered also himself" (Prov. 11:25). It is a matter of faith in God that one can risk the promise, "Honour the Lord with thy substance, and with the firstfruits of all thine increase: So shall thy barns be filled with plenty, and thy presses shall burst out with new wine" (Prov. 3:9,10).

Barnabas had learned the sweet lesson which the Lord gives us in the model prayer. He could pray, "Give us THIS DAY our daily bread," and risk God about tomorrow. He had learned the truth of "seek ye first the kingdom of God, and his righteousness; and all these things shall be added unto you" (Matt. 6:33). So Barnabas could give all he had and be content. He did not fret about the future.

Isn't that the meaning for us in Philippians 4:6,7, "Be careful for nothing; but in every thing by prayer and supplication with thanksgiving let your requests be made known unto God. And the peace of God, which passeth all understanding, shall keep your hearts and minds through Christ Jesus"? That is, one need not worry if he goes to God and prays through and can thank God and have peace.

We see that faith is here a part of goodness, the character of this good man.

2. Barnabas Had Faith That God Would Use the Men, Now Untried Beginners

John Mark had failed somewhat in one trial. He had gone with them out to the island of Cyprus on the first missionary journey, gone as their "minister," that is, their servant. But he may have gotten homesick. He may have felt that running errands, waiting on these two preachers, carrying baggage was a dull business. Maybe he was made fearful by the opposition. At any rate, Mark had quit. He went home to Mamma. But Barnabas had faith that God would bring something out of this young man, and He did.

Barnabas insisted on taking him on a missionary journey, and he became a trusted preacher, useful in the Lord's work.

So Barnabas had had faith that Paul, the fiery young preacher, though perhaps unstable and not yet well settled in the work, freshly back from Damascus where he had barely escaped with his life—perhaps Barnabas saw in him, by faith, a great preacher. So he would not let the man stay after those three or four years down in Tarsus alone but must go get him and get him into the ministry. I am sure that God is greatly pleased when one can look forward and see God has something wonderfully useful in the awkward beginner.

When I felt led of God to give up my ministry as a college teacher and gospel singer, I remember that one preacher told me rather sadly, "You will ruin a good gospel singer to make a poor preacher." No doubt there were others who would have discouraged me. But I remember when I went to Dr. J. L. Ward, president of Decatur College where I had graduated, and told him I was going to preach, he said, "Yes, my wife and I have known for a long time that God was going to make a preacher out of you." Maybe that is part of the reason he loaned me some money when I worked my way in that junior college. He gave me a job milking cows, then waiting on tables, then teaching arithmetic to students not well prepared for college. I am so glad he had faith that God had something for me to do and would use me.

So it was with J. B. Tidwell, teacher of Bible in Baylor University. One day he had announced to a class, "If a girl here doesn't want to marry a preacher, she had better not marry John Rice." He knew my plans to go on to college teaching and my leadership in such matters for which the university gave me a scholarship. But he saw beyond what others saw, even beyond what I saw.

Oh, Barnabas had faith that God would raise up men to preach and he wanted to have part in that. He was full of faith.

III. BARNABAS WAS "FULL OF THE HOLY GHOST"

There is an inspired progression of thought here, a description of Barnabas, even as there is in many Scriptures. So Paul's salutation in his letters to Timothy and Titus: "Grace, mercy, and peace" be to you. First there is the grace in the heart of God, the working of it is mercy, and the result of it is peace.

And so it is with that progression of truth in II Corinthians 1:2,3, "Grace be to you and peace from God our Father, and from the Lord Jesus Christ. Blessed be God, even the Father of our Lord Jesus Christ, the Father of mercies, and the God of all comfort." What kind of a God is He? He is "the Father of our Lord Jesus Christ." God gave His Son, and that means Calvary and atonement and the only way in the world that God could righteously give us mercy. He is the "Father of our Lord Jesus Christ."

Hence, He is "the Father of mercies." That means that out of the atonement, out of the death of Christ, out of the loving giving of God the Father of His Son, now all the mercies of God can be poured out on us who are bought and taken into the family and counted righteous.

So, then, He is "the God of all comfort." No comfort unless there is some way to have peace with God. No comfort unless there is some answer to all our sins. No comfort unless we can come to the dying hour knowing that beyond is the glad resurrection and life in the presence and heart of God.

So here in this text about Barnabas there is a divine progression, inspired progression, of thought. Here there is the godly, loving and generous character of a good man, and then there is faith in God, but a faith without love, even if you could move mountains, is no good, according to I Corinthians 13. He had faith in God which meant surrender to His will, trusting Him about the future and as to his work. This man was filled with the Holy Spirit of God. This good man, with faith and usefulness, of course, must be filled with the Spirit of God.

1. How Could Any Christian Be Worth Much Unless "Full of the Holy Ghost"?

All greatly used people in the New Testament were filled with the Spirit.

In Luke, chapter 1, Elisabeth, the mother of John the Baptist, was filled with the Holy Spirit and witnessed with great joy. The Virgin Mary must have been filled with the Spirit and she speaks with a holy anointing about the blessing that is hers and of "God my Saviour." In the same chapter Zacharias, the father of John the Baptist, is "filled with the Spirit" and witnesses wonderfully that now "the dayspring from on high hath visited us," and now those who sit in darkness and in the shadow of death can have hope.

And when Jesus was brought to the Temple, Simeon "came by the Spirit into the temple," to hold and bless the Baby Jesus. Anna, "a prophetess," one speaking in the power of the Holy Spirit, was there. In Luke 1:15, John the Baptist was "filled with the Holy Ghost, even from his mother's womb."

Oh, being "full of the Holy Ghost" is normal Christianity and anything less than that is subnormal.

We learn that the Lord Jesus, our Pattern, now the perfect, sinless God-Man, but the Second Adam and the Son of Man and the model Man, would not begin His ministry until wet from the waters of Jordan's baptism He prayed and the Holy Ghost came on Him (Luke 3:21,22), and so Jesus began His Spirit-filled ministry.

2. But the Fullness of the Spirit Is Promised All

At Pentecost, in Acts 2:14-21, Peter recalled that blessed promise in Joel 2:28-32 where Joel had said, "And it shall come to pass in the last days, saith God, I will pour out of my Spirit upon all flesh: and your sons and your daughters shall prophesy . . . ." Oh, the Holy Spirit power is for everyone, and they shall prophesy and "whosoever shall call on the name of the Lord shall be delivered [saved]," Joel said. The promise is for everybody.

So in Acts 2:38,39, they asked Peter, "What shall we do?" He commanded that they were to repent, that they were to be baptized for the remission of sins, that is, looking toward, referring to the salvation they got when they repented, and then "ye shall receive the gift of the Holy Ghost. For the promise is unto you, and to your children, and to all that are afar off, even as many as the Lord our God shall call." Oh, the promise is to everybody!

Since the command to win souls is given to every Christian and those who have been saved and baptized are to be taught to carry out the same commission as the apostles (Matt. 28:19,20) and as Revelation 22:17 says, ". . . let him that heareth say, Come," so every Christian must have the power of God to do the work of God. It is normal Christianity, and the Holy Spirit power is promised to all.

That is implied, also, in the symbolism when Christ died. The spear was thrust into His side and "forthwith came there out blood and water" (John 19:34). The blood surely was atonement for sin. The blood surely was for everybody. First John 2:2 tells us, "And he is the propitiation for our sins: and not for our's only, but also for the sins of the whole world."

Well, then, what meant the water? That surely is the same water representing the Holy Spirit pictured in John 7:38,39, "He that believeth on me, as the scripture hath said, out of his belly shall flow rivers of living water. (But this spake he of the Spirit, which they that believe on him should receive: for the Holy Ghost was not yet given; because that Jesus was not yet glorified.)" Yes, the water pictured the blessing of Holy Spirit power upon Christians; a river should flow out from every Christian's inmost being.

That is also what Isaiah 44:3 promised: "I will pour water upon him that is thirsty, and floods upon the dry ground: I will pour my spirit upon thy seed, and my blessing upon thine offspring." As the blood pictured atonement for every poor sinner in the world, so the water pictured that everybody who takes the blood for atonement may take the water for an enduement of power. Oh, the Holy Spirit enduement is for every Christian who will take it.

3. Every Christian Is Commanded to Be Filled With the Spirit

In Ephesians is a blessed command, "And be not drunk with wine, wherein is excess; but be filled with the Spirit." That is, it is a sin to drink wine and get drunk. "Wine is a mocker, strong drink is raging: and whosoever is deceived thereby is not wise" (Prov. 20:1). But if it is a sin to get drunk, then in the same verse is another plain command, and to disobey that, also, is a sin. It is a sin to get drunk, and likewise it is a sin not to be filled with the Spirit, the Scripture says. Oh, the fullness of the Holy Spirit is for everybody, and the command is for all.

So Barnabas was filled with the Holy Ghost.

IV. "MUCH PEOPLE WAS ADDED UNTO THE LORD"

Yes, that was inevitable. When people are filled with the Holy Spirit, they have power upon them, they get people saved. That is what the fullness of the Spirit is for.

1. Plainly Promised That Those Who Are Filled With the Spirit Will Win Souls

In Luke 24:46-49 Jesus gave the Great Commission and with it a blessed promise:

"And said unto them, Thus it is written, and thus it behoved Christ to suffer, and to rise from the dead the third day: And that repentance and remission of sins should be preached in his name among all nations, beginning at Jerusalem. And ye are witnesses of these things. And, behold, I send the promise of my Father

upon you: but tarry ye in the city of Jerusalem, until ye
be endued with power from on high."

They were to get the Gospel out, they were to take the Gospel
to every creature, but they could not do it without power. And so
He said, "Tarry . . . until ye be endued with power from on
high." Power for soul winning.

That is the teaching also of Acts 1:8. Jesus had commanded
the apostles not to depart from Jerusalem but to "wait for the
promise of the Father, which, saith he, ye have heard of me. For
John truly baptized with water; but ye shall baptized with the
Holy Ghost not many days hence." What would be the result?
The eager disciples asked Jesus if He were about to set up the
kingdom of David again. No. He said, "But ye shall receive
power, after that the Holy Ghost is come upon you: and ye shall
be witnesses unto me both in Jerusalem, and in all Judaea, and
in Samaria, and unto the uttermost part of the earth" (Acts 1:8).

Note carefully that those who have the Holy Spirit power on
them will be witnesses for Jesus.

That promise is also in Joel's passage, as quoted in Acts 2:15-
21. The power of the Holy Ghost is come on all kinds of people,
on old and young, on servants and handmaidens, on sons and
daughters, and they shall prophesy or witness in the power of
God, and "whosoever shall call on the name of the Lord shall be
saved," we are told in verse 21.

2. John the Baptist Illustrates This Truth

Of John the Baptist we have the amazing statement that he
was to be "filled with the Holy Ghost, even from his mother's
womb. And many of the children of Israel shall he turn to the
Lord their God" (Luke 1:15,16). One cannot mistake the inevitable connection. One who is filled with the Spirit will win
souls, as John the Baptist did.

3. Fullness of Spirit at Pentecost Led to Winning
of Three Thousand Souls

In Acts 2:4 we find, "And they were all filled with the Holy
Ghost." There were some other incidental miracles at Pentecost.

There was the sound of a rushing mighty wind that filled the house. There were tongues like fire that sat upon the Christian people. They were given the power to speak to others who said they heard the Gospel "in our own tongue, wherein we were born." But these things are more relatively insignificant to the amazing fact that three thousand people turned from sin and trusted Christ, and verse 41 says, "Then they that gladly received his word were baptized: and the same day there were added unto them about three thousand souls."

It shows a bias, a lack of humility, a lack of openness of mind for anybody to read the second chapter of Acts and not know certainly that the command on which they went was to carry the Gospel and that the promise was they should be endued with power from on high and witness for Christ, and the results were that three thousand people heard the Gospel and were saved! So with Barnabas it is said that he was "full of the Holy Ghost and of faith: and much people was added unto the Lord." That was normal. That was to be expected.

4. Even the Lord Jesus Did Not Win Souls Until Anointed and Filled With the Spirit

It is a remarkable thing that up to thirty years of age the Lord Jesus had never won a soul, never preached a sermon, never worked a miracle. He came as our Pattern, our Example, and thus He would not do the work that we are to do until He had the special anointing for it, which we must also have. And so we read in Acts 10:37,38, "That word, I say, ye know, which was published throughout all Judaea, and began from Galilee, after the baptism which John preached; How God anointed Jesus of Nazareth with the Holy Ghost and with power: who went about doing good, and healing all that were possessed of the devil; for God was with him." Note that the Lord Jesus had special power from God, and God the Holy Spirit was with Christ, and His miracles were done as a Spirit-filled Man.

Then we are surely justified in saying that the fundamental reason why God fills anybody with the Holy Spirit is that they may witness for Christ and win souls.

Note the great result with Barnabas, as with Jesus, as with John the Baptist and as with many others is not that they talked in tongues, not that they had a "second blessing," with the carnal nature eradicated. They did not become sinless. It is not even suggested that out of them was formed a church by this fullness of the Spirit. On the contrary, it is clearly told that they won souls because of the power of God upon them; so it was with Barnabas.

O Christian reader, today I would set out to have the power of God like Barnabas had! O God, give us faith like Barnabas had and loving care for others and unselfishness, and let us have the power of God to win souls, as it was with Barnabas.

12

Judas Iscariot

Apostle, Miracle-Worker, Moral Man, Unconverted,
Devil-possessed, Hypocrite, Thief, "Devil,"
"Son of Perdition," Suicide,
Who Went to Hell

*Showing the Awful Danger of Church Membership or
Moral Life Without Being Born Again, the Sinful
Love of Money and the Eternal Ruin of One
Who Puts Anything Before Christ
and Salvation*

The most awful name in human history is that of Judas
Iscariot.

Benedict Arnold was a traitor and to many Americans it is a
term of great reproach. But Benedict Arnold had grievances; he
betrayed only a human cause. He turned from one group of ordinary mortals like himself to another group.

But Judas Iscariot was the arch-hypocrite of the centuries and
he betrayed the lovely Son of God Himself. He sold the Saviour
of mankind for thirty pieces of silver, then that godless tongue
said, "Hail, master," and those wicked lips stained the holy face
of Jesus with the kiss of a traitor.

The Saviour Himself said Judas was a "devil," and "the son of
perdition" (John 6:70; John 17:12). The term "the son of perdition" is only used in all of the Bible of one other being and that
is the terrible Man of Sin or Antichrist who will appear on the
earth in the Great Tribulation time in all the power of Satan.
The apostles spoke of Judas with horror as one who went "to his
own place," that is, evidently Hell (Acts 1:25).

No other man ever had greater privileges, and none ever
abused them so wickedly. Judas returned evil for good, hate for

love, and that to the holiest and purest and most kindly Being who ever walked this earth in human form. So the name *Judas Iscariot* is now a synonym for all that is unholy, vile and traitorous.

Yet, dear reader, you who shudder at the wickedness of Judas Iscariot, are you guilty of the same sin? Some who read this message may be on the road that leads by the same devious ways to the place where Judas Iscariot went.

Judas Iscariot was not always vile. Some mother loved him proudly and dreamed of a great future for the boy who nursed at her breast and then slowly under her fond eyes grew to manhood. Perhaps his parents dreamed as proudly of the future of Judas when they saw him follow Jesus as did Zebedee and his wife when they gave up the stalwart James and John and saw them leave their nets and ships and the fishing business to follow Jesus and so take their places in the hall of eternal fame as the apostles of our Lord.

Judas was loved and respected. He was regarded as a model Christian. He was never suspected by the other apostles. Outwardly he had many of the marks of a Christian. He was a professed disciple of Christ, a preacher of the Gospel, even a miracle-worker. He was evidently chosen by the other apostles as treasurer. To the very last they never suspected him of treachery.

You may be in the shoes of Judas Iscariot, and I earnestly urge you to consider some ten facts about him given below.

I. TEN FACTS ABOUT JUDAS

In Matthew 10:1-8, we find the account of how Jesus called the apostles, named them and sent them out to preach, and gave them supernatural power.

> *"And when he had called unto him his twelve disciples, he gave them power against unclean spirits, to cast them out, and to heal all manner of sickness and all manner of disease. Now the names of the twelve apostles are these; The first, Simon, who is called Peter, and Andrew his brother; James the son of Zebedee, and John his brother; Philip, and Bartholomew; Thomas, and*

*Matthew the publican; James the son of Alphaeus and
Lebbaeus, whose surname was Thaddaeus; Simon the
Canaanite, and Judas Iscariot, who also betrayed him.
These twelve Jesus sent forth, and commanded them,
saying, Go not into the way of the Gentiles, and into any
city of the Samaritans enter ye not: But go rather to the
lost sheep of the house of Israel. And as ye go, preach,
saying, The kingdom of heaven is at hand. Heal the sick,
cleanse the lepers, raise the dead, cast out devils: freely
ye have received, freely give."*—Matt. 10:1-8.

Beginning here, we call your attention to some of the Bible
facts about Judas Iscariot.

1. He Was Called to Be an Apostle

The honor that came only to a few men in the history of the
world came to Judas. His was the same privilege with Simon
Peter, with James and John, that trio of great preachers who
shook the world of their day with the Gospel. Matthew, the converted publican who wrote the Gospel called by his name, was a
companion of Judas, and Judas could have been as greatly used
of God.

We know certainly that Judas publicly claimed to be a Christian, that is, to love and trust Jesus Christ. The very fact that he
followed Jesus as one of His chosen twelve was a profession of his
faith. Besides, he most certainly had been baptized. After Judas
had killed himself and after Jesus had arisen from the dead, the
apostles, meeting together, considered the question of a success-
or to take the place of Judas, and they said:

*"Wherefore of these men which have companied with
us all the time that the Lord Jesus went in and out
among us, Beginning from the baptism of John, unto
that same day that he was taken up from us, must one be
ordained to be a witness with us of his resurrection."*—
Acts 1:21,22.

One who was to take the place of an apostle must have companied with the disciples during the entire ministry of Jesus,
"beginning from the baptism of John."

Judas, then, like the other apostles, must have been baptized when John was baptizing in the river Jordan. If Judas went to Hell, then he went as a church member, went as a professing Christian.

2. Judas Was a Preacher

Not only was Judas called as an apostle, but he actually was sent forth to preach (Matt. 10:5-8). He probably baptized others, for "Jesus himself baptized not, but his disciples" (John 4:2). Jesus gave Judas power over unclean spirits, power to work miracles, commanded him to heal and preach, for Judas was one of the twelve. And Matthew 10:5-8 says, "These twelve Jesus sent forth, and commanded them . . . preach . . . Heal the sick, cleanse the lepers, raise the dead, cast out devils." Judas was commanded to do these things and, as far as we know, he did.

Certainly there have been some preachers who did such things though unsaved, as Matthew 7:22,23 tells us. How strange to think that Judas Iscariot went about daily claiming to be a Christian, even acting as a minister of the Gospel, when he would eventually betray Jesus Christ!

3. Judas Lived in Most Intimate Contact With Jesus

Jesus and the twelve seem to have gone almost everywhere together. In one or two cases, Peter, James and John went with Jesus and saw His miracles when others did not, but we may be sure that Judas heard practically every sermon Jesus ever preached.

He was there when Jesus healed the maniac of Gadara, casting out a legion of devils. He saw the woman at the well of Sychar in Samaria when she was so happily converted that she forgot her waterpot and ran to tell the people, "Come, see a man, which told me all things that ever I did: is not this the Christ?" And he saw the great revival that followed.

He saw the storm on the Sea of Galilee stilled by the voice of Jesus. He, with the other apostles, passed the broken pieces of bread and fish to the multitude when five little barley loaves and two small fishes fed five thousand. We suppose he saw the water turned to wine. He saw lepers cleansed. He saw the dead raised. There could have been in his mind, it seems, no reasonable doubt about the Saviour being all that He claimed to be.

But even more precious than these miracles, Judas knew the compassionate heart of Jesus. He saw Him in His daily walk. He heard the tender tones of His voice, He knew when Jesus wept and prayed, sometimes all night. He knew His compassion for sinners and publicans. He saw Him forgive the harlots, receive the outcasts, give hope to the hopeless, and preach the Gospel to the poor!

I say, Judas knew the intimate heart of Christ by daily contact for three and one-half years. He dipped into the same bowl at meal times and slept, no doubt many times, in the same room at night. In their times of prayer together, surely Judas must have many a time lifted his voice with the others. How could such a man as Judas turn out to be a traitor?

4. Judas Was, at First, a Man of Highest Moral Character, Respected by All

This must have been so. Judas passed for a Christian, and there is not a hint that any one ever suspected that he was otherwise. Though Jesus early in His ministry said, "Have not I chosen you twelve, and one of you is a devil?" yet no one seemed to suspect Judas.

Down to the last night the disciples honored Him. Others were jealous when James and John sought the leadership and had their mother ask that they be given the first places in the coming kingdom, but no such resentment against Judas is ever mentioned. Peter said, "Though all men shall be offended because of thee, yet will I never be offended" (Matt. 26:33). But even then no one accused or suspected Judas.

When Jesus said openly at the table the same night that He was betrayed, "One of you shall betray me," each disciple there said, "Lord, is it I?" Peter had John, who was leaning on the Saviour's breast, to ask Him who it would be. None of them thought it would be Judas. And when Jesus said to Judas, "What thou doest, do quickly," even yet they simply thought that Judas was to buy something for the passover feast. The moral life of Judas deceived all the apostles; in fact, it deceived everyone, I suppose, but Jesus Himself.

Judas was even made treasurer of the band and "had the bag, and bare what was put therein" (John 12:6). The disciples would not have chosen it so had they not been convinced that Judas was all right.

How fearful a truth it is that Judas at first was a moral man of the very highest type, yet fell into such sin and came to such an awful end!

5. Yet Judas Was Never Converted

In John 6:64 Jesus said, "But there are some of you that believe not. For Jesus knew from the beginning who they were that believed not, and who should betray him." Then when other disciples left Him, Peter declared that "we believe and are sure that thou art that Christ, the Son of the living God." But in verses 70 and 71 "Jesus answered them, Have not I chosen you twelve, and one of you is a devil? He spake of Judas Iscariot the son of Simon: for he it was that should betray him, being one of the twelve."

Judas never believed in Jesus as his Saviour! Even from the beginning Jesus knew that Judas had not trusted Him and would betray Him. Thus, early in the ministry of Jesus, Judas was said to be a devil!

Here is a sad truth, then, that Judas was never converted. He was a moral man but not born again. His name might have been on the church book, but it was not on the Lamb's book of life. He was a professor but not a possessor of everlasting life. Judas was not one who was first saved, then became lost. No, he was never saved. He never trusted Christ for salvation, never was cleansed in the blood, never was made a new creature by the Holy Spirit of God. He fooled men but he did not fool God!

6. Love of Money Probably Led Judas to Reject Christ and Thus Damn His Soul

The Word of God tells so much in so few words. In the twelfth chapter of John we see a happy scene around a supper table.

Lazarus has been raised from the dead and they have made a great feast. Mary, the sister of Lazarus, her heart overflowing with love and thankfulness, was taught by the Holy Spirit about the coming death of Jesus, and so with "a pound of ointment of spikenard, very costly" she had anointed the feet of Jesus and wiped His feet on her hair. The whole house was filled with the odor of that precious ointment, and Jesus was touched and pleased so much that He promised what she had done should be told to the whole world wherever the Gospel is preached.

But we are told that Judas was there, and these verses reveal with startling clearness what is happening to his character:

"Then saith one of his disciples, Judas Iscariot, Simon's son, which should betray him, Why was not this ointment sold for three hundred pence, and given to the poor? This he said, not that he cared for the poor; but because he was a thief, and had the bag, and bare what was put therein."—John 12:4-6.

He had become a thief! Trusted by all the disciples, he has betrayed their trust. The love of money has eaten like a canker into his soul; now Judas steals for himself from the offerings given to support Jesus and the twelve and to care for the poor!

The man who tried morality without Christ found his morals broken down. There is no true morality without Christ, without regeneration. The outwardly moral man is not moral inside. Every unregenerate heart is rotten with sin and out of such hearts "proceed evil thoughts, murders, adulteries, fornications, thefts, false witness, blasphemies" (Matt. 15:19). It was immediately after this that Judas went to the chief priests and offered to betray Jesus for money, as you see from Matthew 26:14-16:

"Then one of the twelve, called Judas Iscariot, went unto the chief priests, And said unto them, What will ye give me, and I will deliver him unto you? And they covenanted with him for thirty pieces of silver. And from that time he sought opportunity to betray him."

It seems to have been a clear choice between Jesus and money.

For thirty pieces of silver Judas was to betray the Son of God! It was the price foretold in Scripture (Zech. 11:12,13). It was the price of an injured and mangled servant (Exod. 21:32). For this amount of money—estimated to be between seventeen and twenty dollars in value—Judas committed the terrible crime which has made his name accursed through the centuries.

7. Judas Became Literally Possessed of Satan

In Luke 22:3 we are told, "Then entered Satan into Judas surnamed Iscariot, being of the number of the twelve."

And following this, Judas covenanted with the chief priests to betray Jesus! John 13:2 tells us that "the devil . . . put into the heart of Judas Iscariot, Simon's son, to betray him." He who cast out devils was now possessed by Satan himself! Judas was like the man out of whom the unclean spirit went and then returned "and taketh with himself seven other spirits more wicked than himself, and they enter in and dwell there: and the last state of that man is worse than the first" (Matt. 12:45). This explains, as well as anything else can do, how Judas committed this terrible sin of betraying Jesus.

8. Judas Descended to the Lowest Hypocrisy, Betraying Jesus With a Kiss

Can you imagine the breaking heart of Jesus when this took place?

> *"And while he yet spake, lo, Judas, one of the twelve, came, and with him a great multitude with swords and staves, from the chief priests and elders of the people. Now he that betrayed him gave them a sign, saying, Whomsoever I shall kiss, that same is he: hold him fast. And forthwith he came to Jesus, and said, Hail, master; and kissed him. And Jesus said unto him, Friend, wherefore art thou come? Then came they, and laid hands on Jesus, and took him."*—Matt. 26:47-50.

Jesus loved him, called him "friend," even though He had known all these years that Judas would betray Him. Judas said to Jesus, "Hail, master." Then the mob seized Jesus and bound

Him and Judas collected his thirty pieces of silver!

9. Terrible Remorse of Conscience Seized Judas So That He Brought Back the Money to the Priests and Confessed His Sin

However, these wicked friends were no help. They did not pray for him to have pardon. They could not show him any way of peace. He had sold Christ for money, and now the money burned like fire in his soul, and in utter despair he committed suicide. In the words of the Scripture,

> *"Then Judas, which had betrayed him, when he saw that he was condemned, repented himself, and brought again the thirty pieces of silver to the chief priests and elders, Saying, I have sinned in that I have betrayed the innocent blood. And they said, What is that to us? see thou to that. And he cast down the pieces of silver in the temple, and departed, and went and hanged himself."*— Matt. 27:3-5.

After Judas hanged himself, his body fell and burst asunder (Acts 1:18), a horrible reminder to all the passers-by of the sad fruits of sin.

10. Judas, After All His Opportunities, Went to Eternal Torment in Hell!

The inspired apostles asked God to help them select an apostle "that he may take part of this ministry and apostleship, from which Judas by transgression fell, *that he might go to his own place"* (Acts 1:25). Judas fell, not from salvation, for he never had it, but from the ministry and apostleship, "that he might go to his own place." His own place was Hell, the place of every sinner not born again, whether he is a church member or not, whether he is moral or not, whether he is a preacher or not.

This is what Jesus meant in John 17 when in His prayer to the Father He said, "Those that thou gavest me I have kept, and none of them is lost, but the son of perdition; that the scripture might be fulfilled" (vs. 12). Judas, the son of perdition, was lost. Jesus had kept all those who really came to Him. But Judas never truly came in his heart, so he died and went to Hell.

Judas "repented himself" about the money and brought it again to the chief priests, but he did not repent toward God nor have faith in Jesus Christ as Saviour. So the poor, hopeless, Devil-possessed man who had been moral, who had been numbered with the apostles, who had preached and worked miracles, who had been trusted by all the disciples, died without Christ and now must spend eternity in torment. As Jesus said of him, "It had been good for that man if he had not been born" (Matt. 26:24).

II. LESSONS FOR YOU FROM JUDAS ISCARIOT

Many will read this sermon who are not saved and every soul, saved or lost, needs to give earnest heed to the lessons to be drawn from the life of Judas Iscariot. He has been on a pinnacle of infamy and his name is heaped with the scorn of those who despise his sin, but beware, reader, lest you be guilty as he was, deceived by sin, captured by Satan, at last to suffer eternal remorse in Hell.

Then let us consider the following lessons which God's Word brings to our mind as we consider Judas Iscariot.

1. Lost in the Church

Judas was counted a Christian but he was lost. He was baptized, yet he was lost. He preached the Gospel, yet he was lost. He worked miracles, yet he was lost. He was trusted by all who knew him, save Jesus, and yet he was lost.

It is a terrible thing to go to Hell from anywhere, but what remorse must be the portion of those who go to Hell from a church! More people go to Hell than go to Heaven, for "strait is the gate, and narrow is the way, which leadeth unto life, and few there be that find it." Many who expect to go to Heaven will be disappointed, for Jesus said, "Not every one that saith unto me, Lord, Lord, shall enter into the kingdom of heaven; but he that doeth the will of my Father which is in heaven" (Matt. 7:21). Many who expect to go to Heaven are lost and will not go. The five foolish virgins expected to go into the marriage and yet they had no oil. They had only the lamps of profession and not the oil of salvation.

In my first revival, two young women called me to talk with an old man who sat on the ground near the country brush arbor.

He said, "Brother Rice, I am all right. I never did anybody any harm."

"But have you ever been converted?" I asked. "Have you ever trusted Christ as your own personal Saviour?"

"Why, I have been a church member for a long time. I was superintendent of a Sunday school once. I have prayed in public many times. I am as good as the other church members. You need not worry about me."

I insisted that religious activities were not enough. He must have more than that to meet God in peace. But he said, "Well, I have never done anything very bad. About all I ever did wicked was to cuss a little bit."

"You might just as well say, 'About all I ever did was to kill a few men now and then,' " I said. "You are a sinner and unless Christ has changed your heart you are lost and condemned today. Jesus said, 'He that believeth on him is not condemned: but he that believeth not is condemned already, because he hath not believed in the name of the only begotten Son of God.' And again He said, 'Marvel not that I said unto thee, Ye must be born again.' Has God changed your heart?"

I remember that he looked down quietly for a little bit, then answered frankly, "No, Brother Rice, I don't know that I was ever born again. I guess I have never been saved if that is what it takes."

"Then don't you think it is time you got that settled today?" I said.

He answered, "Yes, I do!" and arose and came with me at once to the altar where he knelt down with tears and prayed for forgiveness and salvation and trusted Christ. Thank God he received it and went home happy! How sad if he had died, this Sunday school superintendent, this man who prayed in public, this moral church member, before he was ever born again!

Some years ago in a Sunday morning service when thirty-seven or thirty-eight people responded to the invitation in public profession of faith in Christ or coming as backsliders to renew their vows, a young woman came screaming from the back of the church house and weeping aloud. She said, "My name has been on the church book but it has never been on the book of life!" She was saved that day by simple faith in Jesus.

Let me warn you with all the solemnity of which I am capable, that you may be in the church unsaved. Maybe you were sprinkled as a baby and all your life have counted yourself a Christian because you were in the church. Or maybe you decided to mend your ways and reform; with others you joined the church, expecting to live a better life and hoping thereby to get to Heaven. Do not be deceived. Millions are in Hell who went there from the churches. Church membership cannot save you.

A woman in Dallas, Texas, came to me, saying, "I have been baptized; now I want to be born again."

In an Oklahoma revival some years ago, a dear girl of Catholic faith looked at me with burning eyes and told in broken voice how she had looked to her church and priest and confessions and prayers and mass to save her soul until she was brought to death's door by illness. Then she declared, "I found that what I had might be good enough to live by but it wouldn't do to die by! I promised God if He would give me another chance I would make sure this time that I was saved."

I remember the agonized heart-searching that went on as I taught her the simple way of salvation by trusting Jesus and depending wholly upon His blood, shed for sinners. When she saw how simple it was to trust in Jesus, what a quiet, deep joy was expressed in her face! I remember that she went to her sister and urged her to make sure of her salvation beyond any doubt, lest she should be damned and lost by being in the church without Christ and having a profession without a real possession of salvation.

The reason Judas was lost was that he did not trust in Jesus for salvation, did not surrender his heart to Jesus and take by faith the salvation freely offered for every sinner, purchased fully on Calvary.

Jesus died to take *your* place. Today He will be *your* Saviour if you will simply trust Him with all your heart, depend upon Him, receive Him, claim Him as yours.

May God grant that no reader of this message may go to Hell depending on church membership, or baptism, or good deeds, as many others have.

2. A Moral Life Utterly Failed
to Save Judas

I suppose there is no doubt that at first Judas was a man of high moral standing. His life deceived everybody but Jesus. The other apostles believed in him and I suppose elected him treasurer. But for all his moral standing, Judas went to Hell.

I said that church membership could not save a sinner. Neither can the lodges. There are doubtless scores of Masons in Hell, not because they were Masons but because they had not been born again. The lodges have done irreparable harm in causing men to depend upon a system of morals.

But the man who has a cultured mind and a tender conscience will go to Hell if he does not have Christ, just as surely as a reprobate sinner. The man who is kind to his neighbors, who pays his bills and keeps his marriage vows, is as certainly lost as Judas Iscariot if he has not been regenerated and given a new heart by the work of the Holy Spirit. It is only by faith in Christ that a lodge member can keep out of Hell, and so with every other moral man.

It was to Nicodemus, a ruler of the Jews religiously, a Pharisee in practice, one of the greatest moral men of his day, that Jesus said, "Except a man be born again, he cannot see the kingdom of God," and "Ye must be born again" (John 3:3,7).

And the sad part is that Judas' morals failed him. After all, there is no true morality outside of Christ. How could Judas really be moral in heart and hate the Lord Jesus Christ? The very fact that he rejected Christ in his heart, did not love Him nor trust Him, is the best possible proof of his own wicked heart.

The Pharisees who crucified Jesus claimed to be moral men, too, but they have gone down in history with Judas Iscariot as the most striking examples of wicked hate and selfishness. The man who rejects Christ is immoral and rotten at heart. "The heart is deceitful above all things, and desperately wicked: who can know it?" (Jer. 17:9).

Outwardly men may be genteel, cultivated, attractive and magnetic. Inwardly we know that without Christ they are whited sepulchres, wolves in sheep's clothing, and hypocrites, even as Judas Iscariot. Jesus Himself is the touchstone of true morality.

Let me know a man's attitude toward the immaculate Son of God and I will know his heart better than in any other possible way. If he hungers and thirsts after righteousness, he will rejoice in the righteousness of Christ. If he has a longing for purity, he will love the pure and holy Lamb of God. If he is merciful, he will be attracted by the merciful Saviour. If he truly loves men, he will be drawn by the compassion of Jesus. There is no godliness, no true morality, no true righteousness outside of Christ

The pretensions of Judas soon fell away and he was revealed as a wicked sinner, a thief, a money-loving criminal, a despicable and cowardly traitor.

I warn you now, moral men, that your morals will end as did those of Judas. Your character without Christ will gradually break down, and one day you will appear outwardly to be what you really are inwardly, a wicked-hearted, Christ-rejecting, Hell-deserving sinner!

Today I beg you, confess your sin and seek Christ's mercy and forgiveness. If Judas had done that he would not have become a thief and then the betrayer of Jesus, a suicide and then an inmate of Hell.

3. Hypocrites Who Betray Christ
With a Kiss

What is purer than a mother's kiss? How much sacrifice and forgiving love it stands for! With a kiss sweethearts pledge their undying love one toward another. How sweet is the kiss of a true wife and of innocent children! A kiss means devotion and loyalty and true love.

But Judas turned the emblem of love and devotion into the

sign of a traitor, saying, "Hail, master." He kissed Jesus that the soldiers and mob would thus know who to take for crucifixion.

Doubtless, many of you who read this do lip service to Christ. You claim to believe the Bible, to believe in Christ, in Heaven, in Hell, in salvation. I wonder if your pledge of devotion is as insincere and hypocritical as the kiss of Judas?

Some of you teach Sunday school classes, yet you have never said good-bye to the picture show and the bridge party. The same mouth that praises Jesus Christ, blows forth cigarette smoke. The same tongue that offers testimony in the prayer meeting, later talks scandal about your neighbor. "Out of the same mouth proceedeth blessing and cursing" (James 3:10).

The same lips that sing in the choir, take God's holy name in vain! If that be so, then you are guilty of hypocrisy like Judas. You say, "Hail, master," and kiss Him but you run with the mob that would crucify Him. Beware lest your praise is only from the lips! Beware lest your service is fraudulent and offensive to God.

The Lord said about certain people, "Ye hypocrites, well did Esaias prophesy of you, saying, This people draweth nigh unto me with their mouth, and honoureth me with their lips; but their heart is far from me" (Matt. 15:7,8).

Our thanks at the table are formal. Our service in the churches too often has no heart, no feeling, no devotion. This cold-hearted, unfelt religion is an abomination to God! No wonder sinners are not moved by our preaching or that God does not answer our praying. Cold churches, professional preachers, formal worship, matter-of-fact service—these, I fear, have taken the joy out of our religion, have robbed Christ of His glory and betrayed Him before the world. We have said, "Hail, master," alas, too many times and kissed Him with a kiss of insincerity, a traitor's kiss like Judas!

May God give us sincerity in our religion! May we awake to our shams and confess our lukewarmness and forsake our hypocrisy!

4. The Love of Money: What a Terrible Sin!

If Judas drank, that is not told in the Bible. If he cursed, it is never mentioned. Judas had no part, we suppose, with the whoremonger or the reveler. No, his sin was much more respectable in the sight of men. He had a money lust, a covetousness, a selfish willfulness that led him to reject Christ and damned his soul for eternity.

This sin, I say, is a respectable sin. It is practiced by the leaders in the church, is conducted from the pulpit. People are encouraged to "make all the money *you* can just so *you* make it honestly," and provided, of course, *they* give a tenth to the Lord!

But that is not the teaching of God's Word. "The love of money is the root of all evil" (I Tim. 6:10). We are warned, "How hardly shall they that have riches enter into the kingdom of God!" (Mark 10:23). It is harder, we are told, to get a rich man saved than to get a camel through the eye of a needle, and only by a miracle of God is it ever done.

How striking that the besetting sin of Judas, the betrayer of Jesus Christ, should be this common sin so little noticed and yet so ghastly in its results!

The love of money is back of every saloon that sells its liquid poison to make murderers, paupers and harlots; to break homes; to thwart mother's prayers; to take roses from the cheeks of wives and take bread from the mouths of little children! For money people sell the booze that fills our asylums and hospitals and penitentiaries and, yea, enlarge the population of Hell!

For money newspapers sell their integrity and advertise the vile stuff. For money church members rent their property for saloons and package stores. For money women sell their bodies and lawyers sell their souls! For money men neglect their wives, neglect their children, their homes. For money men stay away from church, forget to pray, neglect their Bible reading and lose their desire to save sinners. Men so pursue money that, alas, too often like Judas, they lose their souls.

Let it be burned into your soul that it was for money, a paltry thirty pieces of silver, only seventeen or eighteen dollars, that Judas betrayed the Son of God and heaped upon his name eternal shame. What will not men do for money!

Jesus told of the rich fool who said,

"Soul, thou hast much goods laid up for many years;

take thine ease, eat, drink, and be merry. But God said
unto him, Thou fool, this night thy soul shall be required
of thee: then whose shall those things be, which thou
hast provided? So is he that layeth up treasure for
himself, and is not rich toward God."—Luke 12:19-21.

Reader, if you are not rich toward God, how foolish you are
ever to work for an hour to make money, ever to let your thoughts
even center on the money. What good will money do when you
die and go to Hell? No wonder God said such a man was a fool.

Yes, Judas got his money but it could not still the gnawings of
his conscience. It burned his hands until he brought it and offered it again to the priests. They would not have it and said,
"What is that to us? see thou to that." So he laid it on the Temple floor and went and hanged himself. Even yet the money is accursed. It could not be put into the treasury because it was the
price of blood. With it they bought a potter's field to bury
strangers in. And from that day to this in the English language
everywhere "the potter's field" is a name for the spot where they
bury paupers.

What a reminder of the curse that follows the love of money!
Judas tasted part of the curse that was on those who wished to be
rich. James 5:2,3 says,

"Your riches are corrupted, and your garments are
moth-eaten. Your gold and silver is cankered; and the
rust of them shall be a witness against you, and shall eat
your flesh as it were fire . . . ."

If one reads this today who is not converted, I charge you with
the highest folly, in God's sight you have played the fool. You
have thought of food and drink and have neglected your soul. In
Christ's name, I beg you to remember the question, "What is a
man profited, if he shall gain the whole world, and lose his own
soul? or what shall a man give in exchange for his soul?" (Matt.
16:26).

Jesus said, "No man can serve two masters: for either he will
hate the one, and love the other; or else he will hold to the one,
and despise the other. Ye cannot serve God and mammon"

(Matt. 6:24). It is mammon or Christ. The love of money is at enmity with God.

Oh, turn to Christ for salvation! He loves you enough to care for your needs daily. And you who are saved, I beg you, "Lay not up for yourselves treasures upon earth, where moth and rust doth corrupt, and where thieves break through and steal: But lay up for yourselves treasures in heaven, where neither moth nor rust doth corrupt, and where thieves do not break through nor steal" (Matt. 6:19,20).

Judas is an eternal reminder of the folly of desiring money. Out of an honest man it made a thief. Out of a moral man it made a hypocrite. Out of an apostle it made a Christ-betrayer. Out of a proud and honored man it made a dejected suicide. Out of one who walked and talked and ate in the most intimate contact with Jesus it made an inmate of Hell! Beware of the love of money!

5. False Prophets Come in Sheep's Clothing

If Judas Iscariot, the apostle of Jesus Christ, was an unsaved, wicked thief, the son of perdition, possessed of the Devil, then surely we must beware about false prophets. We have many warnings on this subject in the Bible. Jesus said, "Beware of false prophets, which come to you in sheep's clothing, but inwardly they are ravening wolves" (Matt. 7:15). And Paul wrote to the Corinthian Christians:

> "For such are false apostles, deceitful workers, transforming themselves into the apostles of Christ. And no marvel; for Satan himself is transformed into an angel of light. Therefore it is no great thing if his ministers also be transformed as the ministers of righteousness; whose end shall be according to their works."—II Cor. 11:13-15.

One is commanded to "try the spirits" and one of the gifts of the Spirit greatly to be desired is that of "discerning of spirits." If Satan could use an apostle of Christ, he may mislead and use others in high positions. Unless we beware, false prophets will lead us away from faith in a supernatural Bible, the atoning blood of Christ and the necessity for a new birth. Satan and his demons are very real when one studies the catastrophe in the life of this moral man Judas.

III. THE BITTER END OF SIN

How well Judas learned that "the way of the transgressor is hard." Sin promises much but it gives little. The cup of pleasure seems sweet until you come to the bitter, gagging dregs that you must drink.

It is said about spiritual wisdom, "Her ways are ways of pleasantness, and all her paths are peace" (Prov. 3:17), but concerning the way of the Christ-rejecting sinner we are told that "there is a way which seemeth right unto a man, but the end thereof are the ways of death" (Prov. 14:12).

How well Judas learned the sad truth! He was entangled by the goal of morality without Christ. He looked for profit and doubtless part in an earthly kingdom without repentance and regeneration. He looked for wealth as the treasure of the King and of an empire. But he fell to the sin of embezzling the alms of the poor and sold the King of the Jews, the Prince of Peace, the Son of God, for a paltry thirty pieces of silver that burned like fire in his pockets and in his conscience until he threw them ringing on the stone floor, and went and hanged himself!

Where are the friends of Judas? Those smart friends with whom he counseled cunningly and entered into a solemn covenant? Judas doubtless thought that he would be a big man when it was all over, standing well with those in authority. But he failed to count on the remorse of conscience and their scoffing laugh as they said, "What is that to us? see thou to that."

His friends were like the friends of the prodigal boy when he landed in the hogpen. They had helped him spend his money— the wine-drinkers and harlots had—but when his money was gone, the friends were gone. So when Judas had served his day, there was no one who cared for his anguished heart, no one to pray, no one to counsel him, not a friend who loved him.

The girl who would be popular and sometimes throws away her modesty, her reputation and even her virtue to have friends, soon learns, alas! that those kind of friends never do any good when you are in distress of soul.

Suppose you make money: Judas did. It will trickle between your fingers as you go out into the horror of black darkness at death to meet an angry God you have scorned and neglected. When your body is eaten with disease and when youth has fled, what good then is money you got at the price of your soul? Judas learned that lesson too late.

The end of sin is always unexpected. Bob Silver, convicted of murder and sentenced to the electric chair, said to me in the Tarrant County jail one day, "I never thought it would come to this! We only thought of the money. We didn't intend to kill anybody. We thought we had gotten away, but when we were caught, I said, 'It is the hand of God. He is against us!' I never expected to be condemned to die as young as I am."

The end of sin is unexpected to the sinner. It is unexpected because he does not believe the Bible, unexpected because he will not listen to his mother, will not see the tears of his wife, will not heed the warnings of the preacher, will not give heed to the tender pleading of the Holy Spirit. "The soul that sinneth, it shall die," and "Whatsoever a man soweth, that shall he also reap."

Judas learned it, as you will, too, my friend, if you go on in sin without Christ. Please hear this solemn word: the end of sin is bitter, as bitter as gall! You are on Judas' road if you do not turn to Christ for mercy and forgiveness. Turn your heart from sin to accept God's mercy and be saved.

Neglected opportunities mean a hardened heart, offending the Spirit of God and finally eternal condemnation.

These years I have been preaching I have brought the message again and again, "Now is the day of salvation," "Today if ye will hear his voice, harden not your hearts." A thousand illustrations of it have come to mind, some in the Scripture and some from my own experience. But I never knew a more pertinent example of the disastrous results of neglected opportunities than the case of Judas Iscariot.

Judas had a finely developed moral nature. He must have been taught morality, honesty and virtue in childhood. He was respected and honored for his virtues. And even after he had committed such a horrible sin, of selling Jesus for money and betraying Him with a kiss, still the ghost of that moral character returned to haunt him, and his conscience lashed him to suicide.

With that kind of nature, can you imagine how Judas was touched when he saw Jesus bless the little children and heard Him say, "Of such is the kingdom of heaven"? He heard Jesus say that "Except ye be converted, and become as little children, ye shall not enter into the kingdom of heaven" (Matt. 18:3).

The fiery preaching of Jesus when He said, "Except ye repent, ye shall all likewise perish" (Luke 13:1-5) must have stirred him to the depths of his heart. He saw case after case of marvelous conversions. He heard the burning words of Jesus as He preached in the twenty-third chapter of Matthew His scathing sermon to self-righteous Pharisees like Judas who had never been born again. He must have trembled when Jesus said to them,

"Woe unto you, scribes and Pharisees, hypocrites! for ye make clean the outside of the cup and of the platter, but within they are full of extortion and excess. Thou blind Pharisee, cleanse first that which is within the cup and platter, that the outside of them may be clean also. Woe unto you, scribes and Pharisees, hypocrites! for ye are like unto whited sepulchres, which indeed appear beautiful outward, but are within full of dead men's bones, and of all uncleanness. Even so ye also outwardly appear righteous unto men, but within ye are full of hypocrisy and iniquity."—Matt. 23:25-28.

Do you think he could ignore the warning when Jesus said in verse 33, "Ye serpents, ye generation of vipers, how can ye escape the damnation of hell?" He certainly knew the insistence of Jesus that "Ye must be born again."

In my own mind I feel sure that Judas thought, "Some day I will be saved. I dare not wait too long." But he was ashamed to confess his hypocrisy. Like multitudes of others in the churches, he did not want it known that all these years he had been a hypocrite, claiming to be what he was not. Then he felt that he could not be saved without in his heart giving up his thieving, his love for money which had now well nigh mastered his soul. Eventually his heart grew harder and harder, and when Jesus rebuked him publicly for objecting when Mary anointed the Saviour's feet with ointment, his hard heart seemed to turn to stone. The respect and admiration which he must have had for Jesus seemed to curdle into hate. He was too far gone in sin to take warning. His heart was too hard to be touched. He shook off what conviction he had. He must have ground his teeth in vengeful spite as he went to covenant with the chief priests to betray the Saviour to them for thirty pieces of silver.

At last Satan had entered into Judas Iscariot and in person the Prince of Devils, the enemy of mankind, rushed him out of his reason, away from the call of the Holy Spirit, past all the warning signals until at last in anguish and despair Judas hung himself and with the last gasp his soul, like the rich man's, awoke in Hell, tormented in flame.

Every sinner who reads this and says, "Sometime I will be saved," is walking the road of Judas Iscariot. Pharaoh said, "Tomorrow." It was typical of the Christ-rejecting heart, and Pharaoh must eventually have committed the unpardonable sin that we believe Judas did.

Tomorrow your heart will be hardened. Tomorrow you will not listen to the preaching of the Gospel. Tomorrow you will be so involved in sin that you cannot break loose. Tomorrow you may have so long rejected Christ and grieved the Holy Spirit that He will leave you forever. Tomorrow you may have sinned away your day of grace: tomorrow may be too late. Tomorrow may never come.

God help you, sinner, to trust Jesus today. Be saved while you can. Today your heart may be tender and I earnestly plead with you to come while you can. If your heart is hard today, it will be harder tomorrow. If you think you cannot give up your sins today, how can you do it tomorrow after sin has slowly bound you with chains that you cannot break?

Is there any way I can make you see the danger of neglecting your soul's salvation? Judas started the road you are traveling and you see where it took him. And every man in Hell, if you could talk with him today, would tell you, "Yes, I intended to be saved but I said, 'I am not ready yet.' " They went to Hell, every one of the millions there, because they did not repent of their sins and trust Christ while they had time and opportunity. Isaiah calls:

"Seek the Lord while he may be found, call ye upon him while he is near: Let the wicked forsake his way, and the unrighteous man his thoughts: and let him return unto the Lord, and he will have mercy upon him; and to our God, for he will abundantly pardon."—Isa. 55:6,7.

Today is God's time to be saved. The proverb says, "The road of By and By leads to the town of Never."

When Judas dropped to the lowest depths of sin, Jesus called him "friend." However hard your heart, however wicked your life, however many times you have rejected Him, He loves you today. He wants you to be saved. Today, this minute, if you will turn to Him with all your heart, He will save you. Will you let Him do it just now?

It is the burning desire of my heart that by this message sinners may be turned to God and saved from sin and Hell. So with an earnest prayer in my heart, I ask you today to trust Jesus now. He died for you. He loves you. He is ready. The very second that you turn your heart to Him in penitence and trust Him to take you, He will. He said, "Him that cometh to me I will in no wise cast out" (John 6:37).

Then come just now and then write and tell me so that I may rejoice with you. Turn, oh, turn today from the way of Judas Iscariot and be named instead with those who love and trust Jesus Christ and have been washed and made white in His blood.

If you will say, "Yes," to Jesus today, will give Him your whole heart, will risk Him to forgive all your sins, then write to me today. I will rejoice with all my heart. We will have a prayer meeting and a time of praise here in the office and I will write you a personal letter. Oh, the angels in Heaven will rejoice! Do it just now and your letter will be counted confidential and will not be published unless you desire it. Can you sign the following statement and mail it to me today?

(Date)_____

Evangelist John R. Rice
Box 1099
Murfreesboro, Tennessee 37130

Dear Brother Rice:

I have read your sermon on Judas Iscariot and God knows I do not want to go his wicked way. I know I am a sinner and today, right now, with all my heart I turn to God confessing my sin and depending on Him for salvation. I believe that He loves me, that He died for me, and here and now I take Him to be my Saviour, risking Him to take me to Heaven. I believe that He changes my heart and will help me to live for Him. I am glad to confess Him as my Saviour and I write this to let you know.

Signed_____

Address_____

_____

(Of course you should tell others too. Tell your loved ones there and go to the house of God as soon as possible and publicly claim Christ as Saviour. Then we hope you will follow Him in baptism and live a happy life of service for Him.)

13

Cornelius:

How the Army Captain Got Saved at Last

One might have thought that the Italian man with the burning eyes who sat restlessly in his office would have been happy, but he was not. He had a good family, all of them devout, law-abiding, reverent, respectful and obedient. He had good friends. He was known as an honest, upright, trustworthy man. He was a captain in the Roman army, and he had brought with him, when he came from Italy to Palestine sometime before, a company of Italian soldiers.

Now he prayed again and again and pleaded. Oh, he must find God! He must find some way to have his conscience eased and a sense of forgiveness. He knew that he, as all men, must die. He had a wonderful reputation as an upright, moral and devout man, one greatly trusted, yet there was a deep consciousness that he was a sinner, that he needed some way to know the true God.

When he came from Rome, already he had dismissed the idea of any worship to the Roman deities and he had quietly smiled in mockery at the idea of worshiping the emperor. And now among these Jews in Judaea he had come more and more to hear that they claimed to know the true God and to have written words from Him and instructions about righteousness.

How earnestly he had prayed and sought to find God! He had given money to the poor. He had taken great pains to be a good husband and father, a good citizen, and good even to the soldiers who were under him, for he was a captain, a centurion of the Italian band of soldiers, helping occupy and control Judaea for the Roman Empire.

Now it was midafternoon, but he had had no food. His troubled wife had pleaded with him to come and eat, but he would not. He had long and earnestly sought to find the true

God, had prayed very much and had fasted until midafternoon.

He had known only the heathen gods. He had no Bible. He had never heard a preacher preach the Gospel. Would such a man be saved? Would God leave him to go his way and die unforgiven, lost and condemned? He did not believe so. So he earnestly prayed and waited on God.

And now how he learned about the Saviour and heard the Gospel is wonderfully told in Acts, chapter 10. Here we read verses 1 to 8 in that chapter:

"There was a certain man in Caesarea called Cornelius, a centurion of the band called the Italian band, A devout man, and one that feared God with all his house, which gave much alms to the people, and prayed to God alway. He saw in a vision evidently about the ninth hour of the day an angel of God coming in to him, and saying unto him, Cornelius. And when he looked on him, he was afraid, and said, What is it, Lord? And he said unto him, Thy prayers and thine alms are come up for a memorial before God. And now send men to Joppa, and call for one Simon, whose surname is Peter: He lodgeth with one Simon a tanner, whose house is by the sea side: he shall tell thee what thou oughtest to do. And when the angel which spake unto Cornelius was departed, he called two of his household servants, and a devout soldier of them that waited on him continually; And when he had declared all these things unto them, he sent them to Joppa."

I. THIS HEATHEN MAN SOUGHT GOD

It is a wonderful commendation that verse 2 gives us about Cornelius, the Roman centurion. He was "a devout man, and one that feared God with all his house, which gave much alms to the people, and prayed to God alway."

1. Note His Earnest Sincerity

He gave to the poor. He gave "much alms to the people." Obviously, a man who wanted to love God would love the people. He who wanted to have forgiveness would seek to do right.

And again he was "a devout man." That does not mean he was saved, but he was a God-fearing man, one who followed what light he had and earnestly tried to live an upright life and prayed always to the God whom he did not know but whom he sought.

He "prayed to God alway." I would suppose that that meant the heart-cry of his hungry soul not only came again and again as he knelt to pray and went to his secret place to seek the face of God but that all the time his heart was reaching out toward God. Whether he was carrying on his business as army captain, or dealing with his family, he was continually seeking God.

His concern and sincerity is obvious in that he was even fasting here while he prayed until three o'clock in the afternoon.

2. This Heathen Man Had Reason Enough to Seek God

Every poor sinner is without excuse if he goes on without God. Romans 1:18-20 tells us that everywhere there is evidence of God.

> *"For the wrath of God is revealed from heaven against all ungodliness and unrighteousness of men, who hold the truth in unrighteousness; Because that which may be known of God is manifest in them; for God hath shewed it unto them. For the invisible things of him from the creation of the world are clearly seen, being understood by the things that are made, even his eternal power and Godhead; so that they are without excuse."*

One cannot see God who is invisible, but one can see the world He has made. There is abundant evidence of God's eternal power and Godhead ". . . so that they are without excuse" if men do not seek God and do not believe in Him.

Psalm 19:1-4 says:

> *"The heavens declare the glory of God; and the firmament sheweth his handywork. Day unto day uttereth speech, and night unto night sheweth knowledge. There is no speech nor language, where their voice is not heard. Their line is gone out through all the earth, and their*

words to the end of the world. In them hath he set a
tabernacle for the sun."

Those who do not have the Bible have their conscience, so Romans 2:11-16 tells us that when a Gentile, such as this Roman army captain, does not have the law, the Bible, he does have a conscience—"having not the law, are a law unto themselves: Which shew the work of the law written in their hearts, their conscience also bearing witness, and their thoughts the mean while accusing or else excusing one another" (vss. 14,15).

Conscience does not tell a man how to be saved but it tells him he is a sinner. It tells him he must give an account to God. It tells him that sin must be punished.

That little spark of divine fire that God has put in the breast of every sinner is a reminder.

Do you not think lost sinners, even if they did not know the Gospel (and millions even in America do not know the Gospel), have a conscience? Do they not know they must die and they are not ready to face that?

Years ago a western United States marshall lay sick. He had risked his life again and again to arrest bank robbers, train robbers, notorious gunmen of the West. Now he said to the preacher who stood by his bedside, "I'm not afraid of death. You know that. I have risked my life many times. I am not afraid of death. But, O God, what is on the other side of death! That is what I am afraid of."

So this army captain felt his need of forgiveness and salvation although he had never heard the Gospel.

3. But God Was Seeking Him, Too

Yes, in the first place, God seeks every lost sinner in the world. John 1:9 tells us that Jesus is "the true Light, which lighteth every man that cometh into the world." In some sense every poor sinner in the world is lighted with heavenly light to draw him toward God. His conscience reminds him he is a sinner and needs forgiveness. Creation all about him shows that there is a marvelous God who made him, who provided for him, and to whom he must answer.

In John 12:32 and 33 Jesus said, "And I, if I be lifted up from the earth, will draw all men unto me. This he said, signifying what death he should die." Jesus is drawing every lost person in the world toward Him in some way.

We are told in I John 2:2, "And he is the propitiation for our sins: and not for our's only, but also for the sins of the whole world." The Saviour who died for the sins of the whole world is not willing that any should perish.

We may be sure, then, that the hunger of heart which Cornelius had was from God. And, as he turned to seek God, God gave more burden but more light and, then, made clear how he could hear the Gospel and be saved. God was seeking Cornelius.

II. GOD MEETS ALL WHO SEEK HIM SINCERELY

There is a wonderfully sweet lesson for us in the fact that God listened to this heathen man's cry. He saw his burden to know God and to do right, saw his gifts to the poor, saw how earnestly he had led his family to be devout. Let Cornelius be a sweet encouragement to every hungry heart who is away from God.

1. Multitude of Promises Say All Who Seek God Can Find Him

This truth is explicit in Romans, chapter 2.

A. In verse 7 we read, "To them who by patient continuance in well doing, seek for glory and honour and immortality, eternal life."

B. There is a divine law of sowing and reaping. God blesses those who try to do right; God punishes those who willfully go on in sin. God notices "them who by patient continuance in well doing seek for glory and honour and immortality" and they are to get eternal life. Not by their seeking to do good but because if they are seeking to do good and want to do good, God will make a way for them to come in touch with the Gospel.

On the other hand, those who "do not obey the truth, but obey unrighteousness," for them God has "indignation and wrath, tribulation and anguish."

We note clearly that God said through the angel, "Thy prayers and thine alms are come up for a memorial before God." God does care whether people do right or not. The limited righteousness of any man's efforts is enough to save him, but it does please God and means that God is willing for him to have more light so he may find the way to salvation through Christ.

C. This Scripture makes clear that "God is no respecter of persons." It is a slander against God for anyone to think that in God's predestination and election He prefers to send some to Hell and prefers to save some. This does not represent His heart attitude. Oh, He wants everyone to hear the Gospel and be saved.

It is true that He knows ahead of time who will be saved, but God cannot be blamed for those who will not.

Again, God's sweet promise of James 4:8, "Draw nigh to God, and he will draw nigh to you," shows that anyone who turns toward God can find Him if he sincerely seeks the Lord.

Again, God's promise to wayward Israel is pertinent here. He said in Jeremiah 29:11-14:

> *"For I know the thoughts that I think toward you, saith the Lord, thoughts of peace, and not of evil, to give you an expected end. Then shall ye call upon me, and ye shall go and pray unto me, and I will hearken unto you. And ye shall seek me, and find me, when ye shall search for me with all your heart. And I will be found of you, saith the Lord: and I will turn away your captivity, and I will gather you from all the nations, and from all the places whither I have driven you, saith the Lord; and I will bring you again into the place whence I caused you to be carried away captive."*

Anybody who seeks God with his whole heart will find Him. God will hear those who persistently call upon Him with their whole heart.

Again the Scripture says, "Those that seek me early shall find me" (Prov. 8:17). Psalm 34:18 says, "The Lord is nigh unto them that are of a broken heart; and saveth such as be of a contrite spirit." The penitent heart can always find God.

Besides so many explicit statements, there is a whole tenor

and course of teaching involved throughout the Bible in God's "whosoever." There is the "whosoever" of John 3:16. God loves the whole world and whosoever in all the world will believe in Him can be saved. But God certainly must mean that a will to believe in the true God must be respected.

No one can honestly say that in the Bible there is a wall set up against sinners who are penitent, who long for mercy and forgiveness, who want to know the true God and to serve Him! No, the way is open for sinners who want forgiveness and salvation. If they do not have the light, it will be given as they follow on.

Does one doubt about the Bible? Then the thing to do is to choose to have a will to do the will of God, then God has promised, "If any man will do his will, he shall know of the doctrine, whether it be of God, or whether I speak of myself." And Hosea 6:3 says it so well: "Then shall we know, if we follow on to know the Lord."

This eagerness of God to be found of all who seek Him, to answer all who call upon Him sincerely and fervently, is stated in Matthew 7:7,8.

> "Ask, and it shall be given you; seek, and ye shall find; knock, and it shall be opened unto you: For every one that asketh receiveth; and he that seeketh findeth; and to him that knocketh it shall be opened."

2. Many Sweet Illustrations That the Seeker Can Always Find God

An Ethiopian eunuch went up to Jerusalem to worship. Even as Cornelius, he was a seeker after God. He would be called a devout or a God-fearing man. He obtained a copy of the prophecy of Isaiah, handwritten on a scroll, and read it earnestly. Meantime, he did not know whom to see at Jerusalem. The apostles seemed not to have known he was there, and no one seems to have known the hunger of his heart except God.

God called Philip away from his blessed revival in Samaria. He was to go down to the road that goes from Jerusalem to Gaza. He went speedily. There came the chariot with a man reading the Scriptures. When the angel of God told Philip to draw near, he ran to the chariot and said, "Understandest thou what thou readest?" The eunuch answered, "How can I, except some man should guide me?" Then Philip began at the same Scripture in Isaiah, the 53rd chapter, and preached Jesus to him. The man was saved and immediately wanted to be baptized, as told in Acts, chapter 8. Oh, God would not let that seeking man go on without making a supernatural movement that someone should bring him the Gospel.

Another case like that of Cornelius and like the Ethiopian eunuch is that of the wise men of the East who came and found the Baby Jesus. I do not suppose anyone can doubt the sincerity of those men. They, too, were perhaps heathen men and from somewhere in what had been ancient Babylon. They probably had some of the Scriptures that the Prophet Daniel had written in their country telling of the coming Messiah. Even they knew that according to Daniel 9:20-26 the Messiah, the Prince, would come, that He would come some 483 years after the decree of Cyrus that Israel should rebuild Jerusalem. And since He was to be the King of the Jews, they sought Him at Jerusalem. God again took sweet pains to see they had encouragement.

First there appeared a star, some great body in the heavens, that was a mark to them that the time was at hand. They followed what light they had to Jerusalem, for would not the King of the Jews be born in Jerusalem? No, but wicked King Herod was used to inquire of the Jewish scribes where the Messiah would be born. They knew, as the wise men from the East had not known, the prophecy in Micah 5:2 that Christ should be born in Bethlehem. And so they came to Bethlehem. There again, gladly, they saw the star they had seen in the East! Oh, they followed what light they had and God moved bodies in the heavens and wicked King Herod and all the other things necessary to see that they found the Saviour they sought.

Last year a woman in Wisconsin had a burdened heart over her sins. She wanted to be saved. And at the Lutheran church where she attended no one got saved and no one told how to be saved! She had heard about people going to the Holy Land and what blessings they had and she wondered if she should go to Jerusalem and see these places for herself—would she there some way find the light and be saved?

Where she worked there was a Catholic woman who takes THE SWORD OF THE LORD. She told the Lutheran woman, "If you want to go to the Holy Land, Dr. John Rice takes a group every year and that would be a good time to go." She wrote and enrolled in our tour. We did not know the hunger of her heart, but God did, and in Jerusalem in a service in a little Baptist church the Gospel was preached by one of our tour members, the invitation was given and she came forward and was wonderfully saved. Oh, how the tears flowed! And she asked my wife if it was all right for people to weep when they got saved! Then how gladly she came to tell me about it!

The next day she talked about it. Again she said with a happy heart, "Jesus said, 'Seek and ye shall find,' and I sought and I found!"

Oh, yes, the heart that honestly wants mercy and forgiveness can find it. And those who seek God will have a way made clear to God.

3. God Saves No One Without the Gospel

I am glad that God's Spirit eagerly makes a way for people to find the way and be saved if they seek that Truth with all their hearts. But there is no shortcut in it. No one bypasses the Gospel. All the good intentions of Cornelius would do no good if he did not hear the Gospel. An angel from Heaven could not tell him. Some other Christian must bring him the word. So an angel from Heaven told Cornelius to send to Joppa to the house of Simon the tanner to inquire for Simon Peter, "who shall tell thee words, whereby thou and all thy house shall be saved." Ah, God will not save Cornelius without the Gospel.

The Ethiopian eunuch, with a hungry heart and searching the Scriptures, could not be saved until somebody explained the Gospel.

It may be one in a million read the Bible and get saved. I think perhaps one is never saved unless some way the Gospel has been brought to his attention or there was some other impact besides the Bible. But if in some rare case one were reading the Bible and found the plan of salvation and got saved, remember it still had to be the Gospel. Remember still that somebody translated the Bible, somebody printed it, somebody bought it! God never saves anybody without the Gospel. And God never saves anybody without some Christian's helping.

The Scripture says on this matter, "For whosoever shall call upon the name of the Lord shall be saved. How then shall they call on him in whom they have not believed? and how shall they believe in him of whom they have not heard? and how shall they hear without a preacher?"

It is God's plan that the Gospel should come filtered through somebody's love, warning, entreaty, praise and testimony. It is not just the Gospel but "it pleased God by the foolishness of preaching to save them that believe." God wants some human testimony to tell about the Saviour.

And Romans 10:17 says, "So then faith cometh by hearing, and hearing by the word of God." One cannot have saving faith without knowing what the Bible says about Jesus. It may be quoted or read or paraphrased, but the truth must be out that a man is a sinner, God loves sinners, Jesus died to save sinners. He gives everlasting life to those who trust Him.

People are not saved without the Gospel.

So we may be sure there is a moral guilt and wickedness in unbelief. Always one who is not saved could have been saved. In John 3:19-21 Jesus said:

"And this is the condemnation, that light is come into the world, and men loved darkness rather than light, because their deeds were evil. For every one that doeth evil hateth the light, neither cometh to the light, lest his deeds should be reproved. But he that doeth truth cometh to the light, that his deeds may be made manifest, that they are wrought in God."

Oh, the one who does not know the plan of salvation could know it. One who does not have further light could have it if he sought it. The honest, penitent heart seeking for forgiveness can find it, even as did Cornelius.

III. GET ALL YOUR LOVED ONES SAVED!

It is blessed that when Cornelius was saved, all his family was saved. He was a devout man "with all his house." He had concern for those.

1. Godly Man Sets Moral and Spiritual Tone in His Family

We are not surprised that the whole family is included in this wonderful, spiritual time of salvation.

All the family feared God because the husband and father feared God. He had evidently taught them that the heathen gods of Rome were no gods. He had taught them morality and righteousness. He had taught them spiritual truth as far as he knew.

And this was intentional, no doubt, for in Acts 10:24 we find that when Peter came to Caesarea, he found them altogether: "And the morrow after they entered into Caesarea. And Cornelius waited for them, and had called together his kinsmen and near friends." And then again in verse 44 we read, "While Peter yet spake these words, the Holy Ghost fell on all them which heard the word." They were ready to be saved. They were hungry, too. They had been taught to seek the Lord by this man.

Oh, we must face the fact that a man is accountable for his family. And this man knew it. We must face the matter that "like father, like children." Always it is true that a man can lead his family for God if he himself is what he ought to be. It is never true that it is unpredictable about the children of godly men. A godly man who not only lives right but disciplines and controls his family as he ought, can have them serve the Lord, too.

We know that the sons of Eli, high priest of Israel, turned out bad, but he was blamed for it. The Lord said of him that he knew about his sons' wickedness: "Now Eli was very old, and heard all that his sons did unto all Israel; and how they lay with the women that assembled at the door of the tabernacle of the congregation," and that he rather querulously inquired, "Why do ye such things? for I hear of your evil dealings by all this people. Nay, my sons; for it is no good report that I hear: ye make the Lord's people to transgress." But he did not compel them to leave the priesthood, nor did he punish them, as the Scriptures required of adulterers.

The fact is, we learn that these sons of Eli had not been converted. "They knew not the Lord" (I Sam. 2:12). Eli was certainly responsible for that and Eli profited by their bad habits and so God told him, "Wherefore kick ye at my sacrifice and at mine offering, which I have commanded in my habitation; and honourest thy sons above me, to make yourselves fat with the chiefest of all the offerings of Israel my people?" (I Sam. 2:29).

Then the message of God came to him through Samuel, "For I have told him that I will judge his house for ever for the iniquity which he knoweth; because his sons made themselves vile, and he restrained them not." We may be sure that not only a godly example and earnest prayer but honest discipline, taking responsibility for his family, was the way this Cornelius, a heathen man seeking God, reared his family.

There is no promise that if you simply pray but do nothing, your children will turn out right. There is no promise that if you live an upright, moral life yourself, that your children will automatically turn out right. But with honest discipline and teaching, we can claim the promise of Proverbs 22:6, "Train up a child in the way he should go: and when he is old, he will not depart from it."

This man Cornelius lived a godly life and the respect which his children and his kinsmen and neighbors had for him was based partly on his godly authority and the enforcement of righteous standards in his own home.

He was commander of a company of Roman soldiers. He was commander in his own home, also. That is as it ought to be.

2. Other Great Bible Christians Took Responsibility for Their Families

The Lord said of Abraham in Genesis 18:19, "For I know him, that he will command his children and his household after him, and they shall keep the way of the Lord." Note not simply that Abraham lived a godly life but he commanded his children and his household, and God could be sure they would follow Him, so God made His secrets known to Abraham, His friend.

We find the same attitude in godly Joshua. In Joshua 24 we find that Joshua called elders of Israel, heads of tribes and officers, together and laid down the law to them plainly. Would they go the way of the Amorites and serve the heathen gods, or the gods the Israelites had served in the wilderness and brought a curse upon themselves, or would they serve the Lord? He said, "Choose you this day whom ye will serve . . . but as for me and my house, we will serve the Lord." And that meant not only that Joshua was speaking for himself, but also for his family. He had a big family—children, grandchildren, great grandchildren, and many servants. He takes responsibility for them all. I should think he also took responsibility for the soldiers under his control. Oh, a man must give an account to God for his family. He must not only be a good example but must have authority in the home.

A man must be responsible for his family. Lydia, evidently head of her own home, was saved and brought her household also: "And when she was baptized, and her household, she besought us, saying, If ye have judged me to be faithful to the Lord, come into my house, and abide there. And she constrained us," says the apostle in Acts 16:15.

And when the Philippian jailor was saved, the whole family was also saved. The Gospel was preached to him very simply, "Believe on the Lord Jesus Christ, and thou shalt be saved, and thy house." Note that term "and thy house." They could be saved, too, the same way, and the jailor must feel his responsibility about it. And the following verse says, "And they spake unto him the word of the Lord, and to all that were in his house." The next verse says he was "baptized, he and all his, straightway." Then, he "rejoiced, believing in God with all his house."

When a man gets saved, he ought to get his family saved. The man who is devout and upright and who enforces proper discipline and sets the moral and spiritual standards in his home, can win his loved ones and should.

So, then, Cornelius was saved and his kinsmen and friends, too.

Oh, but what kind of a Christian is that man who gets saved, but his children go to Hell? Or his brothers? Or his next-door neighbors? A man who is saved and means business and lives for God ought to be able to get those who love him, even as Cornelius got "his kinsmen and near friends" (vs. 24).

3. Many Times We Have Seen It Proved That a Man Can Lead His Household to God

At Lewistown, Pennsylvania, in a citywide campaign with fundamental churches, I preached on a Sunday afternoon on "The Sins of Men." And I bore down with great emphasis on the sin of a man letting his family go to Hell, letting his children grow up wild and untamed—and unsaved.

Hearing me was a tall, solemn-faced man, with dark hair and eyes, a lined face. He looked much as Abraham Lincoln must have looked as he sat there. He never smiled at a joke. One could not tell what was going on behind that poker face. But something was sure going on!

When the service was over, he went out into the vestibule, put on his topcoat (it was midwinter) and then out on the steps of the building he took from one pocket a meerschaum pipe and slammed it on the concrete and it broke into a hundred pieces. From the other pocket he took a can of Prince Albert tobacco and sailed it down the street and it went into the opposite curb and down the street on the ice, spewing out tobacco. Then he drew his sleeve across his eyes and started walking down the sidewalk. I watched him. He was taking long strides. There was obviously some great purpose on his mind. I said to someone, "Something is going to happen at that man's house!"

That was on Sunday afternoon. The following Friday night this man urged us—my party, Dr. Harry Clarke, my daughter Grace at the piano, my secretary and advance man—to go to his house for supper. I protested but he insisted. There was a special reason. When we got there we found that nine of his family—sons, daughters, sons-in-law and brothers-in-law—had been saved that week. Two more were saved the next day. Oh, he set out to get his family saved.

In Sherman, Texas, a troubled woman of Seventh-Day Adventist leanings told me sadly, "I'll never make it! Every day I find something in the Bible I have left undone." As I laughed at her, she began to weep. "You ought not laugh. It isn't funny."

I said, "I am laughing because I am so glad you found you can't make it. Maybe now you will listen to one who tells you that Somebody made it for you."

She said, "Can you tell me how to be saved so I can know it for sure?"

"I surely can," I said. She asked me to come to her house at 1:30 that afternoon. I did not know why she had postponed it until the afternoon, but when I got to the house I saw cars lined up. She had twenty-three of her loved ones and family there in the room to hear the Gospel. I baptized eleven of that crowd when they got converted and two more later.

Ah, this devout man Cornelius got his family and loved ones in. So must we. We must account to God for our loved ones.

IV. THE GOSPEL THE SAME FOR EVERYBODY

There are some people who think that in Old Testament times Jews were saved by keeping ceremonial law, but they are mistaken. The old Scofield Reference Bible leaves the impression that the Gospel of John the Baptist was different from that of Jesus and the apostles. That is a part of the faulty Plymouth Brethren doctrine accentuating a great number of dispensations when God dealt differently with people, they say. So the note in the older Scofield Reference Bible on Acts 19:1-6 says,

> **"Paul was evidently impressed by the absence of spirituality and power in these so-called disciples. Their answer brought out the fact that they were Jewish proselytes, disciples of John the Baptist, looking forward to a coming King, not Christians looking backward to an accomplished redemption."**

But good Dr. Scofield was mistaken in his interpretation here. When God says "disciples," neither Dr. Scofield nor anybody else has a right to say "so-called disciples." The Gospel that John the Baptist preached was the same as Jesus preached. The baptism that John the Baptist had is the only baptism that Christ and the apostles had.

It is true that their ceremonial law was given in the Old Testament pointing to the coming Saviour and that in the New Testament there is no more ceremonial law, but the Gospel all through the ages has been exactly the same. In Acts 10:43 Peter tells us by divine inspiration, "To him give all the prophets witness, that through his name whosoever believeth in him shall receive remission of sins."

1. Old Testament Saints Saved Just Like People Are Saved Today

Hebrews 11:4 tells us that "by faith Abel offered unto God a more excellent sacrifice . . . ." By faith? Yes, Abel trusted the coming Messiah and was saved by faith, just as people are saved today. The death of Christ was settled in the mind of God before the world began. The Lord Jesus planned it and the Father ordained it. It was already effective, and every Old Testament saint was saved by faith in that atoning blood that would be shed and already counted done by the merciful God.

Remember that Abel is listed among the prophets in Luke 11:51, so he was one who preached salvation by faith in the coming Messiah.

Abraham also trusted in Christ. We are told that Abraham "believed in the Lord; and he counted it to him for righteousness" (Gen. 15:6). Thus he was saved and is held up as an example of those who trusted in Christ and were saved. Romans 4:1-4 tells us about Abraham:

> *"What shall we say then that Abraham our father, as pertaining to the flesh, hath found? For if Abraham were justified by works, he hath whereof to glory; but not before God. For what saith the scripture? Abraham believed God, and it was counted unto him for*

*righteousness. Now to him that worketh is the reward
not reckoned of grace, but of debt."*

You see, Abraham was saved by grace. We do not wonder
that Jesus could say, "Abraham rejoiced to see my day: and he
saw it, and was glad" (John 8:56).

David also understood this plan of salvation for by divine inspiration Romans 4:5-8 quotes David from the 32nd Psalm:

*"But to him that worketh not, but believeth on him
that justifieth the ungodly, his faith is counted for
righteousness. Even as David also describeth the bless-
edness of the man, unto whom God imputeth
righteousness without works, Saying, Blessed are they
whose iniquities are forgiven, and whose sins are covered.
Blessed is the man to whom the Lord will not impute
sin."*

David had righteousness imputed to him without works, as do
we. His sins and iniquities were forgiven and covered. This is
salvation by grace through faith just as we have it in the New
Testament.

Yes, "give all the prophets witness, that through his name
whosoever believeth in him shall receive remission of sins."

2. Ceremonial Law Preached Same Gospel as John 3:16

How many incidents in the Old Testament picture the true
Gospel. That serpent on a pole in Numbers 21:5-9 pictured Christ
bearing the sins of the world. Jesus referred to that, telling
Nicodemus, "And as Moses lifted up the serpent in the
wilderness, even so must the Son of man be lifted up: That
whosoever believeth in him should not perish, but have eternal
life." So one who looked at that brazen serpent, if he had a
spiritual mind and felt his need for forgiveness and salvation,
knew that God was some way providing an atonement that he
could have forgiveness and salvation.

The ceremonies and incidents were not simply some enslaving
way of dealing with people. They were all pictures pointing to
Christ and salvation.

When the children of Israel thirsted in the wilderness and God had Moses smite the rock and out of it flowed a river of water to water three and a half million people and their cattle, that rock pictured Christ broken, smitten for us and the water of life freely given from the wounded Saviour. And when a second time Moses was commanded to simply speak to the rock, not to smite it, the reason was that when Christ is taken as Saviour, He has been smitten one time and settled forever salvation and as far as the atonement is concerned, "it is finished."

The ark was a picture of salvation with Christ also and those who believed the preaching of Noah and entered the ark by faith pictured those who trust in Christ and are saved from the awful floods of judgment of God. So when Noah preached to those people, Christ came through the Holy Spirit and preached to them, too, as we see in I Peter 3:18-20.

Oh, every prophet in the Old Testament preached the same Gospel as we have now.

That is why Jesus seemed to rebuke Nicodemus so strongly when He said, "Art thou a master of Israel, and knowest not these things?" (John 3:10). Should Nicodemus, a Jewish leader and student of the Old Testament, have known about the new birth? Yes, for in Ezekiel 36:26,27 God had plainly foretold, "A new heart also will I give you, and a new spirit will I put within you: and I will take away the stony heart out of your flesh, and I will give you an heart of flesh. And I will put my spirit within you, and cause you to walk in my statutes, and ye shall keep my judgments, and do them."

It had been freely promised that Jews could be "circumcised in heart," which meant, of course, being born again. Yes, the same plan of salvation in the Old Testament as in the New.

Circumcision pictured the new birth. The weekly Sabbath on Saturday pictured a Heaven that could be won by perfect righteousness if man did right all his life. Then the passover Sabbath which brought a blessed Sabbath on the first day after the blood of the passover lamb was put on the door, pictures salva-

tion by grace, undeserved, as at the beginning of the Christian
life. And every priest in the Old Testament pictured Christ particularly, every sacrifice on the altar pictured His bloody
sacrifice for us. The ceremonial law was not a plan of salvation; it
was simply lights and figures and pictures and illustrations
pointing toward Christ. And so "to him give all the prophets
witness, that through his name whosoever believeth in him shall
receive remission of sins."

3. The Great Statements About Salvation Are Quoted Often From the Old Testament

Romans 10:13 says, "For whosoever shall call upon the name
of the Lord shall be saved." But that is a quotation from Joel
2:32!

Again the Scripture says three times in the New Testament,
"The just shall live by faith," in Romans 1:17; Galatians 3:11
and Hebrews 10:38. But that is a quotation from the Old Testament from Habakkuk 2:4! You see, they had the same plan of
salvation in the Old Testament as we have in the New.

We say that people should trust in the Lord, and that is what
the word "believe" generally means in the blessed promises of
John 3:16; John 3:18; John 3:36; John 5:24, etc. But to trust in
the Lord is advised throughout the Old Testament again and
again.

It is said that Ruth the Moabitess, who came back with Naomi
to Israel, learned to trust the Lord and Boaz said to her, "The
Lord recompense thy work, and a full reward be given thee of the
Lord God of Israel, under whose wings thou art come to trust."
That is a wonderful picture of salvation by faith. Oh, yes, Ruth
put her trust in the Lord and depended on Him for salvation and
forgiveness and was a Christian, just as New Testament Christians are who trust Christ for salvation.

We know that believing on Christ, as the Lord used the term in
John 3:16 and in many other places, simply means to put one's
trust in Christ, to rely upon Him for salvation. But the term trust
is used in that sense again and again throughout the Old Testament.

Dear Friend, Are You Ready Now to Take Christ as Your Own Saviour?

Remember, the promise is, "To him give all the prophets witness, that through his name whosoever believeth in him shall receive remission of sins." So now, today, where you are this moment you can turn your heart from your sin honestly and trust Him to forgive you and have the assurance of God's Word that He saves you here and now. Will you do it? If you admit you are a sinner, if you honestly turn your heart from sin and want forgiveness and help, then I beg you, say yes in your heart to God, rely on Jesus today and thus take Him as your own personal Saviour. Then sign the decision form below, copy it in a letter and mail it to me now. I beg you do it now.

Evangelist John R. Rice
P. O. Box 1099
Murfreesboro, Tennessee 37130

Dear Brother Rice:

I have read your sermon, "How the Army Captain Got Saved." I believe the God who saved Cornelius is ready to save me. I believe Jesus died for sinners, as the Bible says. I admit I am a poor sinner who needs forgiveness and I want God to forgive me and save me now. So here and now, the best I know, I turn my heart from my sin, I trust Jesus Christ to forgive my sins and change my heart. I will rely on Him today to make me God's child and take me to Heaven, and I will set out to claim Him and live for Him.

Now that I am taking Christ as my own personal Saviour, will you please send me a letter of encouragement and help?

Date _____

Signed _____

Address_____

_____